# FROM PROGRAM TO PRODUCT

# FROM PROGRAM TO PRODUCT

## TURNING YOUR CODE INTO A SALEABLE PRODUCT

Rocky Smolin

Apress®

*From Program to Product: Turning Your Code into a Saleable Product*

ISBN-13 (pbk): 978-1-59059-971-6

ISBN-10 (pbk): 1-59059-971-3

ISBN-13 (electronic): 978-1-4302-0614-9

ISBN-10 (electronic): 1-4302-0614-4

Printed and bound in the United States of America 9 8 7 6 5 4 3 2 1

Trademarked names may appear in this book. Rather than use a trademark symbol with every occurrence of a trademarked name, we use the names only in an editorial fashion and to the benefit of the trademark owner, with no intention of infringement of the trademark.

Lead Editors: Jonathan Hassell, Dominic Shakeshaft
Technical Reviewer: Martin Reid
Editorial Board: Clay Andres, Steve Anglin, Ewan Buckingham, Tony Campbell, Gary Cornell, Jonathan Gennick, Kevin Goff, Matthew Moodie, Joseph Ottinger, Jeffrey Pepper, Frank Pohlmann, Ben Renow-Clarke, Dominic Shakeshaft, Matt Wade, Tom Welsh
Project Manager: Beth Christmas
Copy Editor: Ami Knox
Associate Production Director: Kari Brooks-Copony
Production Editor: Kelly Winquist
Compositor: Dina Quan
Proofreader: Lisa Hamilton
Indexer: John Collin
Artist: April Milne
Cover Designer: Kurt Krames
Manufacturing Director: Tom Debolski

Distributed to the book trade worldwide by Springer-Verlag New York, Inc., 233 Spring Street, 6th Floor, New York, NY 10013. Phone 1-800-SPRINGER, fax 201-348-4505, e-mail orders-ny@springer-sbm.com, or visit http://www.springeronline.com.

For information on translations, please contact Apress directly at 2855 Telegraph Avenue, Suite 600, Berkeley, CA 94705. Phone 510-549-5930, fax 510-549-5939, e-mail info@apress.com, or visit http://www.apress.com.

Apress and friends of ED books may be purchased in bulk for academic, corporate, or promotional use. eBook versions and licenses are also available for most titles. For more information, reference our Special Bulk Sales–eBook Licensing web page at http://www.apress.com/info/bulksales.

*To my first wife*

# Contents at a Glance

FOREWORD . . . . . . . . . . . . . . . . . . . . . . . . . . . . . . . . xiii

ABOUT THE AUTHOR. . . . . . . . . . . . . . . . . . . . . . . . . . . xv

ABOUT THE TECHNICAL REVIEWER . . . . . . . . . . . . . . . . xvii

ACKNOWLEDGMENTS. . . . . . . . . . . . . . . . . . . . . . . . . xix

INTRODUCTION . . . . . . . . . . . . . . . . . . . . . . . . . . . . xxi

**CHAPTER 1**  WHO WANTS TO BE A MILLIONAIRE? . . . . . . . . . . . . . 1

**CHAPTER 2**  SO WHAT DO I DO FIRST? . . . . . . . . . . . . . . . . 23

**CHAPTER 3**  THE PROGRAM: FROM THE OUTSIDE LOOKING IN . . . . 61

**CHAPTER 4**  THE PRICE OF SUCCESS . . . . . . . . . . . . . . . . . . . 103

**CHAPTER 5**  LEGAL MATTERS . . . . . . . . . . . . . . . . . . . . . . 129

**CHAPTER 6**  SOME FINAL CONSIDERATIONS . . . . . . . . . . . . . . 155

**APPENDIX**  SAMPLE SOFTWARE LICENSE . . . . . . . . . . . . . . . . 185

INDEX . . . . . . . . . . . . . . . . . . . . . . . . . . . . . . . . . . 189

# Contents

FOREWORD . . . . . . . . . . . . . . . . . . . . . . . . . . . . . xiii

ABOUT THE AUTHOR. . . . . . . . . . . . . . . . . . . . . . . xv

ABOUT THE TECHNICAL REVIEWER . . . . . . . . . . . . . . . xvii

ACKNOWLEDGMENTS. . . . . . . . . . . . . . . . . . . . . . xix

INTRODUCTION . . . . . . . . . . . . . . . . . . . . . . . . . xxi

**CHAPTER 1**  WHO WANTS TO BE A MILLIONAIRE? . . . . . . . . . . . 1

So Why Did I Write This Book? . . . . . . . . . . . . . . . . . 1

Why Am I a Programmer?. . . . . . . . . . . . . . . . . . . . 4

The Lone Ranger Rides Again . . . . . . . . . . . . . . . 6

It Takes Two to Tango, Sometimes . . . . . . . . . . . . . 6

Who Are You?. . . . . . . . . . . . . . . . . . . . . . . . . 7

What's the Big Idea? . . . . . . . . . . . . . . . . . . . . . 8

What This Book Is Really About. . . . . . . . . . . . . . . . 8

*How They Did It: An Interview with Software Developer*
*and Entrepreneur Al Vanderpool.* . . . . . . . . . . . . . . 10

**CHAPTER 2**  SO WHAT DO I DO FIRST? . . . . . . . . . . . . . . . . . 23

Define Your Product . . . . . . . . . . . . . . . . . . . . . 23

How to Be Your Own Systems Analyst: Making a System
Specification . . . . . . . . . . . . . . . . . . . . . . . . . 24

Systems Analysis in Sixty Seconds: Input, Process,
Output, Storage . . . . . . . . . . . . . . . . . . . . . 25

What Comes Out? . . . . . . . . . . . . . . . . . . . . 26

A Digression: Data vs. Information. . . . . . . . . . . . 29

What Is Stored? . . . . . . . . . . . . . . . . . . . . . . . . 30

The Inputs . . . . . . . . . . . . . . . . . . . . . . . . . . 35

The Processes . . . . . . . . . . . . . . . . . . . . . . . . 36

Who Gets to Use It? Controlling Access to Data in Your
Application . . . . . . . . . . . . . . . . . . . . . . . . . . 37

A Deeper Level of Control . . . . . . . . . . . . . . . . . 38

Down to the Field Level . . . . . . . . . . . . . . . . . . 39

How Much Control to Build In? . . . . . . . . . . . . . . 41

Navigation: Finding Your Way Around the Program . . . . . . . 41

Go Back Where You Came From! . . . . . . . . . . . . . 44

The Platform . . . . . . . . . . . . . . . . . . . . . . . . . . 46

The Wrap-Up . . . . . . . . . . . . . . . . . . . . . . . . . 46

*How They Did It: An Interview with Jewelry Designer, Software
Developer, and Entrepreneur Barbara Carlton* . . . . . . . . . 48

**CHAPTER 3**   THE PROGRAM: FROM THE OUTSIDE LOOKING IN . . . . 61

What I Don't Want to Talk About . . . . . . . . . . . . . . . . 61

How to Hire a Programmer . . . . . . . . . . . . . . . . . . . 62

What I Do Want to Talk About . . . . . . . . . . . . . . . . . 65

The Opening Form . . . . . . . . . . . . . . . . . . . . . . 66

A Not-So-Foolish Consistency . . . . . . . . . . . . . . . . 69

Type Casting: Selecting the Right Font . . . . . . . . . . . . 74

The Color of Money: Picking the Right Palette . . . . . . . 75

Preferential Treatments . . . . . . . . . . . . . . . . . . . . 78

A Foreign Concept: Getting Ready to Sell Overseas . . . . . 79

Size Matters: Issues in Screen Resizing . . . . . . . . . . . 85

When Good Software Goes Bad: Error Trapping and
Reporting . . . . . . . . . . . . . . . . . . . . . . . . . . 87

A Quick Word About Mice . . . . . . . . . . . . . . . . . . 88

Testing . . . 1, 2, 3 . . . Is This Thing On? . . . . . . . . . . . . 89

And in Conclusion, My Friends . . . . . . . . . . . . . . . . . 90

*How They Did It: An Interview with Jackie and
Doug Murphy of Murphy's Creativity* . . . . . . . . . . . . . 91

**CHAPTER 4**   THE PRICE OF SUCCESS . . . . . . . . . . . . . . . . . . . . 103

A Matter of Definition. . . . . . . . . . . . . . . . . . . . . . . 103

The Thing About Software . . . . . . . . . . . . . . . . . . . 105

    Breaking Even. . . . . . . . . . . . . . . . . . . . . . . . 106

    What's It Worth to Ya, Baby? Perceived Value . . . . . . . . 107

    You'll Never Walk Alone (Well, Rarely):
       Looking at the Competition. . . . . . . . . . . . . . . . . 108

Finding the Peak of the Revenue Curve. . . . . . . . . . . . 110

Pricing Options . . . . . . . . . . . . . . . . . . . . . . . . 112

    Fixed Price . . . . . . . . . . . . . . . . . . . . . . . . . 112

    Annual Subscription . . . . . . . . . . . . . . . . . . . . 112

    Pay per Seat . . . . . . . . . . . . . . . . . . . . . . . . 113

    Pay per Use. . . . . . . . . . . . . . . . . . . . . . . . . 113

    Pay by Capacity. . . . . . . . . . . . . . . . . . . . . . . 113

    Give It Away? . . . . . . . . . . . . . . . . . . . . . . . . 114

Getting Paid: Setting Your Payment Policies . . . . . . . . . . 115

Actually Getting Paid: Dealing with Your Receivables . . .
   and Their Payables . . . . . . . . . . . . . . . . . . . . . . 116

Leasing and Self-Financing. . . . . . . . . . . . . . . . . . . 117

Annual Support: Creating an Annuity . . . . . . . . . . . . . 117

And in Conclusion, My Friends . . . . . . . . . . . . . . . . 118

*How They Did It: An Interview with Arthur Fuller* . . . . . . . . 119

**CHAPTER 5**   LEGAL MATTERS . . . . . . . . . . . . . . . . . . . . . . . 129

How to Talk to a Lawyer . . . . . . . . . . . . . . . . . . . 130

Who Owns Your Software?. . . . . . . . . . . . . . . . . . 131

Never Sell Your Software . . . . . . . . . . . . . . . . . . . 133

The Business Format . . . . . . . . . . . . . . . . . . . . . 136

    Sole Proprietor. . . . . . . . . . . . . . . . . . . . . . . . 137

    Partnership . . . . . . . . . . . . . . . . . . . . . . . . . 137

    Limited Liability Company. . . . . . . . . . . . . . . . . . 138

    Corporations . . . . . . . . . . . . . . . . . . . . . . . . 138

Insuring Success . . . . . . . . . . . . . . . . . . . . . . . . 139

What If You Get Hit By a Truck? Software Escrow . . . . . . . 140

Copyrights . . . . . . . . . . . . . . . . . . . . . . . . . 141

Trademarks. . . . . . . . . . . . . . . . . . . . . . . . . 142

There Be Pirates Out There . . . . . . . . . . . . . . . . . 143

*How They Did It: An Interview with Barry Matfield* . . . . . . . 148

CHAPTER 6    SOME FINAL CONSIDERATIONS . . . . . . . . . . . . . . . 155

When to Stop Programming. . . . . . . . . . . . . . . . . 155

The Version Two List. . . . . . . . . . . . . . . . . . . . 156

Custom Tailored or Off the Rack? . . . . . . . . . . . . . . 157

Manual Labor. . . . . . . . . . . . . . . . . . . . . . . . 158

How to Get Started Writing Your User Manual. . . . . . . 160

What to Say . . . . . . . . . . . . . . . . . . . . . . 161

When to Start Programming . . . Again. . . . . . . . . . . 162

Reference or Tutorial? . . . . . . . . . . . . . . . . . . 163

Back Matters . . . . . . . . . . . . . . . . . . . . . . 164

Online or Hard Copy . . . . . . . . . . . . . . . . . . 164

Online Help . . . Or Not . . . . . . . . . . . . . . . . . 165

It's a Wrap: Packaging Your Product . . . . . . . . . . . . . 165

The Last Word: How to Eat an Elephant . . . . . . . . . . 169

*How They Did It: An Interview with Steve Capistrant
   of Symphony Information Services* . . . . . . . . . . . . . 170

*How They Did It: An Interview with Reuben Cummings
   of Government Finance Consultants* . . . . . . . . . . . . 178

APPENDIX    SAMPLE SOFTWARE LICENSE . . . . . . . . . . . . . . . . 185

E-Z-MRP® Material Requirements Planning System—
   User's Guide . . . . . . . . . . . . . . . . . . . . . . . 185

Copyright Notice . . . . . . . . . . . . . . . . . . . . 185

Trademarks . . . . . . . . . . . . . . . . . . . . . . . 185

License Agreement. . . . . . . . . . . . . . . . . . . . 186

Beach Access Software "As Is" Warranty Statement. . . . . 186

INDEX . . . . . . . . . . . . . . . . . . . . . . . . . . . . . 189

# Foreword

*From Program to Product: Turning Your Code into a Saleable Product* is a book that could have saved me about ten years of pointlessly doing the same thing over and over. More to the point, it might just save you from the same career mistake.

Let me explain.

Every professional programmer in this industry—whether they freelance from project to project or work from job to job—sooner or later arrives at the point when they have to ask themselves, "Is this all there is?" You've gotten to the point when you no longer stumble talking to potential customers, when the earth doesn't necessarily move for you every time the technology advances, when you fit comfortably in your skin as a professional programmer.

Then what do you do? How do you get from the local max of being a competent and proficient programmer for others to being something else? What else is there?

Now there's nothing wrong with doing what you're good at, year after year, project after project. It's fun, you learn new things, you meet interesting people, you may get paid to go to foreign places, and it pays the bills. But it doesn't get you excited anymore.

What Rocky does in this book is explore another way to go than down that predictable career path of freelancing or salaried work: he shows you step by step, issue by issue, how to go from developing software applications for other people to developing something better—a product.

*From Program to Product* lays out the mental and educational process you need to follow to go from software developer to product developer. It is not necessarily an easy transformation. You won't be the same programmer you were after you finish Rocky's book because you'll have learned how to see your software in an entirely different way.

From the bare beginnings where Rocky invites you to see what you're doing in a new and different way, he takes you through defining a product, not just an app; learning how to see your product from the outside in instead of from the inside out; thinking about how to price your product and understanding the core economic reality of selling software; dealing with the legal aspects of selling intellectual property without being mugged; and coping with some of the other tasks you need to master such as internationalization and documentation to get your product truly ready for the market.

By the way, I should make clear here that while I see Rocky's book through code monkey–colored glasses, this is a book not just for programmers. If you've hired a programmer (and Rocky has some great advice on doing just that) to implement your vision of a software application, this book will help you with both the big picture of just how to direct your project into a commercial product and the small but important details, like End User License Agreements (EULAs), you need to get right to protect your investment.

One of the things I really like about this book is that while Rocky shares his experience and insight as someone who has successfully gone from program to product, he goes beyond that to interview others who bring their own insights and experiences to the buffet you get to feast at.

In a lot of ways, Rocky has written the perfect prequel to my book, *Micro-ISV: From Vision to Reality* (Apress, 2006). Where I focus mainly on what to do after you've gotten your product to sell, Rocky covers the hard ground of getting to that point. That's why I said at the top of this foreword I'd wished Rocky had written this book a decade ago—it would have immeasurably helped me go that first step from developer to micro-ISV.

And that's why I recommend Rocky's book to you now. If you've been doing what you do for too long, if you're looking for a clear path to break free from being just a programmer, Rocky is offering you what you need.

It's time to take the red pill.

Bob Walsh
Sonoma, California
February 11, 2008

# About the Author

**Rocky Smolin** wrote his first computer program in 1964 at the age of 16 using computers at the Illinois Institute of Technology in Chicago. He developed and sold his first commercial product three years later while studying for his degree in business administration at Bradley University in Peoria, Illinois, and went on to earn an MBA at San Diego State University in 1974.

After serving as director of information systems for several companies, he started his own small business systems consulting operation in 1980. At the start of the personal computer revolution, he codeveloped PMS-II, the first successful critical path project management system for PCs, and went on to develop and market E-Z-MRP—a manufacturing system for small manufacturers.

Today as owner of Beach Access Software (**www.bchacc.com**), Smolin provides custom databases and applications exclusively in Microsoft Access, as well as continuing to market the E-Z-MRP system.

Smolin lives with his wife of thirty-one years and two sons, 17 and 11, in Del Mar, California.

# About the Technical Reviewer

**Martin Reid** is an analyst with The Queen's University of Belfast and has been working with relational databases for more than fifteen years. Martin is currently working with Microsoft SharePoint Office Server 2007 on a large-scale enterprise deployment. Martin has been technical editor on several Apress titles and is the author of *Pro Access 2007*, also published by Apress.

# Acknowledgments

I would like to acknowledge the invaluable assistance over the years of what is possibly the most generous, friendly, and knowledgeable group of programmers it has ever been my pleasure to work with—the worldwide community of developers at `www.databaseadvisors.com` and particularly those on the AccessD list, who have saved my bacon numerous times and continue to do so to this day.

I would also like to thank those whose interviews are included in this book. They gave freely of their time and experience to help others like themselves become more successful software entrepreneurs, and their contributions are invaluable.

And finally, I would like to express my deep appreciation to everyone at Apress who had a hand in this project—particularly those who made the decision to take the risk of going ahead with this project based solely on the sketchy outline and résumé I submitted to them. I hope their confidence in me was not misplaced.

# Introduction

Programming . . . it's the most fun you can have with your clothes on. At least for a propeller head like myself. And making a pile of dough doing it—well, what could be better?

But getting from an idea and bit of code to a polished product ready for market takes more than great enthusiasm and a couple of cases of high-octane cola.

Through hard experience, sometimes expensive and often painful, I have learned what one needs to do to turn an idea for a software product into reality. And that is what this book is all about. The book begins with your idea for a great program and ends with you at the starting line, product in hand, ready for that first day of business and that first sale.

I'd like to say that this is a top-down cookbook for success—as orderly as a well-written subroutine. But it isn't. The software game is simply not that neat.

So this book is more of a checklist, covering a wide range of topics—from systems analysis, to legal matters, to how to make your program look good to the customer. You'll read about the economics of software—pricing, license arrangements, and the like. And get advice on what makes an effective manual, how to test your software, and many other topics you might not have thought about.

Interspersed among the chapters are interviews with folks just like you who have been successful at turning their ideas into programs, turning the programs into products, and turning the products into profitable businesses. They'll tell you how they did it—what they did right and what they did wrong.

If you have questions or comments about program design, product development, packaging, or any other topics in this book, please contact me through the Beach Access Software web site: **www.bchacc.com**. Really. I would like to hear from you.

A word about color: you'll note that the figures and illustrations in this book are printed in black and white. However, some of these figures are better off seen in color, and for a couple of them, seeing the colors is essential to understand the point I'm trying to make. All of the figures in this book are available in color on the Web as a download, and I would urge you to download these figures and have them handy when reading the book. To download the figures in color, point your browser to `www.apress.com/book/view/1590599713` and look at the "Book Extras" section.

# Who Wants to Be a Millionaire?

Most of us harbor a secret fantasy about being in business for ourselves and raking in a lot of dough. Some of us—like myself—are doing it and are halfway there—we're in business for ourselves.

In the last fifty years, rock star aspirations aside, a popular dream is to be a software entrepreneur who writes "The Next Great Killer Application"—a program that will cause a river of easy money to flow into your life.

What you have is an idea for a computer program that you think would be a popular product. The state of your program may be anywhere from a half-baked scheme to a smoothly functioning program.

What you don't have is a way to get from idea to reality.

You might already have crossed the finish line and be out in the free market hawking this gem everywhere you can think of, and are perhaps not meeting with a great deal of success.

Turning an idea into a professional-looking, saleable product involves a lot more than just writing a good program. There are packaging, and marketing, and legal, and organizational, and technical issues to consider.

And you are probably feeling that you don't even know the right questions to ask.

## So Why Did I Write This Book?

I'm a programmer. I have been since I was a teener. Oh, I've had lots of job titles, but at heart I'm just a geek programmer. Right now, I write custom databases and applications for a variety of small businesses using Microsoft Access exclusively, under the company name of Beach Access Software (www.bchacc.com). It's fun. It's satisfying. And having been doing this on my own on a variety of platforms for nearly 30 years, I'm pretty much unemployable.

One day I got a referral from a colleague to a fellow in Dallas—Jack Stone. Jack is a patent and trademark attorney at Scheef & Stone who had developed some software in-house to help keep the legal matters under control.

Then, being both smart and ambitious, Jack decided that this program would be attractive to a lot of law firms like his, so he hired a programmer and turned his attention to generalizing the application—making his highly customized, home-grown code into a program that would be usable by a lot of other patent and trademark attorneys, and maybe even other kinds of law firms. The program is called DocketWorks™ and, as you can see, Jack has it already trademarked. (Jack and I will talk about trademarks in a later chapter—what they are, how to get them. Jack will give you his business card.)

This, of course, is how many, if not most, new software products begin life—as a highly customized application that the creator wants to make into a best-seller.

After a couple years of development, Jack had become disenchanted with the programmer he had hired, and so Jack was looking around for a replacement. At my request, he e-mailed me the current database and application so I could give him my opinion of the state of the program and what it would take to get across the finish line.

After I looked at it, I had some good news for Jack. The database—the tables where the actual data was stored—was pretty well designed. And in the program itself there was a lot of functionality present.

But the bad news was 1) a lot of buttons weren't hooked up yet (that is, there was much functionality that was not yet implemented—doors leading to rooms that hadn't been built yet), and 2) the forms and reports were not very attractive. They were functional but, well, ugly. No color, controls all crammed together—hard to read and not intuitive.

By the way, I did not charge Jack for this analysis. To me, the first look at a potential application is a job interview. So if you find yourself in the position of having to hire a programmer, my first piece of advice (among many to come) is this: you can make your own judgment about programmers who charge their regular hourly fee just to see if they want to work for you.

My judgment is that it is not appropriate and should raise a red flag in your mind. Maybe they're so successful they need to charge for sales calls just to keep the riffraff away. From that kind of programmer you may not get the attention or timely response you need. Maybe they think that every word that drops from their lips is a pearl of great price. In any event, be cautious about paying someone just to look over your stuff.

Anyway, after looking over the database that he had had designed and the state of the program that he had had developed, I asked Jack for a kind of roadmap document on the design and implementation plan for the product to get a sense of just how far he'd come and how much road was ahead. Jack didn't have that, but he had a database he developed himself of some 150 action items—things the program needed, with priorities, subpriorities, and status. But this was more of a task list of unrelated items—some small, some big. And it wasn't the high-level plan I was looking for.

So I began to ask Jack some probing questions:

- What is the target market? Exactly who needs your product?

- What problem does your product solve?

- How are you going to price your product?

- Will you package it or distribute it electronically?

- How are you going to reach the people who would want it?

- How are you going to protect your software from illegal copies?

- Who is the competition?

- What advantage do you have over them?

- How will you track your leads and sales?

- Will you be asking for annual support fees?

- Speaking of support, how will you provide it—both technical and operational?

- Do you have a manual—planned or in process?

There were a number of technical issues as well:

- Will you use fixed screen resolution or form resizing?

- Will you require users to have Microsoft Access, or will you give them a runtime version?

- Do you have a consistent look for all forms and reports?

- Do you have a logo that appears in the same place on every form and report?

- Will you be using floating forms or full screen?

On and on it went.

And the answers to these questions were mostly that he hadn't yet really thought about these things. His focus was on making the software work. That's not a bad motivation, but it's kind of like starting to build a house without an architect and figuring to solve the problems as they arise. (If you find yourself in this position, you're reading the right book. You will need to reverse the process—to go back and do some serious design work before writing any more code. Keep reading.)

So I opened up a Word document and began to organize an outline of all the action items I could think of that Jack needed to do or think about in order to turn this raw program into a saleable product.

I kept that Word document open for three days. Every time I thought of something Jack needed to consider, I added it to the document. And at the end of that, we had a kind of rough roadmap to the finish line.

Looking over that document, I began to think about all the pain I suffered learning how to ask and answer the many questions that Jack hadn't considered when designing a software product for sale. I thought about all the great ideas for programs that never made it to the product stage or failed aborning for lack of good answers to these questions. I thought of all the folks out there who have a custom application they think would make a great product or just an idea for a piece of software they think would be a winner. And I thought about the path from idea to product and the big black box in between—a box that includes product design, development, testing, and packaging.

I looked over Jack's outline again and thought "Wouldn't this make a great book?"

# Why Am I a Programmer?

As I noted at the beginning of the chapter, I'm a programmer. I was a hacker before it became a criminal activity. A geek. A propeller head. I got my first exposure to computers as a high school student. But in those days, there were no computers in high school. To get near a computer, I had to take a weekend course at the Illinois Institute of Technology in Fortran programming. But I got to write and run simple Fortran programs on the university's massive second-generation IBM 7090 computer. It was behind a glass wall in a temperature-controlled environment. And it had a small fraction of the computing power of that three-pound notebook in your briefcase.

I wrote the programs for it on punched cards with 24-hour turnaround on each run. A misplaced comma meant a lost day. It was, viewed from today, awkward, expensive, clunky, and inconvenient.

But I thought I'd died and gone to heaven. There was something magical about the whole computer thing. I was starting to get hooked.

The college I went to had a computer, too. One. A lovely old IBM 1620 with actual hard drives and a printer the size of a Volkswagen that sounded like it was breaking concrete. It was replaced in my sophomore year by an IBM 360/40—a big box with about a thousand blinking lights on the front. I hung with the IBM engineer, and by the time school opened in the fall, I was the only one on campus who knew how to start and run the beast.

So the director offered me the job of systems manager, apologizing because it didn't pay much. "Pay?" I thought. "They'll pay me for what I'd do for nothing?" Now the hook was in but not yet set.

In my junior year, I decided to go for a proficiency grade in one of the school's few computer classes—do a big project, show you know the stuff, and skip the class work. So I wrote a program. Never mind what it was. It was just a utility program providing a feature for Fortran programmers that IBM hadn't provided. And I got my grade.

Then, I guess because I was a business student and kind of in training to be an entrepreneur, I decided to see if I could sell a couple of these jewels. But I couldn't afford to advertise, being a student, you know. So I sent out a press release to the few computer magazines that were in print at the time.

It got picked up by *Datamation*, and the staff gave me a reader service number so people could circle it if they were interested in my product (no Web at that time—it was 1968 and Al Gore hadn't thought of it yet). They would send me the leads (on sticky labels). I followed up with a letter and an order form.

For $40 (which was a couple of weeks' worth of student groceries in those days) the buyer got a deck of IBM punched cards with my program on them.

Imagine my surprise when people began sending me money. The hook was finally set. I got to play with the world's best toys, and people pushed money at me for doing it. How could it get any better?

Well, it did. My dream was to be rich enough and powerful enough one day to own my own computer. You're laughing. Yes, I now have seven, and a few more in the garage. Computers have evolved from expensive, remote, highly specialized machines, to appliances that almost everyone has and needs. In fact, they've become so ubiquitous, they are now an environmental waste problem.

But as soon as Radio Shack came out with that TRS-80 Model II computer around 1980, I moved from being gainfully employed to being a full-time, independent, self-employed slacker playing all day with microcomputers and thinking about how to get people to send me money as a by-product of all that play time.

The first thing I did was write a program for my wife, who wanted to start a business tracking sales leads for companies and sending out their product literature. That worked out pretty well. I was beginning to think I'd never have to have a regular job again.

Then, the fellow I was sharing office space with—a guy who, like me, was pretending to work while playing with these new personal computers—decided that a micro-based (we called personal computers "micros" in those days, until IBM came along and standardized our language) critical path project management system was something the world needed. Boy was he ever right about that.

The first products were sent out on 8-inch floppy disks and included a manual that was printed in uppercase on a dot matrix printer, with no real packaging. The program was called PMS-II (a lot of software in those days had the -II appended to it—a tribute to the pervasiveness of the Radio Shack TRS-80 Model II microcomputer). And we charged $3,000 a copy.

Those were heady days. There were no set rules for product creation and distribution. We made them up as we went along. So we couldn't really make any mistakes.

And the checks began to arrive.

Of course, eventually, Microsoft came out with Microsoft Project for $69, and the game was over.

But the hook was finally set so deep it would never come out.

Over the years, I have developed and sold other applications. A couple of them I'll use as examples in this book to illustrate points I'm trying to make.

## The Lone Ranger Rides Again

One product I'll often refer to is a venerable old manufacturing system named E-Z-MRP (www.e-z-mrp.com), designed for small manufacturers. Originally programmed in a DOS-based language on the old IBM PC, it was reinvented several years ago as a Windows-based product written in Microsoft Access. So most of the examples I use in this book are based an applications developed in Access. However, this book is not about programming but about creating a product. So, regardless of the programming language you use to make your product, this book will be both useful and pertinent.

By the time I decided to leave the world of gainful employment, I had, through no deliberate plan of my own, gained a lot of experience in manufacturing systems. One of the painfully obvious things about manufacturing systems was that only larger operations could afford the investment in dollars and time to implement manufacturing software.

But after the project management adventure, the rules had changed. I thought to myself "If a simplified interface could be designed so that the complex problem of controlling manufacturing could be understood and used by the lowest-level person in a manufacturing business, I could go after the bottom 90 percent of the market where there's no competition."

It took real hubris to create a product that everyone in the business said was impossible. But then entrepreneurs are not known for their humility. Or their aversion to risk.

Now, to create a good software product generally takes two skill sets. You need someone who knows how to code up a smooth, graceful, effective program. And you need someone who understands the application area.

In the case of E-Z-MRP, I happened to know both sides of the game. So I went alone on that one.

## It Takes Two to Tango, Sometimes

Another product I'll refer to throughout this book is The Sleep Advisor (www.thesleepadvisor.com)—a program for consumers that identifies sleep problems and provides remedies for solving them.

As I noted before, to create a good software product generally takes two skill sets—someone who knows programming and someone who is an expert in the application area. In the case of E-Z-MRP, I could sit on both sides of the table. But I didn't know squat about sleep or sleep problems. So as you can guess, it wasn't my idea to create this program.

In 1994 a colleague called me from Tucson with an interesting proposal. He was a clinical psychologist who had developed a unique expertise in the field of sleep disorders.

"Rocky," he said, "I'm doing these sleep consults every day." He explained to me, "I'm asking the same set of questions. I'm coming up with a predictable range of diagnoses, and offering people a finite set of recommendations for solving their sleep problems. Couldn't we write a computer program to do this?"

Being a software developer, I knew this would be much more challenging than it sounded. Being somewhat of a smart aleck, I responded, "Sure. Just tell me what the questions are that you ask, what the conditions are that you diagnose, and (here's the kicker) what the links are between the questions and the diagnoses. And violà! We've got ourselves a program."

So I went over to Tucson, we spread out the butcher block paper, and started to diagram what would eventually become The Sleep Advisor. After two days, we gave up. Translating the qualitative, intuitive approach of a clinical psychologist into a computer program was just too daunting.

But the idea wouldn't go away. We kept coming back to it. I had my doubts that it could ever be done—that a computer program could accurately identify sleep disorders based on the answers to a questionnaire. But we kept at it, off and on, for over ten years. And we finally got it to work. You can see the result at `www.thesleepadvisor.com`.

Partnering has distinct advantages. If you have expertise in the field that your program is made for, but you're not a professional programmer, you should try to team with a good programmer. If you're a programmer, you'll be way ahead of the game to join with someone who is an expert in the field.

Teaming has its obvious downside. Lone rangers don't have much problem with interpersonal conflicts. A partnership is like a marriage in many ways. You have to like each other, have good communication skills, and be willing to compromise what you think is right or best to achieve the goals of the partnership.

Of course, you can always buy the skill set you're missing. As a programmer, you can consult with experts in the field and pay them for their advice. If you're an expert in the field, like Jack Stone, you can hire the software design and programming skills you need.

# Who Are You?

So, do you want to be a millionaire? Do you have the dream—like Jack—of taking that custom application you developed (or haven't developed anywhere yet but in your imagination) and turning it into a product? Do you have a vision of sitting back and opening the morning mail and sorting out the checks? Do you see a river of money flowing into your PayPal account?

But are you stymied, intimidated, or otherwise reluctant to start down that long, dark road?

You are not alone—in either your dreams or your misgivings. But as the old Chinese saying starts "A journey of a thousand miles . . ."

One of the beauties of software is that you don't have to mortgage your house to develop it. It's largely sweat equity. But, in my experience, more people fail to realize their goals because they fail to start, rather than fail along the way. One of the dark sides of being a software entrepreneur is that you have to be self-motivated to be self-fulfilled. There will be no boss other than yourself who drives you to meet the goals and deadlines.

So you need to start. And I'm hoping that this book will give you the information and confidence you need to guide yourself from an idea to a product in-hand that's ready to sell.

# What's the Big Idea?

As I pointed out earlier, at this point in my "career," I happen to favor Microsoft Access as a development platform. I like the kind of Goldilocks applications that it's good for—not too big, not too small.

But programs come in all sizes. You might have an idea for a simple $39 utility program. Or your idea might turn into a $39,000 enterprise application. It may be a *horizontal* application—one which is used by many people, consumers or a wide variety of businesses, crossing many professional disciplines. Or it may be a *vertical* application—targeting a specific group of users.

Selection of your development platform—the language you choose for your program—is up to you. C, HTML, Access, SQL, Oracle—they're all good choices for the right program.

But regardless of the application, all software products have many things in common. And it is those common, generic topics that I have tried to cover in this book—answers to the kinds of questions that I asked Jack Stone. So that regardless of what the size and nature of your program is, and regardless of where you are in the process—not even in the starting gate or already out there flogging your software—this book will help you to reach a successful outcome and steer you around the many hazards and pitfalls that lurk unseen on the road to your first million.

# What This Book Is Really About

**This book is really about getting to your first day in business.**

It is about taking that raw idea you have for a program and creating a saleable product. And setting up the support systems you need to make your business hum.

If you're going to do this thing, you have to be ready for some tough days. But nothing worthwhile ever comes easy. Sometimes what it really takes is stupid, blind obstinacy—the drive to keep going, stubbornly solving one problem at a time until you get the brass ring.

Once I had a partner who had one of those ghastly motivational posters hung in our office. You know, the kind that promotes leadership and teamwork and quality through the use of tired old clichés and kitschy art. This one was no exception. And yet its corny McCuen-esque message stuck in my mind and has provided a handy boost to me many times over the years. It was a picture of a three-masted sailing ship threading its way between rocky outcropping and small islands. And the message:

*Obstacles are what you see when you take your eye off the goal.*

# How They Did It: An Interview with Software Developer and Entrepreneur Al Vanderpool

*I partnered with Al Vanderpool at the beginning of the personal computer revolution and had a hand in the development and marketing of what was then one of the first commercial applications for personal computers, a critical path project management system named PMS-II—the name reflecting the popularity of the Radio Shack Model II computer, which was the state-of-the-art machine at that time.*

*Although he is no longer developing and marketing software, Vanderpool's depth of experience in the software industry creating profitable products and businesses makes his a voice worth listening to. Pay particular attention to the advice he has at the end of the interview for the wannabe software entrepreneur.*

**Smolin:** You're a software developer.

**Vanderpool:** That's correct.

**Smolin:** And, how did you become a software developer?

**Vanderpool:** Well, I've been in computers since the early '60s with General Electric and I was doing a lot of technical support, and then I had the opportunity to go on my own, and lo and behold I wound up writing software. So it was not a conscious decision, it was an afterthought.

**Smolin:** So, the first commercial program you did was . . .

**Vanderpool:** PMS-II.

**Smolin:** And that was in, if I recall, around 1980?

**Vanderpool:** Yes, late '70s, early '80s.

**Smolin:** And that was a critical path project management system.

**Vanderpool:** Right.

**Smolin:** Why did you want to create a critical path project management system? Where'd the idea come from?

**Vanderpool:** Interestingly enough, I had bought a Radio Shack Model II computer when they first came out, and I was looking for something to play with on it, just something to do, and we decided to track our fertility cycle in the hopes of creating a girl.

**Smolin:** You and your wife.

**Vanderpool:** Yeah. So I wrote some date functions and some methods of calculating forward and backwards from dates and coming up with the right things. And then I thought, "Gee, this is the heart and soul of a critical path project management system," which I'd had a lot of experience with at General Electric and Honeywell in the past. Using, not creating. That was the nub of the idea, and from that I started using it in my consulting business for very simple scheduling. And then it started to grow and started to get embellished. I created reports from it, and I was using it myself in my consulting practice. So that's how it all came about. And then I met Rocky Smolin, and he published an article about it in one of the computer rags at the time called *Information Age*, and the phone started ringing, and we decided to go ahead and make it a full-fledged product.

**Smolin**: So you wrote this in which language originally?

**Vanderpool**: Originally it was written in Microsoft Basic, and then it was converted to a Digital Research language so it could be compiled to protect the source code.

**Smolin**: C-Basic.

**Vanderpool**: C-Basic or CB86, a 16-bit BASIC. And then to make it all happen, because languages and supporting software and utilities were pretty crude and pretty user-unfriendly at the time, I added a library of functions to it, replacing the original stuff. That library was from a company called Minnow Bear, or something like that. It had all kinds of expanded capabilities to it which really made the program capable of doing what it needed to be done, which was managing construction projects for larger construction firms, RCA being the first user.

**Smolin**: So this was the first product you commercialized?

**Vanderpool**: This was the first commercial product that I ever created.

**Smolin**: Who was the target user? Before you started to sell it, who did you have in mind to sell it to?

**Vanderpool**: The original idea immediately went to the construction industry because the need was there and they didn't have any tools, or all the tools they did have were extremely expensive and very hard to use, and so they didn't do what they should be doing with them. So the thought was to give them a lower priced, easy to use desktop computer capability so that they'd be able to do a much better job. That was the target market at the time.

**Smolin**: And the Radio Shack Model II was the state of the art at that point.

**Vanderpool**: That was the Ferrari of the day.

**Smolin**: So you sent the product out on 8-inch floppy disks?

**Vanderpool**: 8-inch floppies, yeah.

**Smolin**: How long did that product run, how many years did you flog that jewel?

**Vanderpool**: Probably, easily ten to twelve years of product life on it. Mostly because of the add-on capabilities and additional products that it gave birth to that were supporting it—resource management, graphics, production support, materials management, reporting systems, that type of thing.

**Smolin:** As the technology evolved, did you change platforms, or was it always C-Basic DOS?

**Vanderpool:** It was always C-Basic DOS, with more capabilities as Windows came online, more features were added to the library to take advantage of what was available in Windows, to whatever extent we could. Windows was pretty crude at the time.

**Smolin:** What eventually stopped the sales, or why did you stop selling it?

**Vanderpool:** I stopped selling the product as a conscious decision because the support revenue from it was exceeding the sales revenue for it, and I saw no sense in spinning the wheel of advertising for zero to negative gain. So by stopping the product sale and concentrating on end-user support and relicensing and annual support contracts, it produced a revenue stream for many, many more years until I finally just told everybody, no you can't renew, and no I'm not going to answer the phone anymore. That was the end of it. That was probably mid '90s before that ended. So it had a complete run of maybe fifteen, sixteen years, which is extraordinary for sure.

**Smolin:** You went on and did a second product?

**Vanderpool:** One of my PMS-II users from the Los Angeles area who had taken the course at Brigham Young—they used to teach PMS-II at Brigham Young University graduate curriculum for construction management—and this young guy was really a cost estimator for a construction company who saw the program, and he called me one day and said, "Hey, I took your class. Is there a way I could come down and talk to you? I have an idea." So I said sure.

He comes down and he starts talking about the problems that the construction companies have in soliciting bids and getting responses from bids. Most of the general contractors had stopped doing anything of a specialty work, they were just contracting. And they needed some support with cost estimating. So he laid out this idea for a fax machine–driven application, and I said that doesn't sound too tough. Give me a fax card that goes in a computer and I'll figure it out.

About six weeks later, we had a product that allowed a contractor to specify what trades were needed on a particular project and then go through their database of subcontractors, select all of the local subs that met the criteria, and send them a fax inviting them to bid on this project. That product was called BidFax. It was a wonderful title. It became the Coca-Cola of the industry. People would say, "Did you say get a BidFax on that?", and that's when you know you've done something right. It was a very, very good product for us. I sold that to McGraw-Hill about 1998, I think.

**Smolin:** You said it was about six weeks to get it from conception to where you were ready to sell it.

**Vanderpool**: Essentially, get it from conception to Beta testing so that we could take it to a live construction company and let them use it on a limited basis.

**Smolin**: How long was it in Beta?

**Vanderpool**: I'd say probably about two months with revisions and enhancements before we felt like we had a saleable product.

**Smolin**: What language was that one in?

**Vanderpool**: That was also written in CB86—the same thing that PMS-II was done in, utilizing the libraries that I'd already developed there, so it was fairly easy to construct a new application using the framework that was already there.

**Smolin**: Did you do all the programming?

**Vanderpool**: I wrote the entire thing, yeah.

**Smolin**: And PMS-II as well?

**Vanderpool**: Yep. Well, not all of the stuff in PMS-II, there were a few contributors along the way, but I did the primary work on it, yep.

**Smolin**: How much did it cost you in dollars, to get that, either one of those, ready?

**Vanderpool**: Well, PMS-II was a, I think, early-on product in the microcomputer revolution if you will. I put $30,000 into the company to start with, and I think I spent $7,000 of it before we had positive revenue, and we had positive revenue from then on out. So the real cost of it was quite incidental to the overall value of it. The second product, BidFax, I would say I probably invested, not counting my time, but just actual out of house investment, probably another $20,000 into that product for the packaging, and you know, all of the legal protection, etc., to put it together. But again, doesn't count my time, I'm cheap [*laughter*].

**Smolin**: Were either of those products copy protected? Or how did you enforce deterrence against illegal copies?

**Vanderpool**: Interestingly enough, BidFax was attacked by that very thing. There was a rip-off copy of it that was created. It was called . . . some two-word acronym.

**Smolin**: Was it a knock-off, or was it actually your code that they stole and made copies of?

**Vanderpool**: The core of it was my code, and then they put a different face on it and just the display part of it was changed just to make it look different. And they advertised it—they even copied our advertising, etc. We had a lot of hassle with them. They . . . [used] negative marketing, which is something no one should ever do; their marketing message was, "Don't buy that; buy this because that's bad." It came around and put them out of business.

When I sold the BidFax product line to McGraw-Hill Publishing to add to their contractor estimating systems, that was the end of that product line, took me a year to get out of it but the copy protection was . . . well almost have to go back . . . BidFax had a different method of distributing. We didn't distribute it via diskettes. It was distributed online. I think it was probably the first online software distribution that had an online update distribution in the industry that I'm aware of. I don't remember anybody doing this before that. But because of the capabilities of the onboard fax cards that the customer already had to have installed, it was a very simple thing for me to send them a key for that computer, once they'd paid for it, and then it would come to my computers and say "Here's my key. Do I have a valid key to get software?" So it was essentially very much like the licensing agreements you see today. Then it would download the system, install it, and run it. Every month it would self-check itself, come back to my system, see if there were any updates, and download those automatically for the user. So they found great value to always having fresh, up-to-date, bug-free software automatically on their system.

**Smolin:** So the problem with somebody giving it to somebody else, could they do that?

**Vanderpool:** I never became aware of anyone copying it as a user and reusing seven copies in their company, because if they did, their key wouldn't work again. I had a secure key that was hidden in a system file on their computer which they didn't even know about. If it wasn't there, then the update service wouldn't work, and it would just turn itself back off. So that was a real crude, I guess you could say that's a very crude, early beginning copy protection system that proved to be pretty effective.

**Smolin:** Was PMS-II copy protected in any way on the user side?

**Vanderpool:** I don't recall ever doing any copy protection on that. The industry was so young. It was so new, you know microcomputers and selling software for microcomputers was so early in the game that I don't think people even thought about stealing things off of computers at the time.

**Smolin:** So how did you price PMS-II?

**Vanderpool:** I wish I could say, you know, that it was a deliberate act and that there were some value considerations going on there, but basically in the early conversations we had with RCA they said, "Well, we want it," and I said, "Well, I don't want to sell it," and they said, "Well, we'll give you $1,000 a copy for it," and I said, "Well, how about $2,000," and they said, "Well, how about $1,500." And we agreed at $1,300, and that's how it got priced, $1,295, and it stayed that price for its entire life.

**Smolin:** And the BidFax, what'd you sell that for?

**Vanderpool:** Well, BidFax was, you know, after Broderbund or whatever their name was, the people that came in and said sell everything for $99 type of thing. BidFax pricing was a different consideration. It was a logical thought-through value analysis type of thing and considered all the distribution costs and all of the things we had learned in the prior years and came to a price on it of $595, which was an extremely good value for people at the time. They were spending more than that every time they wanted to do a bid just in clerical support to send out all of the notices. Postage was that much. So they just, it was never even a moment's thought process. It was never a decision point. It was, "OK. Here. Here's the money. And away you go."

**Smolin:** For PMS-II you had ongoing support revenue stream.

**Vanderpool:** Right.

**Smolin:** Did you have that for BidFax as well

**Vanderpool:** Yes, yes. That was the other side of it. I figured the way I came out with the original number was all of my distribution costs amortizing the hardware necessary to do it electronically and all of that sort of stuff came out to about what we were charging for the product plus the commission for the people that were selling it. So that was a break-even as far as I was concerned and recapturing the investment for what I perceived to be a much smaller market than what actually turned out to be. My revenue stream on it was online support and continuous support. For that we charged $400 a year, and I still have people trying to buy it today.

**Smolin:** So both of these applications were single user, not networked?

**Vanderpool:** Basically, yes.

**Smolin:** OK. So you sold it single-price for a license?

**Vanderpool:** BidFax, we did eventually have a multiproduct package for it. But it was simply multiple keys, you buy six copies of the single at a discounted price, and that was fine with everybody.

**Smolin:** Did the original PMS-II program give rise to variations on that product?

**Vanderpool:** No, but it had ancillary products added to it.

**Smolin:** You didn't have a PMS-III.

**Vanderpool:** No.

**Smolin:** But you had add-ons.

**Vanderpool:** We had add-ons that expanded its capabilities into manufacturing, into facilities management, in different areas where scheduling was still the core but resource management and material flow management were just as important. They had to feed into the schedule at a particular time. So I wrote modules that added those capabilities down the road. Plus, presentation graphics, plotters, things like that the bigger firms needed.

**Smolin:** Where did the ideas for these add-ons come from?

**Vanderpool:** The place that all good ideas for products should come from—from your customer base. These were needs that were identified, verbalized by customers, that you take and create a satisfaction of that need. When your customer base is already established, and they have a need that's not being satisfied, it's almost automatic. It's predefined.

**Smolin:** And the BidFax, same kind of evolution?

**Vanderpool:** Well, BidFax continued to grow, and the only add-on products that became available for it were packaged databases, geographical databases for subcontractors by specialties. Using the Construction Specification Institute's coding structure, we were able to take [data] from existing clients that wanted to get involved in a cooperative process, and these were usually the multiple office type construction companies, the Bechtels, the Fluors, those types of companies, where they had operations that were all over the world. They had these databases, and then essentially we made arrangements to use them.

**Smolin:** So you interfaced BidFax with third-party databases?

**Vanderpool:** Third-party databases. Of subs. Contractors. And that then became a new licensing revenue source without any production costs to it at all. Which is why McGraw-Hill wanted to buy this system from me because that's what they did, they licensed databases. So it was a natural to fit right along with BidFax.

**Smolin:** It sounds like you didn't face any big problems bringing PMS-II to market. The market kind of drew you in once you presented it?

**Vanderpool:** More than anything, I think, when the original article was published, it was incredibly surprising when people started calling and went to the trouble of finding the office phone number and everything to call and say they wanted to buy it. Marketing that kind of a product became much more complex as the industry grew, to the point where the advertising cost far outweighed any other cost.

**Smolin:** I remember at the time it was exciting because there were no channels of distribution. There were no precedents. There were no pricing models. There was no competition.

**Vanderpool:** It was a blank blackboard, fill it out yourself.

**Smolin:** So we had to make up our own rules.

**Vanderpool:** Yep.

**Smolin:** In case of the BidFax, did you have any problems getting that one launched?

**Vanderpool:** Well, BidFax had its own defined distribution channel because the guy that came to me with the original idea where there was no concept problem, he wanted to get involved in software distribution himself. So I sublicensed the system back to him for distribution, and that's where the $495 came out. That covered all of those costs, and I didn't worry about it. He didn't take any part of the ongoing revenue; he just did the original sales. He did a very good job of using the existing distribution channels that were out there. Some of the independent stores were still in business then which are now all gone. But there were also outlets that specialized in different products for the construction industry that just added this to their bag and took it right in. It went national in two weeks. Two weeks to it spread[ing] all over the country.

**Smolin:** So you didn't have to do any research on the market or the competition?

**Vanderpool:** Well, there was no competition. It was a noncompetitive environment. There was nothing to even begin to compare to it.

**Smolin:** Did you trademark both of these products?

**Vanderpool:** Yes. All of it was trademarked.

**Smolin:** Did you write a manual for BidFax?

**Vanderpool:** The BidFax system came with a printed installation card which was two-sided, three-sided at one time, triple fold, that just showed them how to get online and how to get hooked up and get it going. The entire manual was built right into the software so it was distributed right along with the code. The entire user guide, training guide, and everything was online.

**Smolin:** You did have a manual, but it wasn't a hard-copy manual?

**Vanderpool:** Not a hard copy.

**Smolin:** All electronic. And how long did that take you to write?

**Vanderpool:** Probably about five times as long as it took to write the software [*laughter*]. That's a big chore that only the people that have done it have any idea how much resource it takes to create a reasonable user guide, because people are not very intelligent that use software and everything has to be triple supported; otherwise they don't get it.

**Smolin:** Was there a PMS-II manual?

**Vanderpool:** Yes. It was a huge PMS-II manual. It was like the *Webster's Dictionary* type of thing.

**Smolin:** As I recall, it originally went out in uppercased dot matrix, paper that was torn apart.

**Vanderpool:** [*laughter*] Yeah, that was the original.

**Smolin:** Continuous tractor feed paper, yeah, and three-hole punched.

**Vanderpool:** You got it, by yours truly. It finally evolved into about a 3-inch-thick three-ring binder with tabs and dividers, and that was just the PMS manual. Each of the add-ons had a 1-inch manual that went with them. The cost of distributing a hard-copy manual and the cost of maintaining the information that's in a hard-print manual is . . . unbelievable until you've experienced it.

**Smolin:** I guess those days are over.

**Vanderpool:** I hope.

**Smolin:** It's pretty much twentieth century technology.

**Vanderpool:** Yeah, oh yeah.

**Smolin:** How often did you release updates? Was it sporadic or scheduled?

**Vanderpool:** PMS-II had a pretty rigid schedule; I would say at least once every forty-five days there was an update to the system. We kind of worked on that kind of a schedule for it. BidFax, because it was online for distribution, and it was updated automatically through the user's system, that was an ongoing process. We kept that [schedule], pretty much, do a feature, release it, do a feature, release it. Bug fixes are obviously something that has to be factored into the equation early on.

PMS-II was very bug prone when we first released it. But after a couple of years of maturity out there, it was as close to a bug-free piece of software as I've ever seen anywhere. BidFax, being built on that base, pretty much hit the road pretty close to bug free. It did have some hardware glitches with the fax card in its early days, but all of that got resolved with the better drivers, etc. It was about as solid as a Sherman tank going down the road.

**Smolin:** So you didn't use a commercial installer for either one?

**Vanderpool:** There weren't any commercial installers at that point in time. And again, going a different route, looking at the experience that we had with PMS-II and sending things out by post, etc., versus electronic distribution, it just made no sense to do anything beside electronic. Again, it was painless for the end user. They just answered the question that was asked and put in the code and bang, bang, it came up for them. So that's kind of the model that we're on today I think.

**Smolin:** How long did it take your typical user to learn to use PMS-II?

**Vanderpool:** To learn PMS-II, sometimes it required them coming in and actually going to school. It was the subject itself. The use of the software was incidental to understanding the technique and how to apply it to the business model that they were in. So, that was the bigger training issue there, how to schedule, not necessarily how to use the software to schedule. It was pretty much straightforward if you understood what you were trying to accomplish. Then how the software went about doing it was pretty straightforward.

**Smolin:** Two, three days of training? Or a week?

**Vanderpool:** At max, yeah.

**Smolin:** And BidFax?

**Vanderpool:** BidFax was originally created to be done the way they were doing it manually, so the transfer of information, the approach they took, the step they took doing things manually were just automated and simplified. And they took to that like a duck to water. It was like almost no training period whatsoever. Learning the terminology and setting up their database took a little bit more assistance, but to use their software once they got subcontractors set up in a correct database was incidental.

**Smolin**: So implementation time for PMS-II, I know it could take forever, but optimally?

**Vanderpool**: I would say it was probably a two-month minimum cycle for them to come up to speed in PMS-II.

**Smolin**: And how about BidFax?

**Vanderpool**: Maybe a day, two at the most.

**Smolin**: What kind of learning and implementation problems did you encounter with people and what did you do about them?

**Vanderpool**: I think one of the things that most software writers still make a mistake with is putting their system in their terms as opposed to their users' terms. I think a lot of the implementation problems that I've experienced and had to come back and solve were due to terminology that was familiar to me but not familiar to the end user—BidFax being an excellent example of that. There's a Construction Specification Institute and everybody knows that as the Contractor Code. And I, of course, called it the Construction Specification Institute's code, and nobody knew what the heck I was talking about. So it was the technical versus the real-life usage of terminology.

**Smolin**: Did you do custom modifications for either of these products?

**Vanderpool**: PMS-II got a lot of custom modifications coming in from real users across the spectrum from small to huge corporations. Many, many, many parts of its features came from the user base themselves. Custom modifications were actually paid for by the contractor that wanted them with the understanding that they would then be supported as part of the full release. So the exchange for them was this gets supported for me, and everybody else gets to use it too, but I get it first.

**Smolin**: How did you handle the problem of having custom modifications that weren't appropriate for all users? Did you support multiple versions, or did you make it invisible somehow? How did you finesse that problem?

**Vanderpool**: Because so much of the changes to the project management system were techniques and existing improvements in the technology of managing projects with critical path network methods, everybody could take advantage of the features. If they couldn't, if it wasn't a general appeal feature, I made it cost prohibitive to them, and they opted to not do it that way. Or I gave them an alternative that was not cost prohibitive but everybody could use. So a little bartering, a little meeting midway. I think if you have something that does something for everybody, then you have something that doesn't do anything for anybody.

**Smolin:** So all of the custom modifications made for PMS-II became generic or part of the standard package?

**Vanderpool:** Part of the standard offering.

**Smolin:** How about BidFax?

**Vanderpool:** BidFax didn't require very much of that at all because we had a much more extensive Alpha-Beta cycle on it. So it pretty much was ready to go and didn't get much change. The only changes that occurred to it in general were things having to do with the hardware support itself or fax cards as they matured as a piece of hardware that we were relying on better, faster, you know, smarter. Custom mods, other than changing terminology, not that much.

And it also had a much shorter lifespan. BidFax was a four-year product because by the time it had reached its maturity point, technology had already replaced it. The Internet became what we know it is today. It became apparent that that was the way everything was going to go. And in fact, the guy that had the original idea created a company called Buzzsaw, which was going to be huge and everybody got involved with it. But unfortunately they weren't paying attention, and all the money went away [*laughter*]. The dot-com bubble burst, and it got swept aside.

**Smolin:** No business model but plenty of hope.

**Vanderpool:** Lots of money coming in but no revenue.

**Smolin:** If somebody came to you and said, "You know, Al, I've got a great idea for a product. I've got half a program written. I'm going to do this," if you had only one piece of advice to give them to keep them from going off the rails, what would you tell them?

**Vanderpool:** That's an interesting question because I just recently had that question come up using the Nextel push-to-talk telephone systems, which are now available on a lot of carriers. They came to me with a product idea, and I said, "Define your market. Give me a market definition. Who is it and how are you going to reach them and why are they going to buy it from you?" They couldn't do that, and after four years of the owner and his friends pouring their money into it, mortgaging their dad's salvage company, etc., etc., etc., they went away. It was a great idea, a fantastic product idea, but they never defined their market. The market is more important than the product. Market definition.

**Smolin:** It was a solution in search of a problem?

**Vanderpool:** Absolutely. And if you don't know how you're going to get that solution out there, then you have no business whatsoever being in this business. Because this is an expensive business to be in these days. Great rewards, great risks. You can't do it in the old style that I've done it. In today's environment, market definition is the number one thing that I would say. If you don't have that, I'm not interested in the rest of your conversation because you've got nothing.

**Smolin:** I see by the old clock on the wall that our time is about up here. In fact, I just finished the questions.

**Vanderpool:** Great, great. I hope it was useful information.

**Smolin:** I hope it's on the little recorder thingies here.

**Vanderpool:** Might want to check.

**Smolin:** No, I don't want to know.

# So What Do I Do First?

If you have started writing your program, the first thing you need to do is stop. If you haven't started writing it yet, don't. There are a few things you need to do before you get to the code writing stage.

## Define Your Product

To beat on the old house-building cliché once more, you need an architect before you start to build. And even before the architect can start to design, they need a broad statement from you about what you want: "I want a Cape Cod-style house of about 3500 square feet, with three bedrooms but expandable in case we have more kids." There. That gives your architect a starting point—a broad vision of what kind of house you want.

Of course, you're the architect. You'll also be the general contractor, and maybe the subcontractors, and also perhaps the plumber, bricklayer, electrician, etc. So in this process of defining your product, and later in creating the more detailed system specification, you'll be talking to yourself a lot.

Now you may think you know what your program does, but I have found that a couple of well-crafted sentences defining your product not only helps clarify what it does and who it's for, but may reveal to you some surprising information about the product and its market.

Here's an example. Many years ago I wrote and still sell a system for small manufacturers called E-Z-MRP (www.e-z-mrp.com). Here's how I define the product:

> **E-Z-MRP** *is an integrated manufacturing system designed for manufacturers from startup to $20 million. It is designed for people who have little or no experience with manufacturing systems. The primary purpose of E-Z-MRP is to tell users every day what to make and what to buy in order to meet their customer commitments. It provides complete material and production planning and execution, inventory control, a powerful Bill of Materials Processor, will print purchase orders, and includes a Capacity Planning module so that the user can do work center loading and capacity planning as well.*

Yeah, it's a yawner. But it's only for my own internal purposes—to clarify in my mind exactly what my program is really about. Your product definition should include not only a pithy statement or two about the primary purpose of the product and its major functionality, but also who wants or needs it.

Here's another one that I codesigned and wrote (www.thesleepadvisor.com):

> **The Sleep Advisor** *is an expert system that identifies a variety of sleep problems and disorders. It is designed for consumers to be run in the privacy of their own homes and generates a comprehensive customized report of the identified sleep problems and remedies, and recommendations for resolving these problems and improving sleep health.*

Again, I have identified 1) what the primary purpose of the program is, and 2) who (hopefully) wants it.

So now it's your turn. Fashion your product statement, print it out, and keep it around to remind you of what you're doing and where you're going.

# How to Be Your Own Systems Analyst: Making a System Specification

There's nothing like a complete, detailed product specification to have in hand before you write the first line of code. But it's an awful lot of work to do. And you may not need that depth of detail. But like having an architect draw up a plan before you start building your house, you do need some kind of system specification before you start programming.

Or, if your program has already been written, or even if your programming has only been started, you need to go back and do this so you can correct all the problems you created by programming without a plan. That's not necessarily a bad thing. A lot of custom programs get written without a spec. They evolve from legal pad to Excel spreadsheet to program without much forethought.

But now you want to turn your program into a product. That's a whole different game. So in the rest of this chapter, I'd like to show you how to create a product specification which contains just the level of detail you need to write a program that can be turned into a successful product.

Therefore, the next step after writing that brief but elegant definition of your product is to create the software equivalent of an architect's plan—a more detailed specification of exactly what your program does. I know that this might seem a bit boring or tedious, but trust me, it will pay off big down the road. So push through this task. You'll end up with a plan for success.

## Systems Analysis in Sixty Seconds: Input, Process, Output, Storage

In a large organization, defining a program is the job of a systems analyst. The systems analyst stands between the programmer and the end user, and translates the needs of the end user into a specification that the programmer can understand.

Again, if you have already created some customized program that you're thinking of turning into a saleable product, you may believe that this step is unnecessary. After all, the program is done. But just like the previous exercise of defining your product, this process never fails to bring to light or clarify fundamental features and processes that you may have overlooked, poorly designed, or awkwardly implemented in your current program.

The level of detail you want to put into this specification is entirely up to you. It's for your own use, and so you don't have to make it more detailed than you need for your own purposes. I have done this for myself and my clients on many occasions, and it always pays off in the end. It's not nearly as much fun as programming, but it may be the best spent time on your whole project.

So how do you approach this job of creating a product specification? Well, all systems, manual or automated, have common functions and can be modeled as in Figure 2-1.

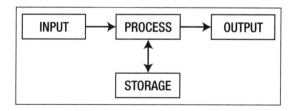

**Figure 2-1.** The Archetypal System

All systems, computer programs or not, can be broken out into these four functions:

1. What goes into the program (**INPUT**)

2. How the input information is manipulated (**PROCESS**)

3. What information is delivered to the user (**OUTPUT**)

4. What data will be stored (**STORAGE**)

Even the simplest utility program can be described by these four functions.

Note that this approach is very **user oriented**, not **programmer oriented**. After all, the program should be defined by what the user needs, not what the programmer thinks is cool. So all of the results of your analysis **must** be governed by what the users must have to solve the problems they're facing. As a systems analyst, the view that I always take is this: my loyalty is to the user, not the programmer. When I come to a design feature that would be "nice for the user," but "difficult for the programmer," the user always wins.

## What Comes Out?

You start this process of defining your product in the **OUTPUT** box. This starting point may look counterintuitive—the **output** looks like the last thing on the Archetypal System diagram. However, all software is designed to solve a problem—to provide information so the user can make a decision or take some action. So ask yourself two questions:

1. What problem is my user trying to solve?

2. What information does the user need out of my program to solve that problem?

### How Detailed Do I Have to Make This Output Specification?

How detailed should your output specification be? It should be just detailed enough to allow you to create these outputs when the time comes. No more. Being a congenitally lazy person, I don't believe in doing any more work than I have to. So I give you the same advice.

In the case of The Sleep Advisor, the answer was fairly simple. Stated in terms the user might use, "I'm not sleeping well. Tell me what my sleep problems are, what's causing them, and how to fix them."

That specification is at the simplest, most basic level. If you're ambitious or see value in being more detailed, you can specify how the reports identifying sleep problems and remedies will be structured—kind of an outline. More rigorous would be to create a sample report showing the format—what font, point size, color, dividing lines, margins, etc. If you're really anal, you can go all the way down to the actual text that will be generated by the program.

In the case of the E-Z-MRP manufacturing system, the answer was a bit more complicated because the application was much more complex. The simplest answer is, "Tell me every day what to make and what to buy so that I can finish on time to ship my products and meet my customer commitments."

But because so many more functions exist in an integrated manufacturing system, many more outputs need to be defined. Manufacturers need inventory reports, purchase orders, production schedules, kit lists, bills of material, cash flow projections—a whole constellation of reports covering many different aspects of their manufacturing operation.

Again, the specification of your outputs might be as simple as a list of reports produced by your program. Or it may go right down to mock-ups of each report showing the size and location of every data field and label.

My opinion? At a minimum, your output specification for each report should include 1) the data fields to be included, 2) the options for sorting the report in different ways, and 3) the kinds of filters or data selection criteria to be offered.

## How Do I Know What the User Really Wants Out?

To know what the user really wants may require a bit of research. The application you are thinking of turning into a product is probably something you already know a bit about, hopefully a lot. So you already think you know what the user needs and, in fact, with luck you may not be too far off the target. If you're fortunate, you're working with a partner who has practical experience in the field and can answer the question with some authority.

Now here's where the good applications get separated from the bad applications. Remember, you are not writing a program, you're fashioning a solution. The people who are going to pay you good money for your solution want a problem solved. They really don't want to buy, learn, and use software. For them, it's a necessary evil. They just want to have their questions answered, and the faster and more completely your program answers those questions, the more money you'll make.

In many, perhaps most, cases, your application, like DocketWorks, began life as a highly customized program written for a specific company. Now you're going to generalize this program to make it work for a number of other companies—hopefully, a very large number.

But how many companies have you worked in or are familiar with that have the same problems and needs as the one using your custom program? Does your program satisfy their need for information? Will they like your current report formats?

There are a lot of ways to find out. Industrial espionage is a good start. Go to the Web and look at the competing products. They'll probably have a list of outputs, maybe some reprints of typical reports. How do your ideas stack up against a product that's already being used? Many vendors will have their user manual downloadable on their web site or will provide a copy of their user manual to you at no charge. Take advantage of what lawyers like to call "free discovery." I am not ashamed to admit that when I did the original design spec for my manufacturing system, E-Z-MRP, I used the manual of a midrange manufacturing system on the theory that their successful product had the suite of reports that most users wanted.

Now I know you want to get on with the programming. That's the fun part. That's what I like. But everyone who writes a program for sale takes their best guess about what outputs the users really need, and they proceed on those assumptions to create their product.

And, because we generally have some experience in the application area, we all hit more or less close to the center of the target. But the difference between a good program and a great one is the one that makes the user exclaim, "That EXACTLY what I need!"

Now, there's one best way to find out what your users need, and that is to take the output spec you've created here—hopefully a batch of well-formatted sample reports, along with the sorting, filtering, and other criteria that govern the order and content of the reports—and go visit your friends and colleagues in other similar companies that either have the problem or have solved the problem your program attacks.

Show them your reports, tell them what you're about, and then LISTEN to what they say. Leave your ego at the door. Don't get hung up defending your design decisions. You're there to hear what you've done wrong. It can be a bit humbling, but what these folks are doing is defining a successful product for you.

While you're there, ask them about the business rules and processes that create the information they use, and the business rules and processes that are affected by this information. You will almost inevitably be surprised to discover some basic business process that you've overlooked or didn't even know about. You'll need information like this for the subsequent steps in the specification process. Releasing a product missing this feature would be at a minimum embarrassing; at worst, it would sink the product. It would betray to the prospects your lack of understanding about their basic business processes and procedures and cause them to lose confidence in you and your program.

Now, go back to the drawing board, list all the things they told you, and then DO THOSE THINGS. These first viewers are defining and refining your product for you. They are telling you where the center of the target is.

If you feel they "didn't understand what your program is about," then you probably don't understand what your program is about or who your target market is. These are both points that you need to clarify NOW, before you go any further. You should come away from these meetings with a positive feeling. A little depressed is OK, but you should feel that the holes and weaknesses you discovered are valuable and can be remedied.

## A First, But Certainly Not the Last, Word About Testing

Carefully defining the outputs of your application will pay double dividends down the road—because after your program's working, but before you go to market, you'll need to test it. OK, you actually need a **lot** of other people to test it.

I'll talk more about this testing process in the next chapter. But for the moment, suffice it to say that you'll need some testers—people who will be willing to put up with some bugs to have your program working for them. These folks will also provide valuable feedback about your program—what's good and bad about it, what's particularly useful, where it's awkward to use, what's missing. In effect, these testers will refine your product definition for you.

And, if your output spec hits close to the center of the target, some of the folks you poll for feedback are going to express a bit of enthusiasm for the product. Great! Ask if they would kindly agree to test your program once it's ready. And put them on your tester list.

## What You Don't Want to Hear

Finally, be ready to hear some really bad news—that your program is so far wide of the mark it's not even on the target. Or that your program is a solution in search of a problem that may not even exist. Could be one of the toughest days of your life.

But business is risk. And if you're going to take a risk with thousands of hours of your life and perhaps thousands of your dollars (or someone else's), you want to lower that risk as much as possible.

The world is full of slick ideas that simply aren't needed by more than a handful of people. On the other hand, the world is full of problems that need solving. And in my experience, once-in-a-lifetime opportunities don't come along more than two or three times a year.

You've got the energy and enthusiasm to write and sell a product, or you wouldn't be reading this book. Just be sure the product you're contemplating has a real chance of success.

The first few folks who look at your design will be your canary in the coal mine. If they start singing, you may be on to something. If they get that glazed look in their eye, you might want to rethink the project.

## *A Digression: Data vs. Information*

Because computers are so powerful and flexible, it's easy to overwhelm your user with output. In fact, there is a somewhat naïve view that says that the more comprehensive the reporting capabilities of my program, the greater will be the perceived value of the product.

This is true, but only up to the point where the system begins to generate outputs that the users don't need or want, but instead have to wade through lots of screens or hit lots of keys to find what they really need. To help determine exactly where to draw the line on outputs, it is helpful to make a distinction between **data** and **information**.

**Data** is passive. It just lays there staring up at you, mute and uninformative. **Information** is data that causes the user to make a decision, change direction, or take some action.

For example, a customer list sorted by company name might be **information** to the user because that's the list they need. But because you also have phone numbers, fax number, e-mail addresses, and street addresses in the customer record, you could easily provide reports sorted by these fields. But a customer list sorted by street address is likely to be just **data** to your users. They'll never use it to make a decision or take some action.

So what's the harm? Well, each feature you add to your program adds a level of complexity. It's a feature that you as the developer have to maintain. It's a feature that you as the developer need to train your users to use (or not to use). And it's a feature that the user needs to learn. It also requires some kind of control on the screen so that the user can use it.

Overstuffing your output spec with cool but arcane reports and options can eventually result in the worst of all possible outcomes—a report suite that produces many reports of marginal value using a process that is so complex and difficult to learn and use that your users don't ever use it. And those who evaluate your program decide to look somewhere else for a simpler solution.

Your admirable motivation to provide comprehensive reporting has backfired. You produced a failing product. (Make a mental note to pay close attention to the section "When to Stop Programming" in Chapter 6.)

So remember that stuff that seems to fall out of your application for free actually has a hidden cost. You must create a balance in your outputs between comprehensiveness and complexity. Ideally, all your outputs provide **information**.

## What Is Stored?

The collection of data stored in tables, files, or whatever is commonly called a **database**. So that's how we'll be referring to this collection from here on. Within the database are collections of related data in what are called **tables**. Note that I call the stuff in your database **data**, not **information**. It's the **processes** that create the **outputs** that turn **data** into **information**.

Many simpler applications do not store enough information to qualify as a database. A utility program that automatically backs up your data might store only a minimum amount of information—what to back up, where to put it, last time it was run, next scheduled backup. Often this type of storage is referred to as a configuration file rather than a formal database. However, even if your program does not have a formal database, much of what follows here still applies. You still need to specify what is stored. Much to the irritation of some purists, I will extend the definition of database to include any kind of information your program needs to store and retrieve.

Referring back to Figure 2-1, it may seem like the STORAGE box should be tackled first. But it's actually the outputs that define what needs to be in your database. Everything that comes out on a report or is displayed on a form needs to come from the stored data either directly or as a result of combining or manipulating data items.

When I do an application design for a client, I always try to impress them with how critically important this step of defining the database is. Much, if not most, of the value of an application is in the specification of the stored data—what fields are included, the formats of the fields (number, character, date, etc.), and the relationships, if any, among the fields and tables. (I like to say 80 percent, but of course it's not really quantifiable that way.) If it is done correctly, the application will be fast, flexible, and elegant, and will run like a spotted dog. If it is done incorrectly, it will cost more to create, learn, and maintain, and will probably run like a stuck pig.

Once the database is correctly designed, any primate can make forms and reports. The real value of the application is in the database design.

I, and many others more qualified than I, have a lot of advice on how to organize the data in your database. But none of it, in my opinion, rises to the status of a "commandment." As Captain Barbosa said in *The Pirates of the Caribbean*, "They're more like guidelines." There are better and worse ways to design a database. But in the programming world, we have a secret motto: "A good program is one that works."

But I digress . . .

So, as the architect of your application, you may need to spend a lot of time thinking about what data to store, how to group it logically, and what the relationships will be among those data items.

## Storing Data at the Atomic Level

In general, you want to hold data in your database at the lowest, most detailed level. This is often referred to as **atomic**-level data, because each of the data items is like an atom. In a report or a **form** (a screen where you input or display data—to be defined later in the section titled "The Inputs"), the atoms can be combined into molecules and compounds, and, ultimately, a complex structure. These summaries are what the user often sees. But "under the hood," everything is stored at the atomic level of detail.

For example, a database containing a table with information about sales orders might include a promised ship date and an actual ship date. So you could easily print a report of sales order items sorted by promised date or by ship date.

But suppose the user needs a report showing the number of days between the promised ship date and the actual ship date. You might be tempted to add a field to your sales order table with this information. Alternatively, you could simply define a field on your report that calculates at report time the number of days between these two dates, and summarize the information on the way out to the printer.

Using the atomic model, the two dates are atoms. The interval between them makes a molecule. In general (and this is a guideline, not a rule), you don't want to store molecules in your database. Just atoms.

Of course, common sense should rule the day. Suppose you have a calculated field—like that interval between the dates, but much more complex—that causes the report to take an unacceptably long time to generate. And it runs lickety-split with the addition of a calculated field to the table in your database. Well then, add the field.

Remember, your product will not be judged by designers on how elegantly you structured your data. It will be judged by the users on how fast and easily it gives them the information they need.

## How to Group Your Data

Assuming your application requires more than just some minimal information, but involves the storage and reporting of a large number of data items, you need to organize them into separate groups or collections in a logical and efficient way. The whole subject of effective database design is beyond the scope of this book. However, let me introduce one concept, perhaps the most useful concept in the whole subject: **database normalization**. From Wikipedia (`http://en.wikipedia.org/wiki/Database_normalization`):

> ***Database normalization*** *is a technique for designing relational database tables to minimize duplication of information and, in so doing, to safeguard the database against certain types of logical inconsistency. When multiple instances of a given piece of information occur in a table, the possibility exists that these instances will not be kept consistent when the data within the table is updated, leading to a loss of data integrity. A table that is sufficiently normalized is not vulnerable to problems of this kind, as its structure prevents it from holding redundant information in the first place.*

Couldn't have said it better myself. Really.

Let me give you a practical example to clarify what might otherwise seem to be a fairly pedantic definition.

Suppose, going back to the customer order table, we have the fields shown in Figure 2-2.

This table is painfully un-normalized. Every order will have the customer's name, address, and phone number repeated. Now suppose the customer changes their phone number. Your program would have to go through each record in the order table, find that customer, and update their phone number.

- Order Number
- Customer Name
- Customer Address
- Customer Phone
- 
- 
- 
- Bunch of other fields

**Figure 2-2.** An un-normalized table

Further, suppose that a feature or function is added later that once again needs the customer phone number. So the phone number gets included in yet another table. No problem, as long as the programmer remembers that if a phone number gets changed in one place, it has to get changed in ALL places in the database that it appears. Which they won't. Guaranteed. In other words, this is a problem.

Figure 2-3 shows a better approach.

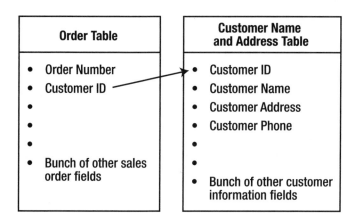

| Order Table | Customer Name and Address Table |
|---|---|
| • Order Number<br>• Customer ID<br>•<br>•<br>•<br>• Bunch of other sales order fields | • Customer ID<br>• Customer Name<br>• Customer Address<br>• Customer Phone<br>•<br>•<br>• Bunch of other customer information fields |

**Figure 2-3.** A normalized table structure

On the left, we have the order table again, but instead of including the customer name and address information, we merely have a pointer (Customer ID) to the table on the right, which is the Customer Name and Address table. In this approach, each customer's information appears in the database only one time—in the Customer Name and Address table.

The Customer ID field is an internal number that the user NEVER sees. It's your database's own private pointer.

When your program displays any order information that will include information about the customer's name and address, your program uses the Customer ID pointer from the Order table to fetch that data from the Customer Name and Address table and include it in the display.

Using this approach, when the customer's phone number changes, it gets changed in only one place. Every part of your application that refers to or displays the customer phone number then automagically displays the updated phone number.

If this whole subject of relational database design and normalization intrigues you, I highly recommend some reading up on it. There are many good sources of information on this subject. One of them is "Get It Done with MySql" by Brawley and Fuller, available on-line at `www.artfulsoftware.com/`. Take a look at the section on normalisation (they're Canadian—don't care much for the letter "z") in Chapter 1. It's a free download. Here's another good tutorial on database normalization: `http://articles.techrepublic.com.com/5100-22-1050416.html`. And from one of the most authoritative voices on the subject, Paul Litwin, a tutorial titled "Fundamentals of Relational Database Design" can be found at `http://r937.com/relational.html` and covers much more than just normalization.

## Busting the Rule

Is there any time you should un-normalize your database, that is, store information which repeats? Well, there are (at least) two situations where un-normalizing your database could be justified.

One reason was given earlier. If normalizing your database makes it run unacceptably slow, then you do what's necessary to make it run fast enough to make your user happy.

The other reason is when you need to store historical data. Suppose you have a table listing items for sale. This table would naturally have in it a description, a sales price, and other item-related fields.

When you create a sales order for a customer, database normalization would dictate that data items like description, selling price, or customer contact information not be stored in the sales order but that only a pointer to the table with this information be included in the order table.

But you can't hold to this rule when storing the completed sales orders for historical purposes. Suppose the selling price or description changes over time, which it certainly will. When you look at an old order, the selling price of the item would be taken from the Item table, which would have the current description and selling price, not the price and description at the time the item was sold.

So when you create the sales order, you must take the current price and description from the Item table, and store it in the Sales Order table. Database normalization is violated (but it's OK) when you need to save a "snapshot" of **current conditions** for **historical** reasons.

## The Final Storage Specification

So at the end of this process of defining your database, what should you end up with? At a minimum, for your simpler applications, you want a list of all the data items you want to store and where you're going to store them. For applications that require a lot of data items to be organized in a logical scheme, you should have a document that details **tables**, **data fields**, and **relationships**. In other words

1. What **tables** go into your database—a table name with a brief definition or description.

2. What **data fields** go into each table—name, data type (number, character, yes/no, etc.), and the length in the case of character data or precision in the case of numeric data (integer, long integer, single- or double-precision decimal, etc.).

3. What the **relationships** will be among the various tables. A diagram like Figure 2-3 is probably the best way to illustrate these relationships. (In Microsoft Access, there is a built-in relationships function that lets you link your tables and then print the resulting diagram.)

As I pointed out earlier, this is the step in the process where you want to take your time. Lots of time.

## *The Inputs*

Given the bang-up job you did defining your **outputs** and **storage**, the contents of the **INPUT** box are pretty much self-defining. You need to have a way for the user to enter, edit, or delete every data item that appears in your database.

A screen where your users input data is commonly called a **form**. So, that's the term I'll use here.

You can make this section of your specification as simple as a list of forms. A level deeper would be a list of forms, a bit of narrative about what each one is supposed to do, and the data fields each will have on it. A more detailed specification would include a sample of each form dummied up showing the placement of the fields on the form.

Generally this list of forms will start by following the way you have sorted out the data into tables in your database—one form for each table. Some forms will have data presented that combine data from two or more tables. And, of course, some forms will not be tied to the data at all. Menus are a good example of this kind of form. Forms that prompt the user for reporting options is another—it's the report that's linked to the data, not the form.

But, once again, you see how spending a lot of time defining the tables, data fields, and relationships of your database governs these downstream activities.

Just be sure that for every data item in your database you have a form that includes that item, so that it can be created, edited, and/or deleted. As noted, you'll also need forms to generate reports, assuming that you want to give your users some parameters by which they can sort the data in different ways and enter criteria (like start and end dates, for example). This way they can filter the reports down to just the data they're looking for.

And, as in the case of E-Z-MRP, you will have some utility functions in forms—user maintenance, options and preferences, etc.

One final input consideration. Sharing data among applications is becoming more valuable, more desirable, and, in some cases, more of a requirement than it used to be. So ask yourself if the inputs to your application are going to involve importing data from some other source. If so, you will want a form that will accept external data.

Specifying the format of this data is the problem. Many developers will lay out a specification defining the exact format in which the data is to be presented. Anyone who wants to push data into the application has to adhere to the format. Some developers, if practical, will allow the user to define the way that the incoming data is organized, so that their application can accept data from a wide variety of sources. The latter approach obviously increases the value of your product. But it can get rather complex.

In any event, importing data from external sources, if it is a necessary component for your product, needs to be thought through very carefully during the design phase. Again, polling potential users and testers will give you the best handle on this.

## The Processes

So now we come to the final step in the technical specification of your product—all the processes that define what goes on under the hood. These processes can be few and simply described but require a lot of definition. In the case of **The Sleep Advisor**, there's only one major process—take the **inputs** (which are the answers the user enters in response to a series of questions about their sleep patterns) and link those answers to the **outputs** (the identification of the sleep problems and remedies). Simple to say, but it turned out to be an expert system containing thousands of lines of code and taking years to perfect.

On the other hand, the processes can be simple business rules. For example, generate a list of every customer with an unpaid invoice that is more than thirty days old.

As in the creation of the specifications of the other three areas, these processes should be defined by the potential users and the problems they are trying to solve, not the program or what the programmer thinks is a neat idea. And once again, some serious time here will pay off big when you actually write the program.

Most importantly, your definition of the internal processes and business rules used by your application might reveal missing pieces in one or more of the other three functions. For example, to effect a certain business rule, you may find that you have to add another data field to a table. This may lead to the modification of a form where the additional information is prompted from the user. Or it may be that a process is defined by your users that generates some valuable information that you haven't yet included in a report. So you'll have to amend the **output** section of the system spec.

A complete definition of your processes will help you to verify the completeness of the rest of your product specification.

# Who Gets to Use It? Controlling Access to Data in Your Application

An important part of creating your system specification is deciding who gets access to each of the forms and functions and perhaps even specific data items in your program.

Your first decision is whether to require some kind of user name and password. In a simple single-user program, you may not need to require a user to sign in with a password. For example, **The Sleep Advisor** collects information from one person, and it's only used by that person. So even though the information gathered is quite personal, it's only used by one person in the privacy of their own home and is not designed to be shared with anyone else. So it's not necessary to password protect this information.

For more complex, multiuser applications where many users are entering, editing, and reporting data, you may want to require the user to sign in with a name and password. Figure 2-4 shows a simple opening form that prompts the user for a name and password.

**Figure 2-4.** The E-Z-MRP login form

## A Deeper Level of Control

If your users need to control access to the data by assigning user names and passwords to those authorized to run the program, then you have to decide if you want a simple user name/password access or if you want to grant some users the right to do anything—some users the right to enter, edit, and report data only, and some users the right only to see data.

In other words, you may want to build in several levels of access:

1. *Administrator*: Users at this level get to do everything.

2. *Read/Write*: These users get to enter and edit data, but they can't do certain high-level functions like add new user names and passwords.

3. *Read-only*: These users can look at data on the forms and run reports, but they can't enter, edit, or delete any data, and, of course, they can't run the functions reserved for administrators.

Figure 2-5 presents an example of a form from E-Z-MRP that allows the user to add, change, and delete users and passwords. The form, of course, requires administrator access.

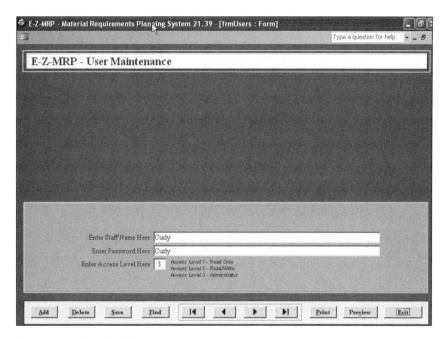

**Figure 2-5.** The E-Z-MRP User Maintenance form

## Down to the Field Level

The kind of scheme just described controls access at the form level. It may, however, be necessary to further refine access down to the function or field level. In other words, a user's access can be restricted to certain functions or perhaps even certain fields on each form.

Figure 2-6 shows a form from the BarTracks Bar Code Tracking and Asset Management System that I developed from the client's system specification. This access design allows an administrator to define access to data at the function level—who is allowed to add, change, and delete data and run the report for virtually every form in the system.

You can even control access down to the field level; that is, on a particular form, you can allow or prohibit certain users from modifying specific fields in a form as shown in Figure 2-7, which presents the BarTracks Manage Permissions function, scrolled down to display this kind of control.

Here, in addition to controlling certain actions involving the transfer of data to and from a hand-held scanner (blue background), the ability of the administrator to control access has been extended to some specific data fields—Funding Type, Purchase Date, Purchase Price, and Modify Existing Asset Notes.

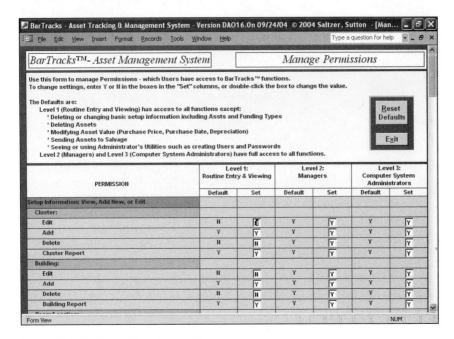

**Figure 2-6.** BarTracks' Permissions Management form

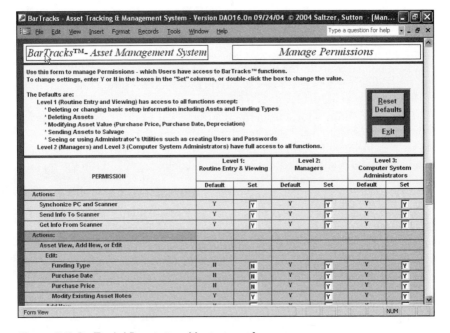

**Figure 2-7.** BarTracks' Permissions Management form

## *How Much Control to Build In?*

So what level of access controls and restrictions do you want to build into your program? Well, the answer should be obvious by now. It's the level of control required to solve the problem that your potential users have or perceive they have. You start with your best guess because you know something about the application. But as you show your system specification to potential customers, ask them about their need to control access to the data. And let them define this part of the program. Finally, if you design some way to turn off these controls completely or partially, then each user can tailor the amount of access and restrictions they want to their own needs. This will enhance the value of your product and relieve you of the necessity of finding a one-size-fits-all solution.

# Navigation: Finding Your Way Around the Program

Another prime topic to consider when specifying your system is **navigation**— or how one moves around in your program to access the various features and functions.

We've all had experience now moving around in web sites. So we all have a feeling for what we like and what we don't like. In general, we like being able to find exactly what we want by clicking a plainly labeled control that links us to the page with the information we want. What we don't like is bouncing around from page to page, hoping to hit on the bit of information we really need.

You've probably also had both good and bad experiences finding your way around packaged products. You can use all this experience to help you design a navigation scheme for your product that is **intuitive**.

Now I put intuitive in bold because it's more important to navigation, in my opinion, than any other consideration. Your customers will NOT read your manual. You'll pour blood, sweat, and tears into it, and they will call asking questions that are answered on page 2. Get over it.

After all, do you read the manual on a new program that you're trying for the first time? Or do you try to figure it out first by hunting and pecking without referring to either the manual or the online help files? OK, then. Your goal, when designing the **inputs** to your product, is to make it so dope-slappingly obvious that the user can at least get started without having to refer to the manual or help files (or have to e-mail or call your tech support).

One key here is to provide a clear way for the user to get back to a "safe" form—usually a menu or switchboard. As noted in the section on consistency in Chapter 3, there's nothing better than a button with the word "EXIT" in bold red letters, placed in exactly the same place on each form.

Another technique is to understand the flow of the process you are mimicking in your program. Remember, just as your database is an electronic representation of what's happening in the real world, the specification that comes out of the PROCESS box of your systems analysis should duplicate and replace the solid manual procedures that have become too time consuming or error prone to do manually. So if a process proceeds from Step A to Step B to Step C, then lead the user through that process with a clear instruction. "Proceed to the Next Step" should be the caption on a hidden or invisible button that appears once all of Step A is completed.

If the organization of your forms into menus and the flow of the individual forms follows the manual processes and procedures of the typical user, users will have an easy time understanding and learning your program and will be guided into doing things in the proper sequence. And (pay attention here) they'll be more likely to buy your software!

The first form the user sees will probably be an opening form of a highly pleasing, welcoming appearance that shows the product name, the version, if needed, a place for the user to sign in and enter a password, and a button that says something to the effect of "Enter." (See Figure 2-4 earlier for the E-Z-MRP opening form.)

Clicking the Enter button generally displays the main menu. Most applications have a main menu, sometimes referred to as the switchboard. It will have a bunch of clearly labeled buttons that will allow the user to open each of the forms. These forms allow entry and editing of data that mirror the way you've organized the data that you are storing. Some buttons will open forms that control the generating of a report. Still others give access to utility programs. You can see the E-Z-MRP Main Menu in Figure 2-8.

Sometimes a button on the main menu will open up a form that is nothing more than another menu—a submenu if you will—with some related functions on it. Clicking the button labeled "Bills of Material" opens up the E-Z-MRP Bill of Materials Menu, shown in Figure 2-9.

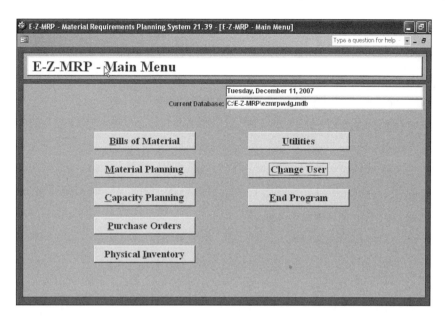

**Figure 2-8.** E-Z-MRP Main Menu

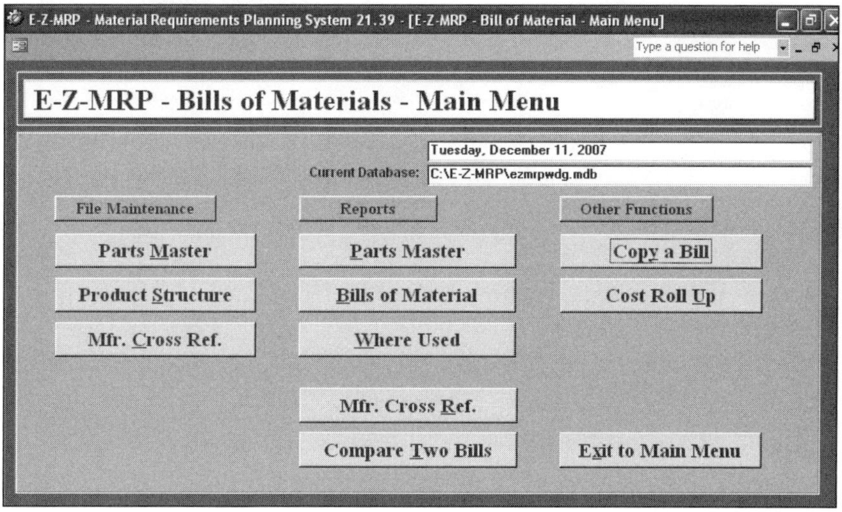

**Figure 2-9.** E-Z-MRP Bill of Materials Menu

## Go Back Where You Came From!

As part of the input specification, make a diagram or document in outline form showing the links among the menus and forms in your application. It will most likely take the form of a tree. In general, it helps your users conceptually to go up the tree to the menu and then down to a different form.

However, sometimes one form leads logically to another form. In that case, you have to decide if and where you want your users to move laterally across the tree—to go from one form to another without returning up the tree to the submenu or switchboard.

Here's an example of lateral movement. On the Bill of Materials Main Menu in Figure 2-9 are three input programs—Parts Master, Product Structure, and Manufacturer's Cross Reference. Initially, to go from one to the other, you had to exit the input form you were on, go back to the Bill of Materials Menu, and click the next input form you wanted. After I heard from several users that they found this inconvenient and wanted to go directly to one of the other input programs, I modified the forms to provide those links. So the altered Part Master form now looks like what you see in Figure 2-10.

**Figure 2-10.** Lateral navigation buttons

So here you see three buttons that allow the user to go directly to three other input forms in the E-Z-MRP system without having to go up the tree to the main menu and then drill down again to the desired form.

In the first release of E-Z-MRP, those lateral movement buttons were not on the form. But enough users called with the suggestion (or complaint) that the program was changed to allow lateral movement.

But go back where you came from! In other words, if a user goes from Form A to Form B without going up to the menu, then, when they leave Form B, return them to Form A, not to the menu. The inclusion of lateral movement buttons is dictated by the way the users do their job. This is critical information you should glean during your initial conversations with potential users and those who are testing your program.

The best way to clarify in your mind how you want your users to navigate through your application is to make an outline or map, similar to site maps you may have seen on more complex web sites.

So here's what the navigation outline for E-Z-MRP would look like. This is just a partial outline, but it's enough to give you the idea. You can see where these items came from by referring back to Figures 2-8 and 2-9—the E-Z-MRP Main Menu and Bill of Materials Main Menu:

- Main Menu
    - Bills of Material
        - File Maintenance
            - Parts Master (direct links to Routings, Product Structure, and Manufacturer's Cross Reference forms)
            - Product Structure (direct links to Part Master and Manufacturer's Cross Reference forms)
            - Manufacturer's Cross Reference (direct links to Parts Master and Product Structure Forms)
        - Reports
            - Parts Master
            - Bills of Material
            - Where Used
            - Manufacturer's Cross Reference
            - Compare Two Bills
        - Other Functions
            - Copy a Bill
            - Cost Roll Up
    - Material Planning
    - Capacity Planning
    - Purchase Orders
    - Physical Inventory

- Utilities

- Change User (opens Main Menu)

- End Program

# The Platform

A **platform** refers to some very technical aspects of your product. What programming language will you be using? What operating system will it be written for? Will it need to run over a network? Will it need to run on the Web? Will it need to be "webbified" in the future?

To answer these questions, you need to think a bit about who will be buying your product. Windows has most of the market for business and personal software. So it would seem natural to develop your application in a language compatible with the Windows operating system.

But Apple has carved out a niche for itself in a couple of areas, like graphics, music, and video production and education. So if you are writing a product that is attractive to graphic artists, the majority of your sales might be for the Mac.

If you are writing an application that needs to be web enabled or run using a browser, obviously you want to choose a web-compatible language.

It is not my purpose here to provide a tutorial comparing and contrasting programming languages and operating systems. What's important for the purposes of your system specification is to identify the kind of hardware and software used by your target market—the folks who are going to pay for your product. And develop your product using the technology that your customers are using.

So, as you go around eliciting feedback about your specification from potential users of your product, be sure to ask them what kind of computers and software they use, and what kind of computers and software their peers and competitors are using.

# The Wrap-Up

So now you should have a pretty complete picture of your application. You've created two documents that define your product—a short one and a long one. The short one, of course, is the one-paragraph product description. The long one is the product specification that includes the following:

- What your users require on the **output** side

- What data you need to **store** in your database to create those outputs

- How you're going to get the user to **input** that data

- Rules or **process**es that govern how your application operates

- The **navigation** scheme—how the users move through your application

- The rules of **access**—who gets to do what in your program

Pretty boring, huh? Pretty tedious at some points, yes? And yet, if you do this job thoroughly, I have no doubt it will lead to some real improvements in your application.

At a minimum, the process of actually creating the program that you want to sell is no longer a dark tunnel. You have a clear roadmap to get from the starting line to a point where you are ready to begin having others test your program. And writing the program becomes much easier. The system specification has broken up the project into well-defined, manageable, byte-sized pieces.

OK, you can start programming now.

# How They Did It: An Interview with Jewelry Designer, Software Developer, and Entrepreneur Barbara Carlton

*Barbara Carlton runs a one-woman shop—Bejeweled Software Company—in Poway, California. Her flagship product, the Jewelry Designer Manager, can be seen at* `www.JewelryDesignerManager.com`. *She didn't start out to be a software entrepreneur. Hers is the classic story of someone who started with a low-tech hobby and a home-grown program for her own use and ended up with a successful software package. Her sagest piece of advice? Test, test, and test.*

**Smolin:** Barbara Carlton, president, chief operating officer, chief cook, and bottle washer of . . .

**Carlton:** Bejeweled Software Company.

**Smolin:** Bejeweled Software Company. So tell me a little bit about the product that you designed and are marketing. What does it do?

**Carlton:** It's a program for jewelry designers to help them price their jewelry and keep track of inventory, their parts inventory, and their finished product inventory. They can print catalogs, price books, costs, do invoicing, bills of material, everything a jewelry designer needs to do in order to be able to sell their jewelry.

**Smolin:** And the name of that product is?

**Carlton:** Jewelry Designer Manager.

**Smolin:** And where did it come from? What on earth made you decide to write a program and try to sell it?

**Carlton:** Well, I was an Access programmer, writing applications for businesses and, as a hobby, I started making jewelry. And I think about the time this program was created, it was at the beginning of this beading frenzy, where everybody and their mother decided they wanted to make jewelry. And bead shows started coming into town every other month. Gem venders would come into town and everybody would go out, and they'd buy all these beads, and there were bead classes and bead shops started opening up. And I was involved in that too. I was making jewelry and doing home parties and selling it to my friends. I had visions of me selling my stuff to Nordstrom's someday, you know, I was really into it. I was going to Tucson, which has the biggest gem show in the world, to buy my beads. And so I needed a way to keep track of all my parts, and so I created this program for my own use. You know, it was just for me to help me as a jewelry designer.

And then I remember going to, I was at the Del Mar Fairgrounds at a bead show with a girlfriend, and I had this little report that I had done in Access. It showed me all my parts and what I paid for it before, what was out of stock and what needed to be reordered. Because you go to these shows and you get so involved in all these beads, and you forget what you came there to buy, and you go home and you don't have the things that you needed. So my girlfriend was looking at my report, and some other people walked by and said "Wow, you are so organized. How did you do that?" And so I thought "Wow," you know, I wonder if other people could use this little program.

So I went on the Internet, did some searches, found some jewelry user groups or chat rooms, and every so often people would say, "How do you know how to price your jewelry?" or "How do you keep track of your part inventory?" And there was nothing out there; there was no program out there. So I remember meeting Jackie Murphy at the user group [the Access Users Group of San Diego—www.augsd.org] and there was another guy who had created some kind of body paint program, for body shops to keep track of insurance jobs, and he told us how he had taken a product and brought it to market.

And I remember thinking, "That would never happen to me!" But then I made a connection where this could be something I could bring to the market, or I could sell to other people. So I just quit consulting at SAIC and just kind of dove into it trying to make it as user friendly as possible, and just to get out there and see what would happen. I thought maybe I could sell . . . 100? You know, if that. I just didn't know what the potential was. I knew there was potential, I just had no idea what it was.

**Smolin**: And when did you first start to sell it?

**Carlton**: June, 2001.

**Smolin**: 2001, so it's a 6-year-old product at the moment.

**Carlton**: Right.

**Smolin**: And who buys it?

**Carlton**: Well, anybody that makes jewelry, or, there's some people that make other crafts where there's assembly involved where you're buying parts or components and you need to figure out a price. But mostly, it can be anywhere from hobbyists, again wannabe designers, people who actually want to do this full time. I have a manufacturing plant in Thailand that purchased it. They may not use all the features of the program, but there's something in it specifically that they like that they use. And I have artists who I see their work in *In Style* magazine and Nordstrom's and Neiman's. It's really across the board.

**Smolin**: What was the initial target market? Who did you think you were going to sell it to at first?

**Carlton:** Probably more people like me, people that do craft shows, home parties. Or again anybody that wants to talk to a Nordstrom's or a Neiman's or a retail outlet, or even wholesale.

**Smolin:** As the market segments began to expand, did you have to modify the program significantly or enhance it in order to satisfy those customers?

**Carlton:** Yeah, yeah, in fact I started with one version. I called it the standard version, and then people that bought it would write to me and give me lots of feedback as far as what to add, what they needed; you know, "This is good, this is bad, can you make it do this, can you make it do that, we want this report, we want that report." And I would add it.

But then it got to the point where it was more of an upgrade than an update. So I decided to come up with another version, and make it more expensive also, and give people the option to be able to upgrade. So, in the past 6 years, I have developed a standard version, a pro version, and a deluxe version. And each one has different features, and they start at $89.95, $129.95, and $259.95. So, depending on where they're at in the business and what features they need, you can decide what version to buy.

**Smolin:** And how do you distribute the product? Is it all direct? Or do you have dealers or distributors?

**Carlton:** I have some, yeah, I have a couple distributors that are . . . they're just really big . . . they distribute everything from packaging to books to displays to components. And I have some bead shops. But most of it, I would say 80 percent, I sell directly through the Internet. People find me through advertising, word of mouth, or just searches, searches on the Internet.

**Smolin:** What discount do you give your dealers?

**Carlton:** They get 45 percent.

**Smolin:** So is it single-user? Multiuser?

**Carlton:** Single.

**Smolin:** Single-user. Is it front end, back end?

**Carlton:** Yeah, it could be installed on a network, you know, because it is the front and back end. But I didn't do anything to it and I'm not going to support any networking issues. But I explain to people how to set it up that way.

**Smolin:** So your license would cover the site?

**Carlton:** No, no, it's just single-user.

**Smolin:** Single-user license and—

**Carlton:** Yeah, and again it's not for business; it's per user.

**Smolin:** Per user, OK. But do you have any controls in there to stop them from putting it on a network with three users and a common back end?

Carlton: Well, there's a security feature built in where they get a CD key or unlock code, and so when I issue a code they get two unlocks, because I assume that most people are going to install it on their desktop and on their laptop. And if they try to install it on another machine, it won't work.

Smolin: OK.

Carlton: So they have to call me and ask for another code. So if it's the person that purchased the program, I will give them another unlock. I wasn't so much concerned about one person giving it to a friend. Although you know I'd much rather have the friend buy it. I was concerned that . . . I'm shipping it to China, you know I'm shipping it all over the place.

Smolin: You'd sell three and find 300,000 installations.

Carlton: Exactly.

Smolin: So how did you pick your development language? You were an Access programmer at the time, yes?

Carlton: Yeah, that was what I was programming in.

Smolin: Have you programmed in other languages?

Carlton: All database languages like dBase, Paradox, Q&A.

Smolin: From the time that you decided you wanted to do this project until you were ready to install it at the first Beta test site, or the first customer, how long did it take?

Carlton: I turned into this like maniac where I couldn't sleep. I was coding all the time. I'd be coding at night. And I'd wake up in the morning and I'd just start again . . . it consumed me, because I could see it. I couldn't stop thinking about it or working on it. Probably about four months.

Smolin: Four months of development, then.

Carlton: Because I already had the basic program, you know, working. I just needed a better user interface, a nice switchboard, and like a look-and-feel, you know make everything consistent, so that anybody could use it, not just me. That is the part that I as a programmer love to do.

Smolin: And did you Beta test it?

Carlton: Oh, yes.

Smolin: And how many Beta sites did you use?

Carlton: Oh. I don't know. I just went on one of the chat rooms and just asked people if they wanted to. I would say maybe twenty.

Smolin: 20! OK.

Carlton: But again, everybody says they want to. I don't remember how many people were really using it. You know I gave them a questionnaire asking them questions: How do you rate this on a 1 to 5 scale? How easy was it to use? What would you pay for this? And I probably got about ten or fifteen back.

**Smolin:** OK so that's a pretty formal Beta testing cycle?

**Carlton:** Yeah.

**Smolin:** So how long was it in Beta testing then?

**Carlton:** Not really that long, because I really wanted to get it out there. I really just had confidence in it, you know, it really just seemed like something that would fly—and I really didn't have anything to lose.

**Smolin:** So you did all the programming?

**Carlton:** Yes.

**Smolin:** And, how much did you have to invest in dollars, if any, to get it going?

**Carlton:** Ah, well, I had to purchase the CDs, because I didn't have any downloads at the time. I had to pay for a graphic artist to design the cover and the back. And I had a friend design the logo, and then another photographer friend took pictures of my jewelry, and so we were able to use that for the cover. I think for all the steps to get the first one out, there's probably about $2,000, and it cost another maybe $1,000 in developer tools—the one-time fee for the SageKey scripts, and install builder . . .

**Smolin:** So about $3,000 out of pocket. And lots of sweat equity. Some small change for Tums and Advil. OK. The usual supplies. So you have some copy protection scheme in there, the CD key—

**Carlton:** Yes, security so they cannot make illegal copies. And it is copyrighted. The logo and the name are trademarked.

**Smolin:** Just out of curiosity, if I take this, and you know, I've got ten machines, you say I can install it twice . . . well, how does it know when I go to the third machine that I've already installed it twice?

**Carlton:** The code for that, I had to buy that. It looks at the serial number of the machine or the fingerprint, and if it's not the one that it initially installed on . . .

**Smolin:** It must write something back to the CD then. Although—

**Carlton:** No it's in the program. It must pick up the serial number or other identifying information about the computer, and after that it's not going to open unless it's the same serial number. And it goes to the Internet on my site and checks it.

**Smolin:** Oh, OK so it's calling home.

**Carlton:** Yes, well it calls home to get the unlock and then every time it opens, it looks to see if it is the same fingerprint.

**Smolin:** OK so when you install it, it calls home. So you've got control through the Internet.

**Carlton:** Right

**Smolin:** Got it.

**Carlton:** And if they don't have Internet access, then I can give them . . . they have to give me the serial number of the machine, and I can give them an unlock.

**Smolin:** Ah, OK. So let's see, the pricing, you've got the three versions . . . how did you decide on your pricing?

**Carlton:** I asked the Beta testers what they would expect to pay for a program like this. I think when I first started I thought like $149 was a good price, but then, based on some feedback early on, I kind of changed it to $89.95 because of my target market, the people, the beaders. Something about going over $99 scared them away. I don't know why. I don't know what it is. I get people who say, "This is unbelievable, you should charge more for it," but then I get a lot of people who say, "I would love to buy it, but it's expensive." So I think that price just seems to be right on.

**Smolin:** So you've been doing . . . so it's been out there for six years. Have you raised the price in that time?

**Carlton:** No. All I've done is created two more versions, so there's an $89, a $129, and a $259 version. The one in the middle, the $129, is probably the best-selling one. But that one has invoicing, where the standard version doesn't. So anybody that is seriously considering selling, it forces them to buy that version.

**Smolin:** OK so your pricing model is single-user license. If they want to put on two boxes . . . well, you let them put it on a second machine, but if they want another one, then they gotta buy another license.

**Carlton:** Um no. If it's there, if they have three computers, and they are using the program, it's just them, I'll give them a third. I'll give them a fourth or fifth. Per user. But I'm not going to argue with them over the phone if, you know, their sister might be using it or something. Again, my concern is more about passing that one CD around to everybody.

**Smolin:** So when you sell one of them to a manufacturer, say in Thailand, if they've got twenty users, they have to buy twenty licenses.

**Carlton:** Right.

**Smolin:** OK. What is your product support policy?

**Carlton:** I have full tech support. I try to encourage them to use e-mail instead of calling me on the phone, but some people prefer calling on the phone. Actually, I would say the majority of the questions have absolutely nothing to do with my program. It's because people don't know how to use their computer, which can be kind of frustrating. But if I don't help them with their computer, then they can't use my program.

**Smolin:** Do you charge for support?

**Carlton:** No, I don't really have a way of doing that.

**Smolin:** Do you find that 5 percent of your users account for 95 percent of your calls?

**Carlton**: Yeah, over the years. I have people who started with me in 2001, and sure enough, they'll call every so often, and it's always like this major catastrophe where everything goes wrong. And again it's nothing to do with my program. But they know to come to me, and you know I think it's sort of like karma. I help them, and they spread the word. You know, if you go on a forum, there'll always be such wonderful things about how nice I was and how much I helped them. And that has helped me sell the product. So maybe I don't see the money right away, but in the long term it really pays off.

**Smolin**: Yeah, well, I've always thought that, you know, anybody can write these applications. If somebody sees it, they can just knock it off. They can duplicate the functionality. The difference I find amongst venders is not whether the program is bug free or bulletproof in its use, but how fast you can get a response when you have a question. Nobody expects a perfect program, but they do want to be able to get back up and running in short order. So I always found that if you don't let anybody off the phone until the problem is solved, that really comes back to you. And the flipside is that if you don't solve the problem, that comes back to you as well.

So what would be, would you say the biggest problems you've faced bringing the product to the point where it was ready to go to market?

**Carlton**: Initially? I think trying to figure out how to get it to install with all the different versions of Access out there, whether I should use the Access runtime or whether I needed some other way to install it. You know my biggest fear was, I don't want to install this program and have people's computers crash or have them calling me and saying, "Your program—

**Smolin**: Screwed up my machine.

**Carlton**: I needed a way so, you know, I could feel like I'm not going to get sued, or I'm not going to get in trouble or tick people off.

**Smolin**: So what did you end up with for installation?

**Carlton**: I used SageKey scripts.

**Smolin**: The **SageKey** scripts. And the Wise installer?

**Carlton**: Right.

**Smolin**: So, what research on the market and competition did you do before you started? Well you told me—

**Carlton**: There was no competition.

**Smolin**: Yeah, there wasn't anything, so . . .

**Carlton**: No. Everything out there was for retail stores, and my customers are not retail.

**Smolin**: They're hobbyists turning semipro.

**Carlton**: Yeah, they have a little shop or something. But they're not a big Tiffany's or a brand name jewelry store.

**Smolin:** How much did it cost, and how long did it take you to get your trademark?

**Carlton:** I hired an attorney to do it for me, and there were some problems, where they wouldn't . . . they didn't approve at first because of the font or something.

**Smolin:** Would you say on the order of $1,000 or $1,500?

**Carlton:** Yeah probably. When it's all said and done. And I did have problems from the beginning where people would try to use the name like The Jewelry Manager. Somebody came out with a program called Bejeweled.

**Smolin:** Have you had to do any enforcement of your trademark?

**Carlton:** Yeah, I mean the same attorney I used for the trademark, he would have to write letters. They hired an attorney. The attorneys went back and forth for a while. The look and feel was exactly like my program. You know the data entry screens were identical.

**Smolin:** Oh, somebody knocked it off.

**Carlton:** They even, you know, they used the same colors I did, they even put in the same mistakes that I did. And then the biggest thing I had a problem with them was on my web site, and when I would do marketing and whenever anybody had written a review, usually I'll say, "This program will help jewelry designers price their jewelry so they can spend more time making jewelry," and they used that exact slogan in theirs. You know, word for word, they copied everything, and they used my marketing, they copied the program . . .

**Smolin:** So it was a straight knock-off.

**Carlton:** [They used] part of my name, so that when people searched for me, they would find them, and at first the guy said, "No, no way, we didn't . . . we thought of this all by ourselves," and then eventually they just they backed off. They're still out there I believe, but they changed enough so that any person, they would look at the screen and go . . .

**Smolin:** There's no violation of trademark and copyright.

**Carlton:** Right. They took away the slogan, they didn't use that anymore. So that's all I could do. But ultimately, unless you have deep, deep pockets, you really can't stop anybody. I mean it's like $60,000 just to file a federal lawsuit. So if you want to start, you've got to be prepared to set down $100,000 or so.

**Smolin:** So there's got to be some real money involved.

**Carlton:** But you have to at least stand up for yourself at the beginning, because if you don't do anything, then you just don't have a chance. So I had probably two people like that, and then just nuisance people—that kind thing. Even now my web site is Jewelry Designer Manager, jewelry is spelled j-e-w-e-l-r-y, so somebody has j-e-w-e-l-e-r-y. So people go there, thinking it's me. And I can't stop that.

**Smolin:** Well, in a way, it's flattering. If you're good, you attract, you know, the imitators. Do you have a manual?

**Carlton:** Yeah, the user guide is on the CD, or now if they order a download, they get a link to a PDF. Probably anywhere, depending on the version, from 45 to 75 pages.

**Smolin:** How long did it take you to write that?

**Carlton:** Not that long.

**Smolin:** As long as to write the program? Or longer?

**Carlton:** No, no much shorter, because again it just goes through each data entry screen, kind of just guides what goes in there. Again, if you're in the jewelry business, you're going to understand what you should put in there. Jewelry part, part name, size, price, vendor, date purchased.

**Smolin:** Right, it's all pretty generic stuff.

**Carlton:** And what I try to teach them again are things specific to using a database, know how to sort, how to filter, how to back up your database. The things that people have problems with are usually more computer functionality, because again, a lot of my customers are maybe middle-aged women that aren't really computer-savvy, so this is a computer program, and they're really kind of new to computers. So I had to just make it really bulletproof.

**Smolin:** And you wrote that manual before you sold the first one?

**Carlton:** Right. It came with the first one. And then I kind of added some things to it, and then again with the different versions I had to make changes.

**Smolin:** Do you have online help in the program? Tooltips?

**Carlton:** Yeah.

**Smolin:** How often do you release updates?

**Carlton:** I would say probably every few months. Updates are free, just little bug fixes.

**Smolin:** How long does it take the typical user to learn to use the product once they open it up and install it?

**Carlton:** You know I think they can start getting data in there right away, start putting in their parts.

**Smolin:** So really not much of a learning curve?

**Carlton:** There really isn't. I think it might take them a while to figure out, when they go through the reports, to see what they want, you know, what information they really need. But for most people, they want a catalog of their work and a price list. And mailing labels.

**Smolin:** How long does it take them to implement the product and, more or less, fully using it, getting their data in and using the reports?

**Carlton:** You know it really depends on how long they've been in the business—

**Smolin:** I know it could take forever but—

**Carlton:** There's people that have, you know, 3,000 beads that they've collected over the years, and I tell them, you know, because, you're not even using all of them. Just enter the ones that you buy now or put in, you know, what you're using now or what is in the pieces that you're currently selling. They need to have something right away. I'd rather them get a price list and a catalog right away. Then later on you can go back in and put in the parts that weren't there.

**Smolin:** So if somebody's motivated and they have their lights on . . .

**Carlton:** They could have a catalog in an afternoon.

**Smolin:** In an afternoon, so it could be theoretically, a one-day or two-day implementation.

**Carlton:** Sure.

**Smolin:** Well that's pretty good. What kind of learning and implementation problems did you encounter with people, and what did you do about them?

**Carlton:** You know I really don't have that problem.

**Smolin:** Well, that's great. Do you do custom modifications?

**Carlton:** Not really, I would rather just do something that's going to benefit all my users across the board instead of just one.

**Smolin:** So anything somebody wants becomes a generic upgrade?

**Carlton:** If I think it's going to be something everybody needs. I mean I've had people say, "Can you make the dollar like four decimal places?" And I'll say, "No," because in real life, nobody's going to look at four decimal places. It doesn't make sense. If it's in a calculation somewhere, yes, I mean you might see that but . . . on a price list? Nobody wants to see that.

**Smolin:** Did the Jewelry Designer Manager lead to any other products?

**Carlton:** Well, one other. I had people say, "I could use this for my crafts." I do corks, or I do candles, or all kinds of other crafts. So I thought, "Oh, maybe I should have another program." So what I did is I created Craft Manager. I took one of my versions, and I took the word "jewelry" out of all the data entry screens and all the reports. The code is all the same. It may say "jewelry" back there, but no one's going to see it. But the user interface just says "craft, part, piece."

**Smolin:** And this is called the Craft Manager?

**Carlton:** Yeah. So, it's really the same, the same exact program, except for the font, and I changed the cover—

**Smolin:** —and some of the nomenclature. And how is it working?

**Carlton**: It's not selling, you know, and I did everything the same. I did advertising, through the craft magazines. And I thought this one would be really, really good. I mean, there's more people—think of Michael's, you know, all the people that go to Michael's. But those people just need crafts for themselves or their friends, they're not really selling it. I mean, it takes time to put the inventory in.

But the people that do . . . I mean my testimonials, they're just incredible, they're like "Thank you." They love it. "Thank you for doing this for us; this is the best thing since popcorn." But maybe I just, I just got lucky [with the first product] with the timing and with the product and all that stuff.

**Smolin**: You have any ideas for another product?

**Carlton**: Yeah, I have a lot of ideas. But I need to do something with this one. It's just hard for me at this point. I think that I've reached my programming limit. I'm not a really good programmer. But I'm learning everything. I'm learning the business. I do the bookkeeping, I do the shipping, I do the Internet, I do the support, and I don't have the time now to just like sit and focus.

**Smolin**: Do you see a limited product life for this product?

**Carlton**: You know, I don't. I don't think it's limited because every day somebody else is getting into the business

People are always going to make jewelry. People are always going to wear jewelry, and people are always going to make it. It's just a matter of is someone else going to come along and knock me off? You know, make it better. I am like the gold standard, and everybody knows that. So, they're going to look at my product first.

So unless somebody else out there is going to go really cheap, or onto something that I just don't have, it will continue to sell. And if they do that, I'm going to have to scramble, and quote whatever they offer or lower my price, but I'm going to try to milk this thing as long as I can. But I have some ideas that could really improve it, or I could probably capture jewelry designers that are on a higher level. But again, I just don't have the time to do the programming.

**Smolin**: That's the life of the lone-ranger programmer, isn't it?

**Smolin**: So if somebody came to you and said, "You know, I got a terrific idea for a product and I think I would like to do it. I laid down and the feeling didn't pass so here I go," what would your most important piece of advice be to that person starting down the road from raw program to getting a product ready to sell? What warning would you give them? What's their biggest pitfall or riskiest point?

**Carlton**: Again, I think it's all about making it really user friendly, and foolproof installation. Because with all the different operating systems . . . Vista, for example, was a nightmare for me. Not because of my Access program, but because of the security. It wouldn't unlock on Vista. You know, I had to wait until the developers of my product's security module had it back-fixed.

And you know my biggest fear, even now, is if someone calls and goes, "I installed the program, and my machine isn't working." Now I *know* it's not my program because I've tested it on every operating system. I've paid people to do that for me, so I know. But I don't want other people to think that it is. So that's my biggest fear. You need to know you've got a really good installation, and it's been tested on all kinds of machines so it doesn't come back to haunt you.

# The Program: From the Outside Looking In

If you followed the advice in Chapter 2, you now have in hand enough of a system specification to start programming your product. Or, if you've already started your program or have a working copy, you can use that spec to start rewriting your program. Or if you're not a programmer, and you're going to hire one, you have a roadmap to show your prospective programmer.

In any event, it's time to take a look at the nuts and the bolts.

## What I Don't Want to Talk About

You are either a programmer or you're going to hire one. In either case, it is not the purpose of this book to teach programming or provide advice on programming techniques. The platform and language you choose for your product depends to a large degree on the application and who is going to use it. In other words, like many decisions, the programming language and operating system you choose for your product must be dictated by the users and market you have already researched and identified. (You have done this already, haven't you?)

In the previous chapter, I touched on the subject of the selection of an appropriate programming language for your product—one that is compatible with the majority of the potential users of your product. And that remains, of course, the most important consideration for the success of your product.

I'm going to assume that you can write a program that works to do what you outlined in the system specification you created or that you're smart enough to hire someone to do that job. This chapter will concentrate on how the program operates from the outside—from the perspective of the user. Where I recommend a specific feature or technique, I'll try to give some guidance about implementation. But, by and large, generating the code—make or buy—will be up to you.

# How to Hire a Programmer

If you're going to do all the programming yourself, you can skip this section. If you intend to hire someone, then you probably already have an uneasy feeling that you're stepping into a potential minefield.

Hiring a programmer is kind of like hiring someone that you know nothing about to do some work on your house. Call in someone to tile your bathroom, and you either end up with an artist who cuts the Italian marble perfectly or a klutz whose tile work looks like a row of crooked teeth. Sometimes you just don't know how it will turn out. But at least in the case of a tiler, you can go and look at their work, and you feel competent to make a judgment. They may do better or worse on your bathroom, but you'll have an idea of their potential.

Programmers are not magicians. We just try to create that impression. Just like bathroom tilers, we have artisans and klutzes. So how do you find the right one?

This programmer you're going to hire will be key to the success or failure of your product. So it pays to do your due diligence.

First, of course, you want to start with referrals. Ours is primarily a word-of-mouth business. The potential programmer can give you referrals. But, of course, they're going to give you the good ones. Finding someone to warn you off of a bad programmer is problematical.

Next, you want to evaluate their work. This is a two-step process.

The first step is easy. Whoever gave you this referral is probably using this programmer's work product. So go take a look. Look for the qualities you're going to read about in this chapter. Is it aesthetically pleasing? Are the forms and reports easily readable, intuitive, and clear? Are the forms and reports consistent? Can you find your way around the application easily?

Ask the referrer about working with this programmer. Did they take direction easily? Were they timely in their response? Did the referrer feel they got good value for the money they spent? If you can find other people who have used this programmer, go look at those applications.

The second step is to evaluate their work from the inside, and this is a bit more difficult. Because you're not a programmer it will be hard to judge the quality of their work when looking at the code they generate. But there are a couple of things to look for. The first thing is comments. Extensively commented code is easier to maintain. But most critically, at some point another programmer will probably be taking over. Why? Stuff happens.

Your new programmer will have a learning curve the difficulties of which will be directly related to how well documented the code is. Here's an example of well-documented code:

```
' *********************************************************************
Option Compare Database
Option Explicit
```

```
'To create a back end for distribution:
'
'1) Create a blank file called DWData_NoData.mdb.
'
'2) Import all tables from DWData.mdb into the new back end,
'    with relationships, but without data.
'
'3) Attach the following tables from DWData.mdb into the new back end:
'
'ActionDates, ActionGroups, Actions, Agents, AgentsCountries,
BaseDateTypes, Country
'DueDateTypes, EntityTypes, FormList, MatterSubType, MatterType, Status,
'WordFormQueries, zsysDateFields
'
'(Attached tables should have "1" at the end of the names).
'
'4) Import this code module into back end, and run FillBackEndTables().
'
'5) Open the front end to create an Options record (or allow it
'    to happen automatically the first time the application is used).
'
'6) When all data looks OK, run RemoveBackEndLinks() to remove the links
to DWData.



Sub FillBackEndTables()

If boolTrapErrors = True Then On Error GoTo Err_FillBackEndTables
    .
    .
    .
```

All of the lines that begin with an apostrophe are comments. Lines without apostrophes are lines of program code. This is not the complete code module, just the heading that the programmer inserted, which reminds the programmer what they were about when they go back months later to look at it. It tells the next programmer what's going on in this module—what the purpose is and how the original programmer went about creating the solution.

Another example of well-documented code is the use of descriptive names for routines and variables. Note in the previous example the name of the subroutine "FillBackEndTables". It gives the reader an idea of the purpose of the subroutine.

Here's an example that combines both—descriptive variable names and documentation (the comment at the end of each line following the apostrophe):

```
'*****************************************************************

Global grsOptions As Recordset 'Options table (used in WordForms form).
Global grsAddActions_Groups As Recordset 'zsysAddActions_Groups table
' (used in Matters Add Actions button)
Global gblnUserLoggedIn As Boolean   'Used by fdlgLogIn
Global gstrTMEmailProfile As String 'Used by TM E-mail Reports function
Global glngNewMatterGroupID As Long 'Used by MatterGroups form
Global glngNewClientGroupID As Long 'Used by ClientGroups form

'  *****************************************************************
```

Variable names like "glngNewMatterGroupID" are much more descriptive and self-documenting than something like "NMGID".

Finally, although you may not be able to understand the code, its appearance can give you a clue as to how orderly and logical the mind of the programmer is. Good code:

```
'  *****************************************************************
If frm.lstBaseDateType <> "U" Then

'Automatically allow user-defined dates
        If Nz(varType, "") <> "" Then
'If there is a basedatefromto type (allow in list if no rule set up)
            varDate = Forms!Matters.Controls(varMattersField)
            If Not IsNull(varDate) Then
  'Allow in list if date to use is null
                If Nz(varDateTo, "") = "" Then
                    If CDate(varDate) < CDate(varDateFrom) Then
                        Exit Function
                    End If
                ElseIf Nz(varDateFrom, "") = "" Then
                    If CDate(varDate) >= CDate(varDateTo) Then
                        Exit Function
                    End If
                Else
                    If CDate(varDate) < CDate(varDateFrom) Or _
                        CDate(varDate) >= CDate(varDateTo) Then
                        Exit Function
                    End If
                End If
            End If
        End If
    End If
```

```
End If

AllowGroup = True

Set frm = Nothing
```

' ********************************************************************

It's a complex nesting of **If**s and **Then**s. You may not be able to read it, but visually it has an orderliness that reveals the programmer's discipline in writing code. Bad code? Imagine the preceding sample without any indents—all the lines left justified. That's bad code. Even if it works, it will be difficult for the programmer to maintain, and even more difficult for the successor programmer to understand.

Finally, you are ready to talk to the programmer. Like any profession, programmers come in a variety of skill levels—apprentice to master, if you will. As their skill level increases, so will their hourly rate. You need to find someone to complement your level of expertise. Your basic coder will need quite explicit direction from you—a detailed specification of how you want each function to operate. The highest-level programmer will double as your systems analyst, translating your vague or untechnical requirements first into a design and only then into a program.

There is only one really critical consideration when evaluating a potential programmer—communication. The programmer will be translating your ideas into a working program. So they have to be flexible and compliant and show you that they understand both what you're trying to accomplish and the roles each of you is playing.

If you cannot communicate your product ideas to them, and they cannot communicate their programming ideas to you, move on to the next candidate.

# What I Do Want to Talk About

What I would like to cover in this chapter are topics you should consider that affect the way your product presents itself to the user.

Arguably the most frustrating and discouraging aspect of programming is that no one will ever know (or really care) how clever you (or your programmer) were in coding up some feature of your program.

What they will judge you on is your product's appearance and how easy and intuitive it is to learn and run. So I'm going to alert you to some features your product should have. I'll describe what they should do. Implementing them will be up to you.

## The Opening Form

It's a cliché, of course, but you only get one chance to make a first impression. The first form your user sees when you start the program doesn't have to be a killer. It simply has to be professional in appearance, tidy, and display certain information. On my opening forms, I have

- The product name (seems obvious)

- The name of the company that produced this jewel

- The release or version number and date

- A copyright notice

- A button clearly labeled "Start," "Begin," "Enter," "Click Here to Start," or something equally obvious

- Optionally, a place for users to enter their name and a password

Figure 3-1 shows the opening form for E-Z-MRP.

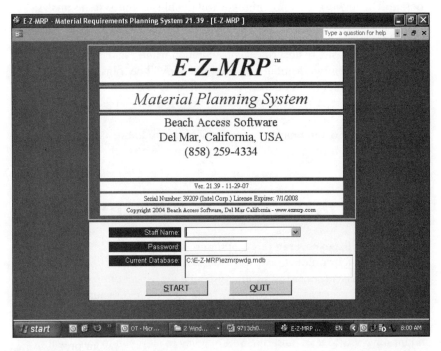

**Figure 3-1.** E-Z-MRP opening form

No, it isn't sexy. But it is functional. It tells the user what the product name is, notifies the user of the copyright, and shows to whom it's licensed (in this case Intel Corp.) and the expiration date of the license. The phone number for technical support is also clearly displayed, and having all this information makes it easy for tech support to identify the caller, and the version and expiration date of their software.

What doesn't show, because this is a picture of the screen, is that the cursor is positioned in the box where the user enters their name. But, trust me, it's there, ready to accept the user's login. As much as possible you want to take the guesswork out of what the user is supposed to do next.

E-Z-MRP is for small manufacturers. They are practical people who value functionality. Aesthetics are often a secondary consideration. The Sleep Advisor, on the other hand, is purely a consumer product. So its opening form needs to be a bit more inviting to the eye. But still, it needs to cover the basics, and you can see in Figure 3-2 that it does.

**Figure 3-2.** The Sleep Advisor opening form

Here, because of the nature of the application, there is a legal disclaimer displayed (there will be more on legal matters in Chapter 5). Since it's a single-user consumer program, no sign-on or password is required. But the basic elements are still there—product name, version, copyright, and, most importantly, a clear instruction on what to do next.

What you place on your opening form, like every facet of your product, is dictated by the customer. There are no hard-and-fast rules. There are applications that don't use an opening form. WinZip just opens right up to the business end of the application. Same with Norton Ghost. Same with Word and Excel.

You probably have a couple dozen applications on your computer. But you may never have paid much attention to their opening forms. Take a few minutes to look at them now. Note what you like and don't like about them. You'll get some good ideas about how you want to make your own first impression.

I would advise you to avoid a couple of things, however, in your opening form.

First, no music or sound effects, please. You take a chance with music. Even if a customer likes your selection, eventually they'll tire of it. A whooshing sound as your opening form materializes on the screen? Spare us.

Second, no animation and no opening movie. Please. It's so cool to see the jigsaw puzzle pieces of your opening form fly in from the perimeter of your screen and assemble themselves. Or to have a short film of happy users getting great benefits from your product and a soothing voice-over welcoming your customer to your program. Especially the first time. Not so much the second time. Less the third.

Have you noticed that more and more web sites with really great music and movie or animation intros also have a button that reads "Skip Intro"? Take a hint.

Third, no opening form delay. By this I mean displaying an opening form for a fixed amount of time and then closing it to display your main menu or switchboard. I love the Wise Installation System. It allows me to package my applications in a professional manner and makes the user's task of installing my application a one-click, wizard-based, task. However, when the program starts, their opening form is displayed for five to seven seconds, during which time I just have to wait. I have encountered this in other programs. I am forced to read their disclaimers, warning about piracy, or whatever, every time I start the program. It's a bit annoying. And the one thing you DON'T want to do is annoy your user. Especially right at the start.

Now to give Wise the benefit of the doubt, perhaps it takes that long to load the program. But if your application takes more than a couple seconds to load, put "Loading program . . . " on your opening form, perhaps turning off and on in one- to two-second intervals. You might combine that with a "progress bar" showing how much of the opening work has been done, giving the user an idea of how much longer it will take to open your program. This lets the user know you're actually working for them while they're waiting.

Finally, if your application is a fairly simple utility type program, you might even consider a "Don't show this form again" check box on the opening form and take the user right to the form they're looking for. But don't do this if it means losing the advantages of having the opening form information displayed as noted earlier.

# A Not-So-Foolish Consistency

Professional software has the same "look and feel" throughout. The forms all look pretty much the same—same colors, graphics, fonts. The reports all follow the same format. It's important that your product reflect consistency for two reasons. First, it makes the product look professional. That, of course, is the image you wish to project. But second, and much more importantly, it makes your program easier to learn and use. And that's what will really make you money.

## Consistency in Forms

Most forms that maintain a set of data will have common functions: add data, edit data, delete data, find data, report data. And an exit button. If you create a template or model for your forms and follow the model consistently, your application will be much easier for your user to learn and use. The button for a certain function will be in the same place on every form.

For example, in E-Z-MRP, I decided to put a menu bar along the bottom of the form. So the menu bar along the bottom of the form for the maintenance of parts, as shown in Figure 3-3, is quite similar to the menu bar for entering the manufacturer's cross-reference data, as you can see in Figure 3-4.

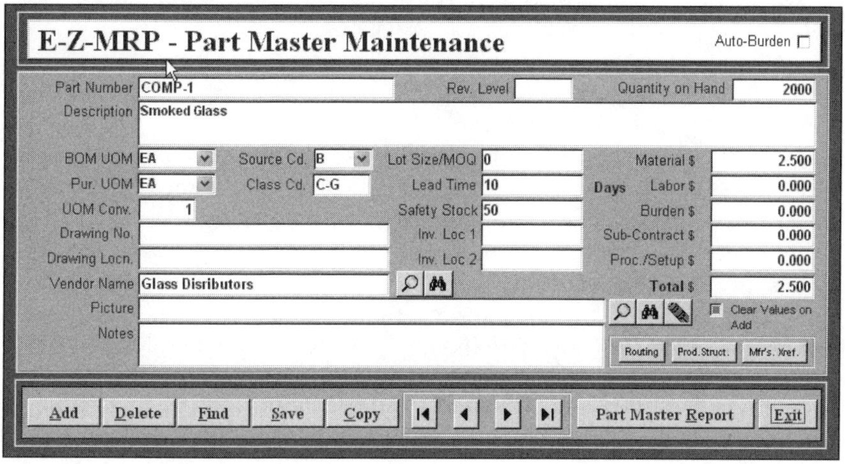

**Figure 3-3.** E-Z-MRP Part Master Maintenance form

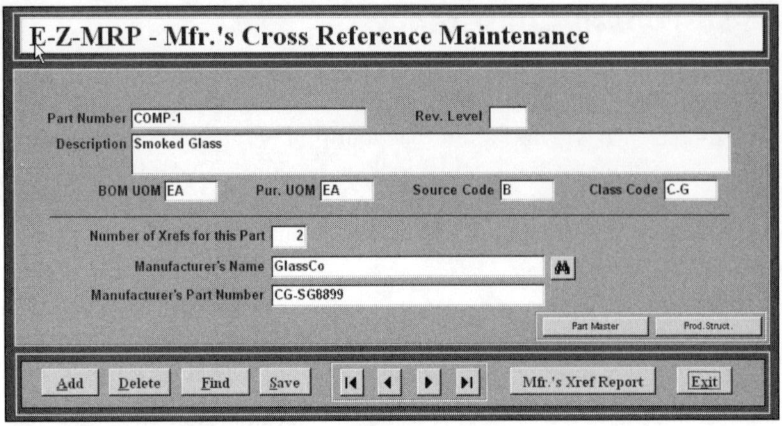

**Figure 3-4.** E-Z-MRP Manufacturer's Cross Reference Maintenance form

The first four buttons along the menu bar at the bottom of the form are Add, Delete, Find, and Save. The button on the bottom right is always Exit. The button to the left of the Exit button is always the report button. The four navigation buttons representing first record, previous record, next record and last record, respectively, are always in the same place from one form to another.

Repeating this pattern consistently over the entire application makes it easier for your users to learn, understand, and use.

Similarly, at the top of every form in the application is a banner clearly stating the function of the form. The general rule—be consistent in the use of color, font, and appearance of controls.

In a form or report, color, as will be discussed at more length later, creates conscious and unconscious associations in the mind of the observer between the color and a function or property of the object so colored. Where there is no difference in function, a difference in color is a distraction. So, for example, you'll notice that the background color for every E-Z-MRP form is the same. To see these figures in color, please go to the book's web site: **www.apress.com/book/view/1590599713**. Then click the Book Extras link and download the file containing the figures.

Note also the consistency of the font and the font color for command buttons, data fields, and data labels. Throughout the application, command buttons on the menu bar are Times New Roman, 10 point, Bold. Data labels and data fields are Arial, 9 point. I like those two fonts because they are easy to read and common to all systems. But there are lots of good fonts. Pick a couple you like. But stick with them all the way through your application. I'll discuss guidelines and recommendations for font selection in more detail a bit later in the section "Type Casting: Selecting the Right Font."

This consistency is not a federal law. You might want to vary from your template on occasion. But when a control, label, or data field varies from your convention, be sure you are doing it to draw the user's attention, consciously and/or unconsciously, to a difference in function.

Here's another approach to the menu bar but displaying the same consistency. The legal matter tracking system—DocketWorks—puts its menu bar at the top of the form as you can see in Figure 3-5, the form that maintains information about persons, and in Figure 3-6, the form for clients.

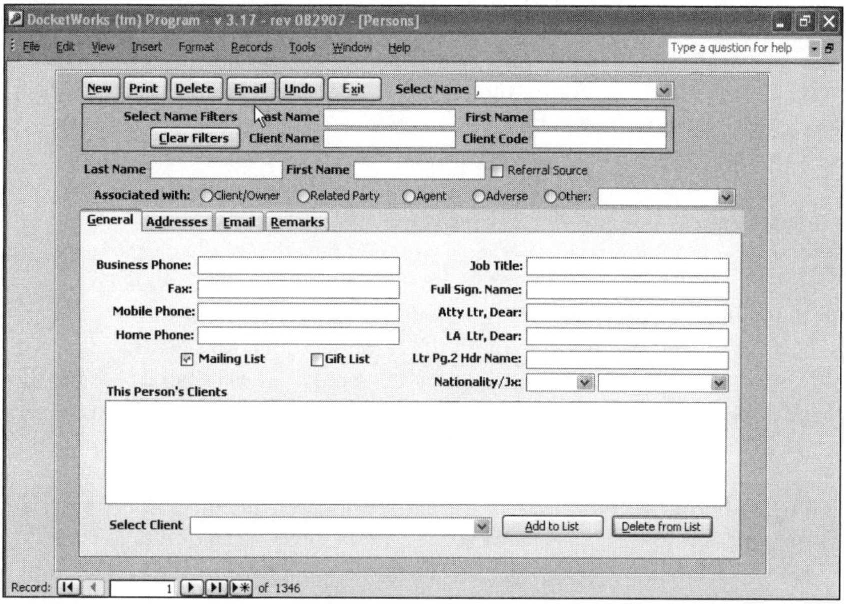

**Figure 3-5.** DocketWorks Persons form

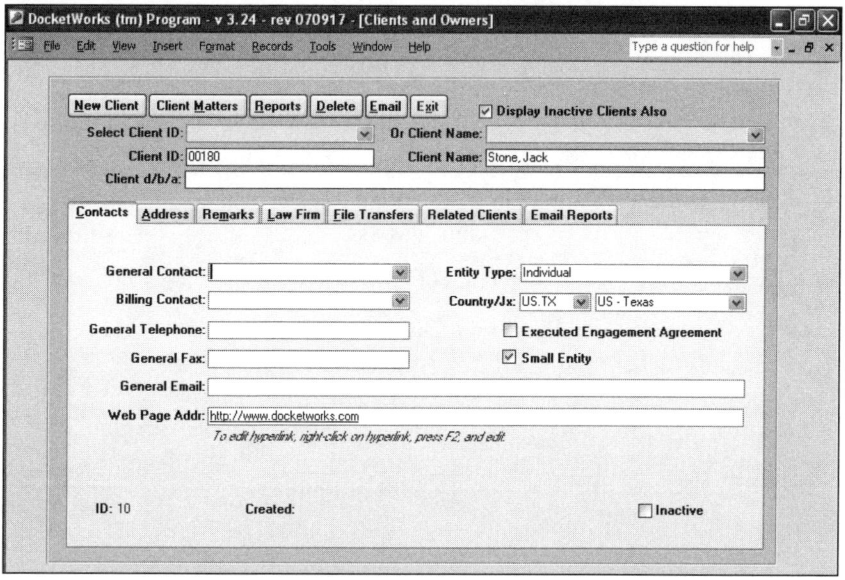

**Figure 3-6.** DocketWorks Clients form

However, note that while the format of the command buttons is consistent, the order of the buttons and the captions are not consistent between the two forms. In the Persons form, the New button should probably be labeled New Persons.

Since this is a product under development, the developer still has a chance to correct this before the product is launched.

A lot of designers like to use little graphics or icons on their command buttons. There are some semi-standard graphics for certain functions but no universally accepted ones. For example, on the Exit button of a form, you'll often see a graphic of an arrow pointing to an open door. But not always.

Careful use of icons can really enhance the eye appeal as well as usability of your program. Check out Ben Cage's use of icons in activ8's Pathways 9 product (**www.activ8.com.au**). On the Pathways 9 product page (click the What's New in V9 link), you can see a well-composed, visually pleasing, balanced form with icons that the user quickly comes to associate with a particular function. The labels underneath the icon clear up any ambiguity.

My personal preference is still for text labels. No matter how popular your icon is, your user will still have to learn its meaning. Icons or labels—it's a fielder's choice. Let your decision be governed, as always, by your customers.

But whether you use icons or text labels, just use the same ones throughout your application for the same function. To close a form, always label the command button Exit or Close or Done or Adios. Whatever caption you pick for the first form you create, however, should be used on all of them. Then, once users learn how to exit from one form, they've learned how to exit from all of them.

## Consistency in Reports

Much of what was said about consistency in forms applies to consistency in reports. Some guidelines:

- Decide on a font and a size for data fields and labels, and use them consistently on every report.

- Try not to use smaller than 9-point type, especially if a large part of your demographic is wearing reading glasses.

- Be consistent on your selection of colors for data and labels.

- Don't use a colored background; in general, higher contrast between text and background makes the report easier to read.

- Design a report header, which should include the product name and a descriptive report name—and use it on every report.

- Put a date and time stamp and a page number on each page of each report.

- If your report can be sorted in different ways and/or filtered by the user (such as specifying a date range), include those sorting and data selection criteria on the report—either in the header or on the last page of the report. Printing any filtering or data selection criteria somewhere on your reports is very important, as it alerts the reader that they may be looking at a subset of the data and not the entire dataset.

- In my applications, I have a preference to give the option to the user to display every report on the screen or send it to the printer. The choice is not always appropriate, but I make the suggestion here and leave it to your judgment whether or not that's a good idea for your application. But if you do it, do it for all reports where it is appropriate.

## Consistency in Operation

Of the three—forms, reports, and operations—consistency in operation is arguably the most important. At this point, you probably know what I mean by consistency in operation—common operations among your forms should operate the same way. Let me give you a concrete example.

Figure 3-7 shows a form from the E-Z-MRP system where the user will spend most of their time. On this form, they can adjust inventory, enter purchase orders and work orders, receive purchased parts, release inventory to manufacturing, complete work orders, and many other operations.

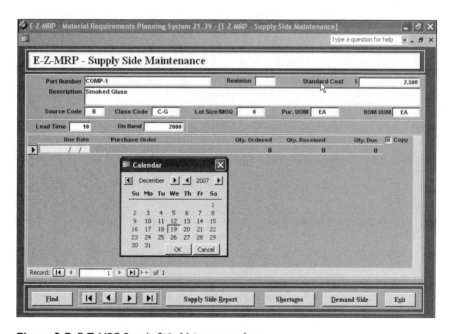

**Figure 3-7.** E-Z-MRP Supply Side Maintenance form

Entering dates can be a tedious operation in any application. In E-Z-MRP, double-clicking a field where the user enters a date pops up the calendar control as shown in Figure 3-7, and the user can then select the date they want by clicking the calendar. Convenient.

But, it must be implemented that way on ALL date fields in the application. Once the user expects the calendar to pop up in response to double-clicking a date field, they will expect that behavior on any and all date fields.

Here's another example. On that Supply Side Maintenance form, there are three fields where the user can enter a number to change quantity on hand (labeled "On Hand"). When the user clicks the On Hand field, they can enter information one of three ways:

1. If they want to **increase** the quantity on hand by a known amount, they enter a **+** (plus) sign before the number, and that amount is **added** to the current quantity on hand.

2. If they want to **decrease** the quantity on hand by a known amount, they enter a – (minus) sign before the number, and that amount is **subtracted** from the current quantity on hand.

3. If they want to **replace** the quantity on hand with a known amount, they enter the new quantity without preceding it with either a **+** (plus) or a – (minus) sign. The number they enter will **replace** the current quantity on hand.

There are three other fields on that form where the user enters numeric information—Quantity Ordered, Quantity Received, and Lead Time. Those fields all follow the same three rules.

That method of changing a numeric field is applied to every numeric field in the system. Because once the user is trained on how to make changes to a numeric field like On Hand, they're going to expect those rules will hold for every numeric field in the application, where appropriate. I can't think right off of a need to violate this rule in my application. But there may be some case where numeric information is not adjusted by incrementing or decrementing by some quantity. In that case, the preceding three rules should not be implemented.

Rules are good, and consistency is important. But blind adherence to the rule simply for the sake of consistency might reduce rather than enhance the usability of your program. Remember Emerson's advice: "Foolish consistency is the hobgoblin of little minds."

## Type Casting: Selecting the Right Font

If you're not sure what font to use, start with two—**Times New Roman** and **Arial**. The first is called a **serif** font because of all the little "hooks" and "feet"—small decorative embellishments—that appear on each letter. The second is **sans serif**—it doesn't have those decorative embellishments.

One of the best things about those two fonts is that they will display correctly on every computer. There are thousands of typefaces available. Many of the more exotic ones will not display correctly if that typeface is not installed on the target computer. So if you want to use one of those nonstandard typefaces, you'll have to install it as part of installing your application. Who needs the headache?

Unless you have a compelling reason to use some other typeface, start, and maybe end, with those two. They have the additional advantages of being readable, familiar, professional, and dignified. And they keep your life simple.

Resist the temptation to use interesting fonts like **Braggadocio** or Papyrus or *BrushScript* or hard-to-read fonts like *Edwardian Script* or *Mistral*, unless the theme of your application dictates it or your audience really thinks it's cool.

But, in any event, try to limit the number of fonts to a maximum of two. And use them consistently—perhaps one for labels and the other for data.

And test your font and point size selection at various screen resolutions. Sometimes your characters will become broken or difficult to read as the screen resolution changes.

## The Color of Money: Picking the Right Palette

There are two reasons to pay close attention to the use of color in your product: aesthetics and functionality. Both considerations go to the heart of the matter: will color choice affect sales?

### Aesthetics in Color Selection

The first, and obvious, reason to give careful consideration to your color scheme is aesthetic. You want your program to appear pleasing to the eye. Pleasing is in the eye of the beholder, of course. So you have to know your audience.

There is a whole science of color in marketing and advertising. Blue is supposed to be the color of trust and wisdom. Pharmaceutical products use it extensively. They want you to trust them. Check the web sites for Ambien, Lunesta, and Sonata.

Green is the color of nature and healing. Black is sophistication. Orange is the fall color and evokes strong emotions about home, and holidays, and food.

A little of research on the science of color in merchandising and advertising is a good thing. It can't tell you what colors will be best for your application, but it can help you avoid making obviously stupid mistakes, although I wouldn't make a career out of it. In the end, your customers are buying a solution. Bad color choice can ruin your application. But a good color scheme is a break-even proposition. It's the solution they'll be judging you on, not your choice of colors.

I was about to tell you that soft pastels like those you see in the opening form of The Sleep Advisor (shown earlier in Figure 3-2) are pleasing and inviting. At a minimum, they aren't jarring or off putting. And so you should avoid primary colors.

Primary colors may be good for products like laundry detergent and break-fast cereal. (Take a fresh look at the laundry soap and breakfast cereal sections the next time you're in the grocery store. They're all shouting for your atten-tion.) But, of course, you're not competing with a lot of other products for your users' attention. So a lot of that bold coloration is probably not a great thing for software that someone will be looking at all day.

But suppose you're writing an application to catalog punk rock music. Your audience will not be attracted by a Laura Ashley theme. They'll be looking for something chaotic that more resembles a mosh pit. Violent splashes of red and yellow might be just the ticket.

Nevertheless, there are a few things you should not do. Don't put blue type on a red background. It makes the letters vibrate and gives you a headache. Don't put blue type on a black background. You can't read it. And in general, dark type on a light background is easier to read than light type on a dark background. Regardless of your user's aesthetic sense or mental state, if they can't read it, they can't use it.

Otherwise, the only hard-and-fast rule to follow on the aesthetics of color selection is the same one I keep coming back to for so many of your applica-tion's design decisions—know your market and let the users make the final decision.

## Functionality in Color Selection

As you have probably noticed, the figures in this book are all printed in black and white. In this section on the functionality of color, I refer to the use of color in a couple of figures; this won't be very instructive unless you download and look at the color version of the figures in this book. So to understand bet-ter the points about the use of color, you should first point your browser to the web site for this book: **www.apress.com/book/view/1590599713**. Then click the Book Extras link and download the file there containing the figures.

The judicious use of color in your application can improve its functionality considerably. The DocketWorks program has a form where the user enters time information for billing purposes. Figure 3-8 shows what it looked like as originally designed.

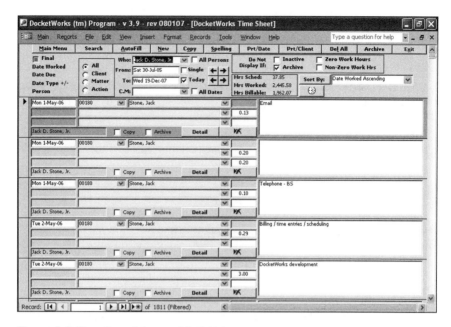

**Figure 3-8.** Time Sheet form—original design

And Figure 3-9 shows how it looks as redesigned.

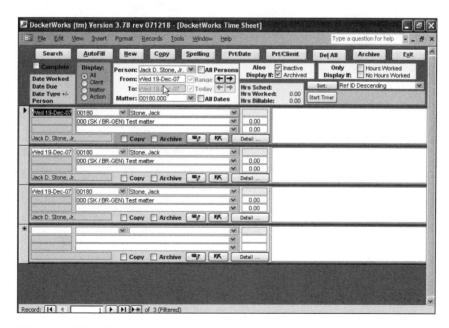

**Figure 3-9.** Time Sheet form—redesign

This form has the disadvantage of being very "control rich." There's a lot of information that needs to be collected and presented. And a lot of different options in the header that the client insisted upon.

To overcome this problem in the redesign, the various controls were grouped by color. And where the controls or labels in the heading had corresponding data fields in the detail section, the same color was used in both places (as in the pink and green sections).

Note also that both forms' headers use the same amount of "real estate"— space on the screen. Both have a lot of controls squeezed into the same small area. But the use of color in the redesign gives the impression of a more spacious arrangement. It's more readable and easier to find the controls or data you're looking for.

Note also in the redesigned Time Sheet form that the background of the selected record is turned from that neutral color to a bright blue. This is a visual cue telling the user what record they are currently working with.

## Preferential Treatments

Everybody likes the feeling of walking into their favorite pub and hearing the barkeep say, "The usual?" I'm always a little flattered when I walk into the China Café and the owner says, "Ah, Mr. Rocky. Bean Curd Szechwan?"

It's no different with software. We all appreciate a program that remembers what we like. Building this feature into your application is one of the easiest things you can do to increase both the perception and the reality of value.

In a multiuser system, you want these preferences or options to be local to the user so that each user can tailor the system to their own likings.

To do this, simply set up a table to save the values of all the switches, options, date forms, sorting choices, data ranges, etc., anything the user chooses.

For example, some reports allow the user a great many options. They may run the same report repeatedly. So they want to see the options they entered the last time they ran it. Figure 3-10 shows a form from the E-Z-MRP system that generates a report which tells the user what they have on hand and what's on order.

The user here has lots of options. They can select up to three levels of sorting on various fields. They can filter the contents of the report by entering ranges of data on nine different fields. Down the right side they have several more options. And they probably want to run the report pretty much the same way every time.

So I created a table in the program that saves the value of each of those controls when the user clicks the Exit button. The next time the user opens this form, I go and fetch those values from the preferences table and set the controls to whatever they had them set to the last time.

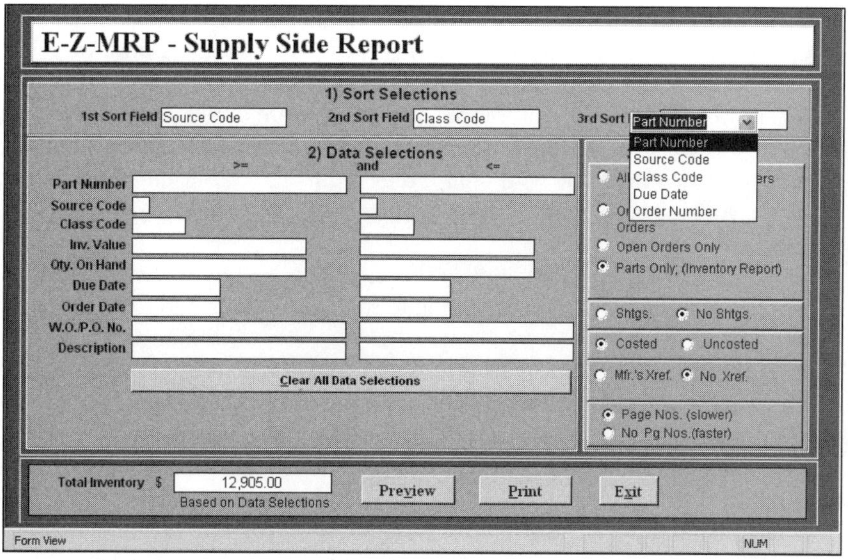

**Figure 3-10.** E-Z-MRP Supply Side report

These are all local values—particular to the user. So they stay with the user's copy of the program on their computer. There are some preferences that are "global" in nature. These, like the office thermostat, should only be changeable by one person—the administrator. A global preference might be the currency symbol. Everyone who works with your application's database will be working in the same currency. The database, which is shared by many users, will reside on a server. And that's where you want to put the preferences table for global preferences.

Implementing this feature is easy if you set up the preferences table before you create the first form. Then, as you add controls to new forms in your application, add the control name to your preferences table, and add the two lines of code that save and fetch the value of that control.

The preferences are not limited to data values or sort selections. As in the Supply Side report earlier, they can set the value of option buttons. They can determine formats or how data is displayed—a date format, a telephone number, whether commas separate the thousands in your numeric data, or the number of decimal places, the currency symbol—just about anything for which the user may have a preference.

## A Foreign Concept: Getting Ready to Sell Overseas

When I launched E-Z-MRP, there was no Internet. If you're under thirty, you may find that hard to believe. But it's true. Selling to other countries was just not on the radar of many small software developers. After all, the United States represented a market about the same size as or perhaps bigger than the rest of the world. There was no e-mail to speak of, so it was snail mail and expensive long distance phone calls. Doing business overseas was awkward at best.

There were lots of other problems, too. There were duties and customs problems to deal with (we used to send diskettes—none of the governments seemed to know what to do with them), they didn't work the same hours as we did, they wouldn't speak English, and payments were a problem. Who needed the headache?

But, in spite of solely marketing in the U.S., I got an inquiry from a dealer in Belgium who said that if he was going to sell E-Z-MRP, it had to be in Dutch.

OK. Never one to shy away from a challenge, I wrote a little program that would strip out the English literals from my program, and package them in text files that I sent off to Belgium. He put the Dutch translation under each English line and sent it back. Then another program I wrote would replace all the English with Dutch and Prachtig! E-Z-MRP in Dutch.

Of course, whenever I had to change the English version, I had to change the Dutch version. Two systems to maintain, but a manageable problem.

Then, of course, it wasn't long before the dealer, being Belgian, needed a French version as well. OK, no problem. We've got the translation programs and the system down pat. A few translations, and I had E-Z-MRP in French (Merveilleux!).

Then I had a chance to make a Spanish version (Maravilloso!). Followed quickly by Portuguese (Maravilhoso!). And finally, just before the end of the DOS era, Chinese (美妙!).

By the time I was ready to redesign and rewrite E-Z-MRP in Microsoft Access, the world had changed. No more hard-copy sales and product litera-ture. No more diskettes and hard-copy manuals. No more UPS and FedEx. Everything went over the Web. And everything came in through the Web. This meant that Poland was as close as Los Angeles. All marketing, promotion, and sales activities were international.

Now I may not be too smart, but I'm trainable. I figured that foreign lan-guage versions of the new package would be needed in fairly short order. So I needed to devise a way to have one package that would support multiple lan-guages. And it had to be easy for someone to make the translations. And it had to be easy to update.

And, most importantly, it had to be thought out BEFORE I started pro-gramming. It had to be part of the design specification.

Now I didn't break any new ground here technologically. There's lots of software available in multiple foreign languages. It's become fairly standard for web pages. So I cooked up my own solution. You can use mine, make your own, or crib someone else's.

But unless you're absolutely positive that you'll never need or want to sell your application in a foreign language, you should anticipate during the design process that you'll need foreign language versions and allow for it.

Here's what I did. The text that appears on the screen and in printed reports falls into two broad categories—captions that appear on labels and command buttons, and messages that are displayed on the screen ("Enter starting date before running report"—stuff like that) or are printed on reports ("The contents of this report have been filtered by the following fields," etc.).

So I created two tables. The first one holds the translations for the controls. The second one holds the translations for the messages. Figure 3-11 shows what the fields look like for the table that holds the translations for controls.

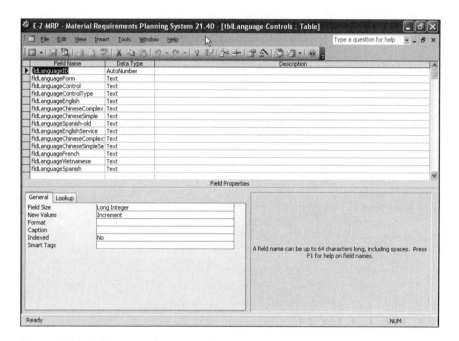

**Figure 3-11.** Fields to translate controls into multiple languages

For each control on a form or report that needs to be translated, a record is created containing the name of the form, the name of the control, the control type, and the English caption.

Figure 3-12 shows what the data in this table looks like.

When a new language is needed, a field is added to the table, and the table is exported to another Access database or a spreadsheet. This is sent to the foreign dealer or whoever has agreed to do the translation. They fill in the blanks under the new column for each control needing translation and send it back. I import it into the E-Z-MRP front end, and Bob's your uncle—new language.

| fldLanguageID | fldLanguageForm | fldLanguageControl | fldLangu | fldLanguageEnglish | fldLanguageChineseComplex | fldLanguageSpanish | fldLanguageFrench |
|---|---|---|---|---|---|---|---|
| 1 | frmMainMenu | Label46 | 100 | System Date: | 系統日期 | Fecha del Sistema: | Date système |
| 2 | frmMainMenu | Label10 | 100 | E-Z-MRP - Main Menu | 易利製造管理 - 主選單 | E-Z-MRP - Menú Principal | EZ MRP - Menu Général |
| 3 | frmMainMenu | Label47 | 100 | Current Database: | 目前資料庫 | Base de Datos Actual: | Base de donnée ouverte |
| 4 | frmMainMenu | cmdBillsofMaterial | 104 | &Bills of Material | 材料構成表&B | &Lista de Materiales | &Articles |
| 5 | frmMainMenu | cmdMaterialPlanning | 104 | &Material Planning | 材料規劃&M | Plan. de &Materiales | Prévision &Matériel |
| 6 | frmMainMenu | cmdCapacityPlanning | 104 | &Capacity Planning | 產能規劃&C | Planif. de &Capacidad | Prévision &Capacité |
| 7 | frmMainMenu | cmdPurchaseOrders | 104 | &Purchase Orders | 採購單&P | &Ordenes de Compras | &Ordre d'Achat |
| 8 | frmMainMenu | cmdLaborDistribution | 104 | &Labor Distribution | 人力分派&L | Distribución de la Mano de &Obra | C&harge |
| 9 | frmMainMenu | cmdPhysicalInventory | 104 | Physical &Inventory | 實際盤點&I | &Inventario Físico | &Inventaire |
| 10 | frmMainMenu | cmdBatchReportGenerator | 104 | Batch &Reporting | 批次與報表&R | rpt por lote | &Batch / Etats |
| 11 | frmMainMenu | cmdAutoCADInterface | 104 | &AutoCAD Interface | AutoCAD 介面&A | interfase autocad | Interface &AutoCad |
| 12 | frmMainMenu | cmdUtilities | 104 | &Utilities | 工具作業&U | &Utilidades | &Utilitaires |
| 13 | frmMainMenu | cmdEndProgram | 104 | &End Program | 程式結束&E | &Terminar el programa | &Fin |
| 14 | frmMainMenu | Label13 | 100 | ™ |  | ™ | ™ |
| 15 | frmMainMenu | cmdChangeUser | 104 | C&hange User | 更改使用者&H | Cambiar Usua&rio | &Changer Utilisateur |
| 2328 | frmBillofMaterials | Label46 | 100 | System Date: | 系統日期 | Fecha del Sistema: | Date Système: |
| 2329 | frmBillofMaterials | Label47 | 100 | Current Database: | 目前資料庫 | Base de Datos Actual: | Base courante : |
| 2330 | frmBillofMaterials | cmdPartsMaster | 104 | Parts &Master | 料件主檔&M | &Maestro de Partes | &Code Article |
| 2331 | frmBillofMaterials | cmdProductStructure | 104 | Product &Structure | 產品結構&S | &Estuct. del Producto | &Nomenclature |
| 2332 | frmBillofMaterials | cmdMfrsXref | 104 | Mfr. &Cross Ref. | 廠商對照參考&C | Ref. Cruz. del &Fabr. | &Réf. Fournisseur |
| 2333 | frmBillofMaterials | cmdPartsMasterReport | 104 | &Parts Master | 料件主檔&P | Maestro de &Partes | Code &Article |
| 2334 | frmBillofMaterials | cmdBillofMaterialsReport | 104 | &Bills of Material | 材料構成表&B | &Lista de Materiales | N&omenclature |
| 2335 | frmBillofMaterials | cmdWhereUsed | 104 | &Where Used | 用途表&W | Puntos de-&Uso | Ca&s d'emploi |
| 2336 | frmBillofMaterials | cmdCopyABill | 104 | Cop&y a Bill | 複製料表&Y | Cop&iar una Lista | Co&pie Nomencl. |
| 2337 | frmBillofMaterials | cmdCostRollUp | 104 | Cost Roll &Up | 成本累算&U | &Acurnul. del coste | Reca&lcul coûts |
| 2338 | frmBillofMaterials | cmdExitToMainMenu | 104 | E&xit to Main Menu | 離開至主選單&X | &Salir al Menú Principal | S&ortie |
| 2339 | frmBillofMaterials | Label64 | 100 | File Maintenance | 檔案維護 | Manten. de los Arch. | Programmes |
| 2340 | frmBillofMaterials | Label65 | 100 | Reports | 報表 | rpt | Etats |
| 2341 | frmBillofMaterials | Label66 | 100 | Other Functions | 其它功能 | Otras Funciones | Autres fonctions |

**Figure 3-12.** Data in the language table for controls

The language is stored as a preference (see the section "Preferential Treatments" earlier in this chapter) through a form in the application that looks like what you see in Figure 3-13.

This language preference is stored in a local table so that, in a multiuser environment, one user could be using the system in one language, and another user could be using the system in a different language.

Translations are done on the fly. When a form or report opens, one of a handful of translation subroutines is called. The form or report name is passed to the translation subroutine, and the subroutine looks at each control on the form or report, checking to see if that control name appears in the table that has the translations for the controls. If it finds a record for that control, the caption of that control is changed programmatically to the language specified by the local language preference.

That's a kind of wordy description of what, you can see, is a very simple approach to translating your application. The Asian languages are a little trickier. First, they require that the users install the Windows East Asian Language support. And second, they may require you to use Unicode. But these are all trivial problems for a crack programmer like you. Right?

The other table—the one that contains the messages—is structured just a little differently, as you can see in Figure 3-14. But the principle is the same.

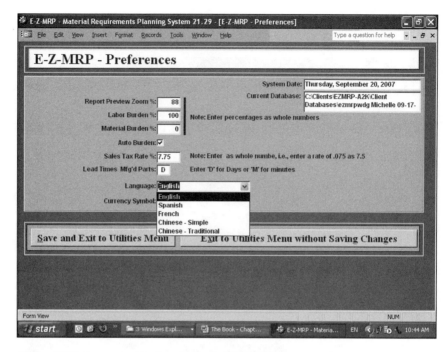

**Figure 3-13.** Language selection on the Preferences form

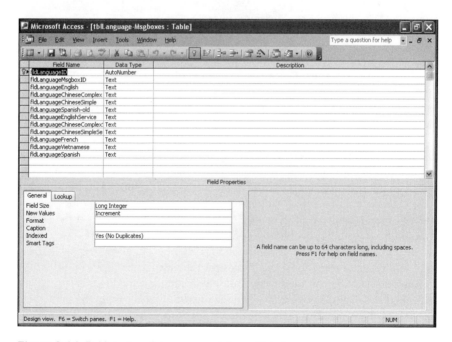

**Figure 3-14.** Fields to translate messages into multiple languages

And the data looks like what appears in Figure 3-15.

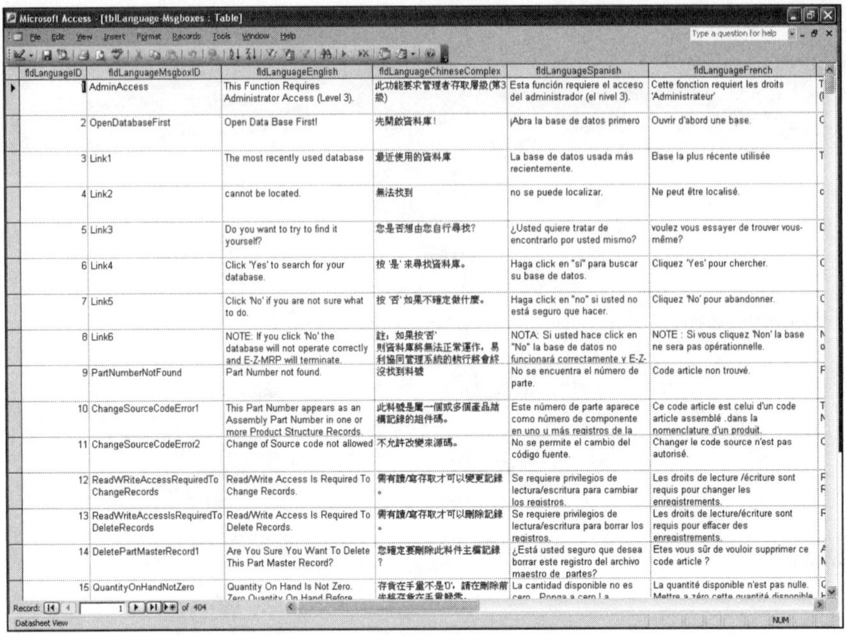

| fldLanguageID | fldLanguageMsgboxID | fldLanguageEnglish | fldLanguageChineseComplex | fldLanguageSpanish | fldLanguageFrench |
|---|---|---|---|---|---|
| 1 | AdminAccess | This Function Requires Administrator Access (Level 3). | 此功能要求管理者存取層級(第3級) | Esta función requiere el acceso del administrador (el nivel 3). | Cette fonction requiert les droits 'Administrateur' |
| 2 | OpenDatabaseFirst | Open Data Base First! | 先開啟資料庫! | ¡Abra la base de datos primero | Ouvrir d'abord une base. |
| 3 | Link1 | The most recently used database | 最近使用的資料庫 | La base de datos usada más recientemente. | Base la plus récente utilisée |
| 4 | Link2 | cannot be located. | 無法找到 | no se puede localizar. | Ne peut être localisé. |
| 5 | Link3 | Do you want to try to find it yourself? | 您是否想由您自行尋找? | ¿Usted quiere tratar de encontrarlo por usted mismo? | voulez vous essayer de trouver vous-même? |
| 6 | Link4 | Click 'Yes' to search for your database. | 按 '是' 來尋找資料庫。 | Haga click en "sí" para buscar su base de datos. | Cliquez 'Yes' pour chercher. |
| 7 | Link5 | Click 'No' if you are not sure what to do. | 按 '否' 如果不確定做什麼。 | Haga click en "no" si usted no está seguro que hacer. | Cliquez 'No' pour abandonner. |
| 8 | Link6 | NOTE: If you click 'No' the database will not operate correctly and E-Z-MRP will terminate. | 註: 如果按'否' 則資料庫將無法正常運作, 易利協同管理系統的執行終會終 | NOTA: Si usted hace click en "No" la base de datos no funcionará correctamente y E-Z- | NOTE : Si vous cliquez 'Non' la base ne sera pas opérationnelle. |
| 9 | PartNumberNotFound | Part Number not found. | 沒找到料號 | No se encuentra el número de parte. | Code article non trouvé. |
| 10 | ChangeSourceCodeError1 | This Part Number appears as an Assembly Part Number in one or more Product Structure Records. | 此料號是屬一個或多個產品結構記錄的組件碼。 | Este número de parte aparece como número de componente en uno u más registros de la | Ce code article est celui d'un code article assemblé .dans la nomenclature d'un produit. |
| 11 | ChangeSourceCodeError2 | Change of Source code not allowed | 不允許改變來源碼。 | No se permite el cambio del código fuente. | Changer le code source n'est pas autorisé. |
| 12 | ReadWRiteAccessRequiredTo ChangeRecords | Read/Write Access Is Required To Change Records. | 需有讀/寫存取才可以變更記錄。 | Se require privilegios de lectura/escritura para cambiar los registros. | Les droits de lecture /écriture sont requis pour changer les enregistrements. |
| 13 | ReadWRiteAccessIsRequiredTo DeleteRecords | Read/Write Access Is Required To Delete Records. | 需有讀/寫存取才可以刪除記錄。 | Se require privilegios de lectura/escritura para borrar los registros. | Les droits de lecture/écriture sont requis pour effacer des enregistrements. |
| 14 | DeletePartMasterRecord1 | Are You Sure You Want To Delete This Part Master Record? | 您確定要刪除此料件主檔記錄？ | ¿Está usted seguro que desea borrar este registro del archivo maestro de partes? | Etes vous sûr de vouloir supprimer ce code article ? |
| 15 | QuantityOnHandNotZero | Quantity On Hand Is Not Zero. Zero Quantity On Hand Before | 存貨在手量不是0，請在刪除前 先把存貨在手量歸零。 | La cantidad disponible no es cero. Ponga a cero la | La quantité disponible n'est pas nulle. Mettre a zéro cette quantité disponible |

Record: 1 of 404
Datasheet View

**Figure 3-15.** Multilanguage showing translations

The field **fldLanguageMsgboxID** is the key by which a message is retrieved. In VBA the call to display a message looks like this:

```
MsgboxUni Me.hWnd, TranslateMsgbox("PartAlreadyInDatabase"), ,
vbExclamation
```

The routine **TranslateMsgbox** looks up the message in the table using the key and passes the right translation to the message box. The ID can be a number or an abbreviation, but I choose to have rather descriptive IDs because it makes the code more self-documenting and easier to read. The ID for this message could just have easily been PAID or PM200. But looking at the code, it would have been impossible to tell what the message said.

So you can see how easy it would be to add a new language. Simply add a field to the end of each of the two tables for the new language, and send it off to your translator. If you want to get fancy, you could even add a field for dialects of English—British English has some different phrasing than U.S. English, and if it means more sales, then it's probably the easiest way to make your software look friendly across the pond.

## International Date, Time, Number, and Currency Formatting

The two other places where your international edition will differ from your domestic release are 1) date formats and 2) currency symbol. Fortunately, both of these problems have been largely taken care of through Windows' Regional and Language Options dialog box (see Figure 3-16).

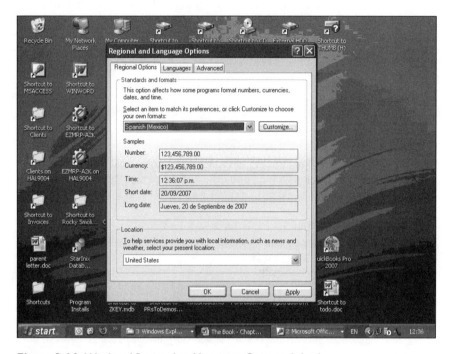

**Figure 3-16.** Windows' Regional and Language Options dialog box

Here your user can pick their country and the date, number, and currency fields will be displayed in the local format.

## *Size Matters: Issues in Screen Resizing*

*I can tell you what drives me nuts about web pages—pages where I have to scroll just a bit to get to a link—that drives me nuts. Or a page where there's only garbage at the top and I have to scroll to see the real information. The important information and action links/buttons need to be on that first screen—not just 1/2 inch off to the right or below. To me, that just smacks of bad design/programming.*

Susan Sales Harkins—notorious Apress author

Whether on the Web or a local application developed in Access, VB, C, or any other platform, your users will have displays set to various resolutions.

This means that, absent any adjustments by you inside your program, the forms you display on the screen will appear either bigger or smaller than they do to you on your machine. Whether bigger or smaller depends on whether the target machine's screen resolution is higher or lower than the screen resolution of the machine on which the form was designed.

If your form goes to a machine with a higher resolution, your form will shrink. If it goes to a machine with a lower resolution, your form will appear larger.

I have always tried to develop my product to the lowest common denominator of user so that they don't have to add any hardware or software or make any adjustments to their system just to run my product. That's just being friendly.

So I run my displays and design my forms in 800X600. First of all, that makes the icons and the controls and text nice and big for my presbyopic eyes. But more importantly, in the absence of screen resizing code in your application, your forms will appear smaller at higher resolutions—although on some super hi-res monitors this will have the effect of shrinking your form down to a maybe a quarter of the screen size. At least you'll be able to see the whole form.

If you develop your forms in a higher resolution, like 1280X768, and give your application to someone who is running a lower-resolution screen, your form will be bigger than their screen. To see what's on the bottom or right side, they'll have to use the scrollbars. Assuming that you put the scrollbars on your form. Annoying AND unfriendly.

The solution is to include in your application some kind of code that will change the size of each control on a form in proportion to the difference between the resolution in which the form was designed and the resolution of the user's screen.

Yes, it's tricky coding. But chances are someone has already written that code for the platform you're developing in. I develop in Microsoft Access. So I use the screen resizing code included on the CD packaged with the *Access 2000 Developer's Handbook* by Getz, Littwin, and Gilbert (Sybex, 1999). Just drop the module into your application, and call the screen resizer in the Open event of every form. You can find similar resizing routines in other languages as well.

One user I visited had my software up on a 22" widescreen monitor. My screen resizing function filled the screen with the opening form. It was very much in your face—pretty dramatic. You could read it from across the room. The designer of the DocketWorks program has included a local preference to use or disable the screen resizing code. So that way your user gets the best of both worlds.

# When Good Software Goes Bad: Error Trapping and Reporting

Bugs happen. Can't be helped. No one expects software to be perfect. I mean if a megacorp like Microsoft can't put out a bug-free application, how can you expect to?

Problems will occur. The differences among software vendors is how fast they respond to a problem. There's nothing more unfriendly than a cryptic error message and an abrupt return to the desktop. Further, when the user calls to tell you something has gone wrong, they won't be able to tell you what it is, where it occurred, or what the error message was. And frankly, that's not their job. It's your job.

Every module, routine, or what have you in your application must have error trapping code—something that will create a clear explanatory message both for you—so you can fix the problem—and the user—to let them know you're on the job.

In E-Z-MRP, I modified a terrific piece of code that creates error handlers in all of the modules in an Access database. The module—named VBErrorHandler—is available for download at **www.databaseadvisors.com/downloads.asp**—and is described on the site as

> . . . *a wizard that allows you to insert error handler code into existing functions and subs. It will insert the "OnError goto" statement, plus an "Exit function" section and then below that, an error handler. The error handler can be a simple msgbox or a completely formed case statement. There is an installation doc in the zip, plus a write-up of using it.*
> *Glen Grubb, Seth Galitzer, John Colby . . .*

I modified the module so that instead of displaying an error message, it opens a form describing the error and giving the user the option of printing the report or sending the report problem to Beach Access Software via e-mail. Since there are no more bugs in E-Z-MRP (casting eyes toward ceiling in innocence), I artificially generated one by dividing a number by zero, just to show you what the error form looks like (see Figure 3-17).

As you can see, this error message gives an indication of where the error occurred, and displays the error number and description.

Just as importantly, it gives the user a clear instruction on what to do next. If you are not developing your application in Microsoft Access, looking at this code might still be instructive. It is a convenient way to build standard error trapping and reporting functionality into every module in your application.

Don't skimp on this. Error trapping, reporting, and clear messages must be a very high-priority element of your application design.

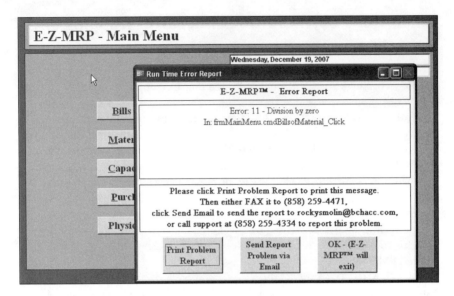

**Figure 3-17.** Error message

It is also important to spend some time on the exact text of each message. For example, "Error 5, File not found." is more irritating than it is helpful. Your user has no idea what to do about it, except possibly to call you for support. And when you get the call, it will be difficult for you to give a good answer.

Include in your error report what function the program is attempting to perform, the full path and file name that cannot be found, and a suggestion as to what the user should do to correct the problem. The complete message should be in terms that the user understands, no geek speak, please, except do include a message ID code you can use to locate the exact message if you need to find it in the source. It is amazing how many support calls can be resolved by an informative error message.

## A Quick Word About Mice

I'm a mousophobe. I don't like mice. They are a necessary evil, I suppose. But when I design an application, I try to implement it in a way that it can be run entirely without the use of a mouse, strictly from keyboard commands, hot keys, and shortcuts.

This is especially important for applications involving a lot of data entry. The operators are going to be much more efficient if they can keep their hands on the keyboard. Every time they have to move from the mouse to the keyboard decreases their efficiency. So I recommend strongly that you make your application as keyboard friendly as possible.

## Testing . . . 1, 2, 3 . . . Is This Thing On?

It seems obvious to say, but before you release your product, you have to test it thoroughly.

Of course, you'll be the primary tester—the first line of defense, as it were. You are what you might call the alpha tester. Of course, you know all the right moves to make. So testing your own software can go just so far.

You need some naïve users to do the rest. And this second rank of testers are called Beta testers. And where they test are the Beta test sites.

Users are great. You never know what they're going to do next. I've had users report odd errors to me. And when I asked them how they did it, they often described a sequence of keystrokes that's so illogical, so senseless, it makes you wonder how they found their way to work in the morning.

However, the fact that MY software allowed them to do it and MY software generated an error when they did it is MY fault, and it's MINE to fix.

The naïve user—your Beta tester—will find all of the invalid paths and sequences of operation that you never thought of, let alone thought possible. This, of course, is where the first use and value of your error trapping and reporting will come into play. Because at the Beta testing level you EXPECT bugs. And you want them faithfully documented and reported.

But Beta test subjects have another even more valuable role to play. They will give you feedback on what your program is doing right but can be improved—places where the Tab key tabs to a control that's out of sequence for the work they're doing, places where a keyboard shortcut would be handy so they wouldn't have to move their right hand from the keyboard to the mouse.

It's time-consuming and often inconvenient, but there can be nothing more valuable than sitting with your beta tester and watching over their shoulder as they run your software. They don't always have the technical knowledge to know what the options and possibilities are in software design, to ask the right questions, or make good suggestions. But they know what they like.

As a software designer, you think you know what the problem is, and you design and implement what you think is a real good solution. You take your best guess, and you always hit somewhere (hopefully) close to the target. Your Beta testers will tell you where you've missed the mark. If you pay close attention to the first few Beta testers, they will refine your aim and score a bull's-eye for you.

A note of caution with Beta testers. It is a rare Beta tester who will deliberately go through each function of your program just to see if it works. Most testers will set up the program for just the functionality they need, and that is all that gets tested. If you have five testers and they all test the same two functions of the program, they have been a big help, but the job is not done. It is still up to you to spend your time to exercise every input, every calculation, and every report in your Alpha testing process.

Recruiting Beta testers can be a tricky business. In return for putting up with the inevitable bugs and lack of operational polish in your program, they'll want to get something of value in return. It goes without saying, therefore, that when you give your program to the Beta testers, it should be as operationally smooth and polished and bug free as you can make it. Beta testers are easily frustrated. So if your software doesn't yield something of value for the time and effort they'll be giving you, you'll quickly lose them.

On the upside, if they're satisfied, pleased with your software, and are receiving good value from using it, they will become your first references. Nobody wants to be first. And the prospects that evaluate your product will want to see testimonials and perhaps ask for references to someone who's actually using your product in a working environment. Having that reference will be invaluable as you launch your product.

# And in Conclusion, My Friends . . .

OK, that was a lot of stuff. There are a lot of different issues regarding the appearance of your product, any of which could make or break your product depending on how you implement them.

Before you start programming, I suggest you scan through this chapter and make an action item list of all the design and implementation issues presented here—and any more you think of yourself. Keep this list at your elbow to remind you of issues that otherwise might slip through the cracks. From time to time, do a more detailed review of your progress on each item. In this way, you'll stay on the glide path to a successful conclusion.

# How They Did It: An Interview with Jackie and Doug Murphy of Murphy's Creativity

*Jackie Murphy started Murphy's Creativity (****www.murphyscreativity.com/****) in 1993 to do mailing lists and envelopes. She developed and released her first product in 1999 and was joined by husband Doug in 2000 after he retired. They avoided one of the developer's worst nightmares by watching a colleague's mistakes. The value of their advice on testing cannot be overestimated.*

**Smolin:** You guys are in business here writing and selling software, doing some custom work, but you also have a couple of products.

**J. Murphy:** Right.

**Smolin:** Looking at your web site, I see two products there—Wedding Management for Professionals and Show Producer. Let's talk about Wedding Management for Professionals first. What on earth possessed you to . . . no let me rephrase that . . . why did you create this product? Where did you get the idea? How did it start?

**J. Murphy:** One of the master wedding planners from the Association of Bridal Consultants came to me and said we need software, and I said OK, what do you need?

**Smolin:** And that was it?

**J. Murphy:** That was it. She actually started out just with a database. She said, "I need to work more efficiently," and so we built the database. And then we kind of got it all done and she [said], "Wow, you know, this should be software," and so . . .

**Smolin:** So this woman was from . . .

**J. Murphy:** The Association of Bridal Consultants. She was a master wedding planner.

**Smolin:** Did she hire you initially to create an application for her?

**J. Murphy:** Yeah.

**Smolin:** So you did the database and then a front end?

**J. Murphy:** Right.

**Smolin:** And was it highly customized for her requirements?

**J. Murphy:** It was. In that all the information we had at that point to create the database came from her. But, as it turns out, because she was a master wedding planner and she'd been at this for so many years, everything that she was doing was also the same knowledge she was passing on to the younger wedding planners. And it was actually pretty much industry standard of how they managed information. So it was actually very beneficial because the design we came up with has pretty much worked across the board for everybody.

Smolin: What year was that?

J. Murphy: That was 1999.

Smolin: You did this in Microsoft Access?

J. Murphy: Access.

Smolin: And did you consider any other platforms for this?

J. Murphy: No. Why would we? You know Access is easy to develop in, right? And that's what we had been working in. So, you know really . . . why change?

D. Murphy: I looked briefly at VB [Visual Basic]. But Access is so convenient to develop in. The reporting is so great. So we stuck with Access.

Smolin: Right. Now you guys do have expertise in other platforms?

D. Murphy: .NET and SQL Server and that stuff. But .NET, you know, if you're going to start all over, that would probably be the way to go, because it's much friendlier to install than Access is now.

J. Murphy: What we're finding with our friends that write software, a lot of them wrote it with VB. And now they're now having to rewrite it in .NET because their VB is not Vista compatible.

Smolin: Do they lose something working in VB not having the automation with the other office modules?

D. Murphy: No, you know Office can be pretty much automated from almost anything.

Smolin: So you finished this application, and she began to use it, and then what made you decide to, like, sell the second one?

J. Murphy: [*Laughter*] It was basically just "Hey this is great let's sell it!" But you can't just sell an Access database. I mean, you can, but then it's just a nightmare to keep it up, and then you've got issues. And so we talked about it and decided, you know, let's just make it software.

Smolin: Make a product?

J. Murphy: Make a product of it.

D. Murphy: She turned it into an MDB—MDE actually. Compiled. But, there's a lot of, well, you know, refinement you have to do to something that's custom to make it into something that's generic. So that was the big project there.

Smolin: Did the wedding consultant you worked with . . . did she know any programming?

**J. Murphy**: No, no she can barely turn her computer on.

**Smolin**: OK, but she knew what the application needed to do. So you had sort of a one engineer and one architect?

**J. Murphy**: Right.

**Smolin**: So you did all the programming? Both of you?

**J. Murphy**: Yes.

**Smolin**: How long would you say it took for you . . . how many hours to do the first one for her to the point where she was up and running and more or less happy?

**J. Murphy**: I would guess the database one was about 40 hours, maybe.

**Smolin**: And then how much more time did you put in to convert it into a marketable product?

**J. Murphy**: That was huge. And you wouldn't think it would be, but that was huge. It probably, with both of our programs . . . half of the time seems to be developing the database part and getting that all running, and then the other half seems to be doing everything else you need to do to make it into a product—you know, the extra code to add menus and all kinds of things that, you know, when you install something it has to go and put fonts in, and do all of that. I actually calculated about how long that took us, because it was a tough project. We figured it was—

**D. Murphy**: Two or three person-months.

**J. Murphy**: We figured it was like . . . 240 hours.

**Smolin**: OK.

**D. Murphy**: That's really hard to do more than estimate. Because we didn't actually record our time, I mean, you know how it goes . . .

**Smolin**: If you were doing it full time, it would have taken you a couple of months.

**J. Murphy**: Oh yeah, yeah.

**D. Murphy**: And you know Jackie developed this thing with Martha [the wedding planner] and then they started thinking about making it broadly available. You know, it's the feature creep thing—well, we gotta have this and we gotta have that, and so there's a lot of that.

**Smolin**: And you have navigation and consistency and all that.

**D. Murphy**: And it's gotta be bulletproof so people don't screw it up.

**Smolin**: Right. So is it single or multiuser?

**J. Murphy**: Single. It can be networked, I mean it's one of those things that most of them are used to, our users do not have networks, so it's built to be single user, but it can be networked.

**D. Murphy**: The way the [back-end database] relinker works . . . it's a standard relinker. You can make it multiuser. Jackie has to lead people through doing that, installing it, and setting it up for multiuser.

**Smolin**: So who buys this wedding program?

**J. Murphy**: Professional wedding planners. It's priced higher than what a bride would pay for software, so it's professionals.

**Smolin**: So it's mostly to individuals? Do any of these wedding planners have organizations where they have staff of people, and many planners, or do you sell it mostly to individuals one at a time?

**J. Murphy**: It's mostly individuals. Some of them will have like two or three people in the office that may or may not be using separate computers and need it networked together. We have a couple of places that are a little bit larger, that are like venues, that will have, you know, they do the whole wedding package thing and then they have six or eight people in the office, but mostly it's just one person in a single office.

**Smolin**: So was this the first product that you commercialized?

**J. Murphy**: Yes.

**Smolin**: Most of these things are sweat equity. Did you have to invest any hard dollars to get it to the point where you could start to sell it?

**D. Murphy**: Oh yeah.

**J. Murphy**: Oh yeah, oh yeah. Our computers needed hardware upgrades and more computers. We needed lots of software.

**D. Murphy**: The first version was pretty much just what we had, was Access 97. And then we ran into some issues because we were outputting reports, and at that time Snapshot format was popular. There was an issue there, and some versions could not put out Snapshots. There was a second edition and a first edition. So at that time, and she was just getting ready to release this at a trade show in like three weeks, when we realized this— that it wouldn't work for some people's computers. So then it was go buy a new computer, go buy Office XP at that time, Office XP Professional and install her, go buy the Wise installer and the SageKey scripts. So it was new computers, new Office, and all that stuff. So there was a lot of money there—

**Smolin**: So to get to the starting line, how much did you invest?

**D. Murphy**: I'd guess for that go around, just to do the development it was like five grand.

**Smolin**: OK.

**J. Murphy**: And in that one, we have about a total of hardware/software costs of about ten grand, between the two products we sell.

**Smolin**: OK. What do you do about copy protection?

**J. Murphy**: Oh, yeah. We bounced that one around, I mean how do you deal with it really. We talked to everybody we knew it seemed like. And everybody's got a different view.

What we did is we decided that our market was small. The largest organization of wedding planners in the world has 4,500 members, so we knew our market was small. So what we do is before we send out a CD, we have an encrypted file that has their company name in it. When we burn their copy to a CD and send it to them, and when they install it, their company name goes on it, and they can't get it off. So they can't give it to their friends and have their friends use it, because they can't put their own company name and logo on it.

**Smolin**: OK and that company name is on the reports that they give to their customers, so . . . and that provides a deterrent . . .

**D. Murphy**: Somebody, if they want to put enough effort into it, they could probably figure it out and break the code. I mean it's not a large market, and it's not a real expensive product so—

**Smolin**: Did you ever find anybody with an illegal copy?

**D. Murphy**: You know, I think Jackie's found people that have handed it around, and they'll call up and say, you know, they'll try and get her to fix it for them—

**J. Murphy**: Yeah, and I did have someone come to me at a conference and say, "You know, the software . . . can we change my name because every time we print out a report I have to white out the company name and I have to put it on my letterhead and I have to run it through my printer again," and I'm like "OK, well, you know . . . " and at the time I didn't realize she wasn't a customer because my customers change their company names and so I said, "Call me at the office and we'll get that all set up for you," and she never called. But I looked her up and she's not one of my customers, so there are very few of them out there because they want their own name on it, and it's a lot of work to, you know, to get around it.

**Smolin**: Well that's a good, good theft deterrent, for your market. So how do you price the product?

**J. Murphy**: When we first started it, I said to Martha, who was the wedding planner, I said, "How do we . . . what price should we put on this?" And she said, "We need to have it low enough that the wedding planners can see themselves buying it, but we need it high enough that it gets enough respect that they see it as a professional tool." And that's what we did. We looked at what our competitors were doing, and we looked at what software for brides cost, and we looked at what, like, the big companies that do catering and stuff are using, and then we priced it accordingly.

**Smolin**: And how much do you sell it for?

**J. Murphy**: It's $365.

**Smolin:** $365. So, it costs you a buck a day to use it.

**J. Murphy:** Yeah, that's what we tell people. A dollar a day, and you've got software.

**Smolin:** Nice. The products that brides buy . . . what price range is that in?

**J. Murphy:** They're actually lower. They range from between $20 and about $60.

**Smolin:** OK, and then the high-end stuff . . . ?

**J. Murphy:** The high-end stuff is up in the thousands, $5,000 or so. And we knew that was way out of the market for us.

**Smolin:** So you sell at a single-user license. Take it, use it, perpetual license. Do you charge for product support?

**J. Murphy:** No.

**Smolin:** No annual maintenance fee?

**J. Murphy:** No, and that's one of the things that we looked at when we were pricing it, because one of our competitors . . . their software's cheaper than ours, but then they have a yearly maintenance fee. And they have a fee for customer support, and everybody was grumbling about this because they were almost impossible to get a hold of on the phone, and then they charged for this customer support and we decided it would work better for us to just lump it all into one package and say, it's free. They're happy with that.

**Smolin:** Got it. Did this original wedding management program, did this give rise to any variations? Do you have more than one model of it? You know a big size, a small size, a just-right size, or is it one size fits all?

**J. Murphy:** It's a one size fits all. We have a couple of companies that had us do modifications to theirs, but no, it's pretty much a one size fits all.

**Smolin:** What would you say was the biggest problem you faced bringing this product to market? And I'm thinking of from the time you decided to make it into a product till the time you got to the starting line.

**J. Murphy:** The biggest thing? Getting it to work on all the possible systems out there. Wedding planners are not always up to date on everything, and we still have people using Windows 95 . . .

**Smolin:** Oh, that hurts.

**J. Murphy:** . . . not with the most current version of our software, mind you, but with the older versions. Some people are still using version 3 where we're on version 5. And we have now people using Windows Vista. So we have to have it be able to have it install correctly on every operating system, and that was part of the hardware issue. We had to get removable hard drives and hard drive drawers, and we set up computers with different operating systems on them so we could test each installation. That and getting the trial version to cooperate, not to let them install it more than once and to do all of the things to protect us there.

**Smolin:** Did you research the market and the competition before you started?

**J. Murphy:** Because it started out as a database, we kind of knew what the market was doing, what our competitors were doing. The wedding planner that we worked with said, "Look at these [other products] and tell me what you think." But other than that, we didn't really pay attention to what they were doing. Their software was written for brides and then made available so that wedding planners could plan multiple weddings. So it's not really the way wedding planners plan things, and so I didn't want to have ours even slightly resemble theirs. So, we looked at what they were doing, but it didn't impress us much.

**D. Murphy:** It wasn't an extensive market research operation. Trying to build this thing for Martha, and then Martha was impressed enough that she thought if it worked the way wedding planners would work, then she would be behind in putting it out to the rest of the world.

**Smolin:** So she knew where to find the first customer?

**J. Murphy:** Right.

**Smolin:** In how many places and for how long did you Beta test it?

**J. Murphy:** Our daughter is really big on computers, and she did our Beta testing; also she usually tests everything we do. She does all of our databases, and she's good. She's good—nobody can pick through things like she can.

**Smolin:** The first few people that you sold it to, did you get some calls? Did you have some fire drills?

**J. Murphy:** Yeah, we had a couple of little things that were problems. You know it's like anything. You build it, then you go through and you think you've fixed all the buttons and entered data and all the fields. But somebody will call and say, "Hey, you know this doesn't work or that doesn't work." So we released version 1 and then it was about two months later, we released version 1.5, because we had just little issues. It wasn't . . . nothing was a catastrophe; it was just little things that didn't work.

**Smolin:** You never know what users are going to do.

**J. Murphy:** Yeah.

**D. Murphy:** We had one of those the other day. Somebody found a field you could put an apostrophe in, and it screwed up the query.

[*Laughter*]

**Smolin:** I have that issue too. Did you trademark it?

**J. Murphy:** No.

**Smolin:** You thought about trademarking? Or why don't you trademark it?

**D. Murphy:** You know about the time you're going through this, David Himmelstein [a trademark and intellectual property attorney], who occasionally addresses the Access Users Group, said, really, when you start out, you have an implied trademark.

**Smolin:** Yes.

**D. Murphy:** And I kind of remembered him saying that going through the formal process, unless it's a really big deal, it's kind of a waste of money. So that was part of the reason.

**J. Murphy:** And we thought the wording he recommended to put into the code, that kind of helps—warns them not reverse engineer this or we'll take your house.

**Smolin:** Do you have a manual?

**J. Murphy:** Yes.

**Smolin:** How long did it take to write the manual?

**J. Murphy:** That was about a forty-hour project.

**Smolin:** Is the manual online or do you deliver hard copy?

**J. Murphy:** We give them the option of buying a hard copy in an effort to save some trees. Our user manual is built into the software, so it's just a button on the screen. You click it, and it opens up the whole user manual. And then you can search it. It's in a PDF file.

**Smolin:** OK, so it's not like online help.

**J. Murphy:** No.

**Smolin:** OK, or you don't have a help button, you know where you get the little blurbs—

**J. Murphy:** Right, no, they call me.

**Smolin:** They call you. How many calls a week do you get from folks?

**J. Murphy:** Probably about three, which is amazing considering we've got a couple thousand copies out there.

**Smolin:** Well, must be pretty easy to use, and pretty solid at this point. So it's been going for seven years.

**J. Murphy:** Yeah.

**Smolin:** That's a good product. How often do you release updates?

**J. Murphy:** Right now we're at about every two years.

**Smolin:** And you're using the Wise/SageKey combination to install the product?

**J. Murphy:** Yes.

**Smolin:** How long does it take your typical user to learn the product, to use it?

**J. Murphy:** You know, the way we built it is it's all intuitive—that they install and then they may call me with a couple of questions, but they're often running and they're doing their first wedding within minutes of installment.

**Smolin:** Oh, OK, so there's not much learning curve?

**J. Murphy:** No.

**Smolin:** So, you don't have to do any training, onsite training?

**J. Murphy:** No.

**Smolin:** Do you have any learning or implementation problems with the software? There's always one user that calls 50 times in the first month, but other than the outliers.

**J. Murphy:** No, then again, we have one little problem area. Sometimes it's hard to figure out how to label things so people understand what they are. For example, we have a form, and it has people you can select from a combo box to create a new record for a vendor for a wedding or something, and then you've got this other box that has this list of vendors that have already been selected for the wedding, and people get those two boxes confused. But other than that, you know, it's been really easy.

**Smolin:** So no onsite training. Do you do custom modifications?

**J. Murphy:** When we first started we did. We made quite a few with the first one. But we decided . . . you know . . . every time you upgrade to a new version, you have to go back and then make all those modifications to that person's stuff. And so we just said, "Alright, that's it, we're not doing this anymore." We have a couple of places that we do modifications, but we said we are no longer going to upgrade you to the new version when one comes out. If you want those changes, you have to pay us to put them in your software.

**Smolin:** So you do have some out there that have custom mods?

**D. Murphy:** They're unique operations, and they're big operations. They're a lot of work. I mean, they paid us quite a bit to modify them.

**Smolin:** So when you come out with a new version, you'll sort of have to handcraft those again?

**D. Murphy:** Yes.

**Smolin:** When I do custom mods, I hook them to the software, embed them in the serial number, so that if it's a button or a function, it doesn't trigger unless it's that serial number. So that way I have one version, and all the custom mods are in there, but they're all hidden.

**J. Murphy:** Yeah, and some of them are just so unique to these people, and it just so modifies everything else.

**D. Murphy**: One of them was a huge venue back in Atlantic City. They started using Jackie's software, and then they wanted to expand it to their whole operation. So there were so many things that we did to customize it for them that it's just a separate program.

**Smolin**: So then you did another product instead of . . .

**J. Murphy**: As if that wasn't painful enough.

**Smolin**: —instead of laying down until the feeling passed, you have a product called Show Producer. And is this a modification of the Wedding Management, or is it based on it, or is it a brand new, fresh thing, what is it?

**J. Murphy**: It's the bastard child, is what it is. Actually what happened was—I had wedding planners that called me and said, "You know, I'm trying to use Wedding Management to help me plan a bridal show. A lot of them live in little towns, and when they do bridal shows, they bring in the vendors that they like to use, and then everybody wins. The brides come in, and they select vendors. So they have these little bridal shows. And they were trying to use Wedding Management because it had all their vendor lists in it to do these bridal shows. So we said, "OK, fine." So we started working with someone who does a great big bridal show. We came up with Show Producer. So if they have both software packages, they can use one vendor list, or they can keep them separate.

**Smolin**: So they share a database?

**J. Murphy**: Yeah, they can share or not depending on what they want to do.

**Smolin**: And how long did it take you to put that one together?

**J. Murphy**: That one was a little bit quicker because we were able to cockroach a lot of stuff from Wedding Management. And, you know, there was less of a learning curve to do that. So that was probably half the number of hours of Wedding Management.

**Smolin**: And how much do you sell that one for?

**J. Murphy**: That one's $389. Which was about the cost of a trade show booth.

**Smolin**: This is for the show managers, right? The show producers?

**J. Murphy**: The show producers.

**Smolin**: So they generally buy both packages then?

**J. Murphy**: No.

**Smolin**: They just get the one?

**J. Murphy**: They just get the one or the other.

**Smolin**: How big is the market for Show Producer would you say?

**J. Murphy**: You know what? That's a really good question. And I didn't really look at that very seriously. I probably should have, but I didn't. I'm guessing it's a lot bigger than I imagined because probably 50 percent of the wedding planners also do small bridal shows. So I'm actually getting a lot of interest in it.

**Smolin**: How long has it been on the market then?

**J. Murphy**: Two months.

**Smolin**: Oh, this is a brand new product, then?

**J. Murphy**: Brand new.

**Smolin**: If you had to give a piece of advice to someone like yourself starting out, they've got a brilliant idea for a product, and they want to do what you did, put it together, make some copies, turn the money faucet on, what would you tell them? What was your best piece of advice, or the biggest thing they ought to look out for?

**J. Murphy**: OK. Do you remember W____ B____? When we first started the Access Users Group, way back in version 2.0 Access, he was writing some software for . . . some industry . . . I can't remember exactly. Anyway, he was working very hard on it, to the point of mortgaging everything he had, to build the software, and he was building it in an NT environment I believe.

**D. Murphy**: It was one of the first versions of NT.

**J. Murphy**: NT. So, he got it to the point to where he felt it was done. And he sent out trial versions to his entire market. Now he hadn't tested it on every system out there. And what it did is it overwrote critical files on people's systems and completely crashed them and made them unusable. So—

**D. Murphy**: He did it in Access 97. And he used the installer that came with the Developer Edition of Access. I don't know if you ever researched that thing, but there was an extensive series of problems with it and modifications were needed to make things work. Now W____ just used it. So it pulled in some DLLs and things off of his NT machine, and then people would install this thing under Windows 98 and 95.

**J. Murphy**: No, it was Windows 3.1.

**D. Murphy**: So it overwrote some critical machine DLLs, and their machines blue-screened.

**Smolin**: So he hosed his whole market first pop out of the box.

**D. Murphy**: He thought he was going to lose his house. I mean he got sued. Several times. It got down to where he I guess worked out some deal, so somebody bailed him out, and so he didn't lose his house. And then after that, he went out and he just started doing SQL Server.

**Smolin**: So your sage piece of advice for the readers?

**J. Murphy**: Is to do the testing. That's why we hooked up all the removable hard drives and the computers and set up all the systems, so that we could test on every environment we could possibly have our software installed on. Because even doing that, we occasionally have people where their husband's a tech guy, and he does this fancy whatever with their system, and it causes a couple of issues, but nothing has ever totally trashed anyone's system. So test—test on all the operating systems available.

**Smolin**: Do you have liability insurance for that? Professional liability or errors and omissions or whatever?

**J. Murphy**: In our license agreement, it says that you have to agree to before you install this operating . . . it says we're not responsible for anything more than the cost of the software. We had a lawyer go through our license agreement and make sure that it was going to, you know, stand up. In fact, we may have copied Microsoft.

**Smolin**: I think we all did.

**J. Murphy**: But that's what the license agreement says, and they have to click OK before they can go forward and install the software. Basically the license agreement is just so that if they pass it on to their friends, we can go back and sue them. You know, that's basically what it's for.

**D. Murphy**: So the biggest liability we have and the reason we're paranoid about testing is we don't want to have our software get installed on somebody's machine and wipe out their business files.

**Smolin**: Seems sensible.

**J. Murphy**: Yeah, and even when our uninstaller goes in and uninstalls, it will take the software out, but it will leave the backup file with the data file in it, just in case they go, "Oh no!"

**Smolin**: Very clever.

**J. Murphy**: That'll save them.

**Smolin**: Cool.

CHAPTER

# 4

# The Price of Success

So now you've got your product deep into Beta testing. You're frantically fixing bugs and adding features that your testers insist are needed (they're probably right), because you want to keep them from bailing out on you.

This is a good time to start thinking ahead about sales and marketing. And your first consideration—the first thing many prospects will ask you—is how much you're going to charge for this jewel.

There are a lot of things that can make or break your business. The price of the product is right up there on the top ten list. Overcharge and you won't sell many. All you'll hear is crickets. Undercharge and you'll do a land office business. But, you won't cover your costs. The more you sell, the broker you'll get.

So I think, even though there's a lot of words and not many pictures in this section, it's worth devoting an entire chapter to the question of how much to charge for your product.

## A Matter of Definition

In order to answer the question of what price to put on your product, we have to talk a little business and economics. (Please try to suppress the yawn. This is important stuff.) First, some definitions. You probably know something about these concepts, either explicitly or intuitively, but a little review never hurts.

- **Revenue**: Revenue is all the money that folks pay you for the privilege of buying your product, plus any other money that comes in from other activities. For example, to keep the cash flow going while you get your product ready for market, you may be doing a little consulting or custom programming. After you start selling, you might have a revenue stream from extended annual support and maintenance fees. This all falls under the heading of revenue.

- **Expenses**: Expenses are all the money you pay to others to keep the lights on in your business. They are also referred to as **costs**. All of your costs can be broken into two broad categories:

  1. **Variable costs**: These are the direct expenses you incur in manufacturing your product. They include the costs such as

     - CD or other media

     - Labels

     - The box into which you put the media, manuals, and other supporting materials

     - The shipping carton

     - The expense of shipping (either from your suppliers or to your customers)

     Variable costs are expenses that vary directly with the number of units of product you manufacture.

  2. **Fixed costs**: These are costs you incur just to keep the doors open. You have to pay these even if you don't sell a single item! They include things like

     - Rent

     - Utilities

     - Telephone

     - Salaries and benefits (yours, for sure)

     - Internet service provider charges

     - Web hosting charges

     - Office supplies

     - Legal expenses (things like obtaining a trademark, for example)

     - Marketing materials

     - Advertising expenses

     - Car payments on the company car (you should be so lucky)

     - The bill from your graphic designer for that snappy package design

     - The bill from your web site designer for an equally snappy web site

     - Computers (of course)

- And printers, routers, modems, ad infinitum (if you can't buy a lot of toys, what's the point, right?)

- Whatever you might have paid to outside programmers to write your product, if you didn't do it all yourself

Fixed costs are expenses you would, and WILL, incur before you make your first sale, and bills you will continue to pay even if you never sell a single copy.

And now, where the rubber meets the road, your raison d'être:

- **Profit**: Profit is what's left over after you subtract all **expenses** from total **revenues**.

There are two other definitions you need:

- **Gross margin**: Gross margin is **revenues** minus **variable costs**. It's usually expressed as a percent. If you express it in dollar terms (that is, selling price minus variable costs) it's called **gross profit**.

- **Net margin**: **Profit** expressed as a percent of total **revenues.** Expressed in dollar terms, it's called **net profit**.

Why are these terms important? You may never have a need to actually calculate your margins, although your best-guess projections are important during the planning phase of your business just to make sure you're not setting up an obvious money loser.

These basic ideas are important to help you visualize your nascent business. So now that we have a common language, we can use it to discuss pricing your product.

# The Thing About Software . . .

The software business is somewhat unique among product-based businesses in that variable costs are so very low. So gross margins are very high. When a computer manufacturer sells a computer to a distributor for $500, they might have $300 of variable costs—parts and labor—in that box. So they have a **gross margin** of 40 percent. Healthy. But, when they spread their fixed costs over the number of computers they sell, that might add another $100 to the total expenses, giving them a **net profit** of $100 or a **net margin** of 20 percent.

That's pretty good. Grocery chains average net margins of around 2.5 percent. Tough business.

Other computer manufacturers making competing products are likely to have similar costs. So they will also be selling their machines for about $500.

The general price range of conventional products then (computers, refrigerators, cars, shoes) is largely determined by the underlying costs. Competition can drive the price down, but it can't drive it below the point where it's not profitable to be in that business.

The thing about software is that almost all of your expenses are going to be fixed. The variable expenses are going to be a small percentage of your selling price. So, unlike more conventional consumer goods with substantial variable costs, the price of your software will be much less constrained by your need to cover your variable costs.

If you're selling a product for $1,000, and your variable costs are only $10 (not unrealistic), it would seem that you could easily discount your product to make a sale. Cut the price in half, and you've still got a gross profit of $490.

But, of course, there's a problem. You have to use that gross profit to cover ALL of your fixed expenses. So while it may seem expedient to cut your price to make a sale or get a distributor on board, in the end you may be "selling 90-cent dollars." And you can't do that for long.

So what determines the selling price of your software? There are three factors that come into play here.

## Breaking Even

As noted previously, you must price your software so that it will **cover your fixed costs**. That, of course, means projecting your sales. And that is a very difficult thing to do.

My only advice here is to be realistic. On the one hand, I have always lived by the rule "Plan for success." If you don't have a goal, you never go anywhere. If you make some conservative assumptions about a selling price and your variable costs, you can easily calculate your gross profit. Then if you make some equally conservative assumptions about your fixed costs, you can project how many units you'd have to sell to get to that magical **break-even point**.

The formula, if you want to get quantitative about it, is pretty simple:

**Break-Even Point = Fixed Costs / (Average Selling Price – Variable Costs)**

So, for example, The Sleep Advisor sells for $60. The variable costs of production are about $5. That yields a gross profit of $55 or over 90 percent (nice). If it costs, say, $1,500 a month to keep the lights on (rent, utilities, supplies, Internet service provider, merchant account, etc.), we only have to sell 28 of them to get past the break-even point. Piece of cake.

If we want to do some sales and marketing, perhaps we set up a PR and advertising program that costs $3,000 a month. Now we have fixed costs of $4,500 and have to sell 82 of them to get past the break-even point. Not a huge number.

Suppose two of us would like to give ourselves $5,000 a month each to cover luxuries like food and housing. Now we have a monthly nut of $14,500 to cover, which we can do handily by selling about 250 copies. Better hope that advertising begins to work.

These projections have (at least) two underlying assumptions:

1. All sales are of hard-copy product. If we sell one through download on the Internet, the variable costs are zero. So that lowers your break-even point a little, but not by enough to make a difference in your planning.

2. All sales are at retail. As will be discussed later, sales to other resellers involve discounting your product—sometimes as little as 20 percent, sometimes as much as 80 percent.

So when you want to set a price for your product, you have to think about how you're going to reach your customer—direct sales? Through resellers? Through distributors who will sell to other resellers? The mix of ways you get your product to the customer, and the discounts you will have to give to resellers, will determine the **average selling price** in the break-even formula shown earlier.

Can I repeat my advice here about being realistic? Many businesses fail because of wildly optimistic projections of sales coupled with a fixed cost plan based on those projections. It is said that the downfall of every person in sales is when they begin to believe their own sales pitch. When planning with a colleague, there's a tendency to dream of great success. Nobody wants to rain on the parade. So plan for success. But don't make a plan that is likely to fail.

## What's It Worth to Ya, Baby? Perceived Value

Nobody wants to break even. That's setting the bar too low. Of course, you don't want to lose money on this business, but it's more fun to think about how much you can make. So let's consider the upside.

The second even more important factor in determining your product's selling price is **the perceived value of your product by the prospective customer**. In other words, there may be no correlation between the selling price you set and the amount of time and effort it took to create your product. Or the fixed costs. Or the variable costs.

If your software can save the user $1,000 a year, they might be willing to pay $500 for it. That means the software pays for itself in six months. But if your software can save them $10,000 a year, they might be willing to pay $5,000 for the very same program. By the same token, two programs that took the same time and cost to develop and incur the same marketing expenses may have selling prices that differ by a factor of 100 based solely on the user's belief about how much using the software will save a company.

Unless you are already intimately familiar with the cost structure and other internals of the users who will be evaluating your program for potential payback, the best way to find out what the program is worth is to ask. And your Beta testers would be the likeliest focus group for this research.

Seems obvious, doesn't it? But I have found it to be a tough question to spring on someone. First, they don't always think in terms of return on investment, or they don't know the numbers well enough to do that projection in their head. Second, many of the advantages of a good software application are either intangible or difficult to quantify.

For example, the E-Z-MRP system helps manufacturers prevent shortages and stock-outs. This means less time chalked up to the Idle Account as manufacturing people stand around waiting for parts to arrive. That number can be determined by a good cost accountant. A reduction in inventory frees up working capital and reduces interest expense. That can also be calculated.

But delivering product on time to the customer has a beneficial effect on the business that can't be easily quantified. Similarly, the benefits of a more orderly business and a calmer, less stressed-out work force can't be precisely calculated. And even if your prospects understand that they could save thousands of dollars a year in less sick time and higher productivity, they may only give lip service to these intangible benefits. Which means that a product you think is worth $1 may be perceived to be worth only $.50 by your prospect.

So, don't expect to get a straight answer to your question. You'll have to tease the answer out of the Beta testers. But an accurate answer to this question is absolutely essential to pricing your product as high as possible.

## You'll Never Walk Alone (Well, Rarely): Looking at the Competition

The third consideration in pricing your product is . . . **the competition**. The software business is the original home of the better mousetrap. All developers have a truly unique product. A technological breakthrough. A new, exciting, innovative, never-before-thought-of solution to a widespread problem. To hear them tell it.

At worst, even if you believe that there is someone out there purporting to solve the same problem, you know your product is better—it actually does the job the others only pretend to do, right?

And that's good. You have to believe in yourself and your product. You have to believe that you're onto something—that you have something of real value to offer.

Now it's possible that you **have** created the equivalent of VisiCalc, which Wikipedia describes as "the first spreadsheet program available for personal computers. It is considered to be the application that turned the microcomputer from a hobby for computer enthusiasts into a serious business tool. VisiCalc sold over 700,000 copies in six years."

But it ain't likely. Chances are, you're not alone out there—that there are products already available which do, to one degree or another, exactly what yours does. In fact, those folks are way ahead of you in this horse race. You're starting in last place.

Of course, if you did a little research on the competition during the design phase, you've got all their good ideas built into your product, you've eliminated all their bad ideas, and you've added all the great missing features. So you might really have a better mousetrap.

But the competition still has something real important that you don't—a track record. History. References. Who hasn't been burned by software? And once burned, twice cautious. So, put yourself on the other side of the table. Would you buy a 100 percent but unproven solution to your mission-critical problem from an unknown startup venture? Or a mature, debugged, but maybe 85 percent solution from someone with lots of history and references? Be honest, now.

So check out the competition's selling prices. If you want to charge more, you'll have to present a very compelling reason why you're worth more. Be brutally frank with yourself. Is your product REALLY more valuable? THAT much more?

Now I have had marketing people tell me that a high selling price can work in reverse—you're creating the expectation in the buyer's mind of great value. It's true to a degree. Look up the history of Pond's Cold Cream and how J. Walter Thompson increased sales by creating the impression of high value without actually changing the product.

But that's just anecdotal. The folks who give this advice generally are not trying to make a living selling your product. They make a living giving advice.

So, unless you've got an obviously better mousetrap, you have to undersell the competitors. But not by so much that you raise the "Why is it so cheap?" question in the mind of your prospects. If the competition sells for $1, don't price your product at $.25, even if your projections show you can make money at that price. People will simply not believe there's a dollar's worth of value in a product that sells for a quarter.

In the end, the price you decide on will be a result of many factors tangible and intangible. In this process, there is a place for intuition or "gut feel," because those judgments are often borne of experience. As Malcolm Gladwell wrote in *Blink: The Power of Thinking Without Thinking*, "Truly successful decision making relies on a balance between deliberate and instinctive thinking."

So, as in so many areas of business and life, you need to strike a balance—between high and low selling price, between knowledge and instinct. As the Roman playwright Terrence famously said, "Moderation in all things."

# Finding the Peak of the Revenue Curve

OK, I want to present one last concept in this chapter—the **revenue curve**. It's actually pretty simple. We all know intuitively that demand varies inversely with price—that is, the higher the price, the lower the demand. Lower your price, and your demand (sales) go up.

As your selling price drops to zero, your sales go way up—but you can't make any money. As you raise the price, demand for your product falls. Raise it high enough, and your demand falls to zero.

Starting from a very low price, as you increase your price, the increase in total revenue more than offsets the drop in unit sales. At some point, however, increasing the price causes a drop in unit sales large enough so that total revenue is less than the total revenue generated by the lower price.

Look at the numbers in Table 4-1—which I've admittedly doctored in order to make my point. I also use big numbers because it's more fun to think about making millions than thousands. Your results may vary . . .

**Table 4-1.** Data for the Revenue Curve

| Unit Price | Demand | Total Revenue |
|---|---|---|
| $50 | 10,000 | $500,000 |
| $100 | 9,500 | $950,000 |
| $150 | 9,000 | $1,350,000 |
| $200 | 8,500 | $1,700,000 |
| $250 | 8,000 | $2,000,000 |
| $300 | 7,500 | $2,250,000 |
| $350 | 7,000 | $2,450,000 |
| $400 | 6,500 | $2,600,000 |
| $450 | 6,000 | $2,700,000 |
| $500 | 5,500 | $2,750,000 |
| $550 | 5,000 | $2,750,000 |
| $600 | 4,500 | $2,700,000 |
| $650 | 4,000 | $2,600,000 |
| $700 | 3,500 | $2,450,000 |
| $750 | 3,000 | $2,250,000 |
| $800 | 2,500 | $2,000,000 |
| $850 | 2,000 | $1,700,000 |
| $900 | 1,500 | $1,350,000 |

| Unit Price | Demand | Total Revenue |
|------------|--------|---------------|
| $950 | 1,000 | $950,000 |
| $1,000 | 500 | $500,000 |

As you can easily see, as the selling price goes up, demand falls off steadily. But total revenue rises for a while, peaking at a sales price between $500 and $550 dollars. After that, total revenue begins to fall off. For those who like pictures, the graph in Figure 4-1 illustrates the data in Table 4-1.

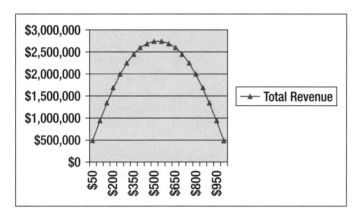

**Figure 4-1.** The revenue curve

Your ideal selling price is at the peak of the revenue curve—**the minimum amount of work for the maximum amount of dollars**.

The data presented in Figure 4-1 creates a nice, neat, symmetrical curve. The real world is certainly not so neat. As your price rises, your sales may not drop off in a smooth curve. That curve may flatten out for a while or drop off suddenly like the edge of the continental shelf.

It would be nice if there was some way to calculate precisely the demand and total revenue as unit price changed. But there isn't. You can approximate the revenue curve by using the experience of similar products. But that data, if it exists, is hard to come by. And how many products are there similar to yours?

But this idea of a revenue curve is still a useful concept when trying to decide on a selling price. Remember, your goal is not to **sell as many as possible**, but rather to **generate as much revenue as possible**.

I had a partner once who suggested that instead of selling our product at $1,000 to $3,000, depending on options, we should price it at $1,000,000. It would be a tough sell. But we'd only have to sell one. We gave it some serious thought.

# Pricing Options

There are a lot of ways to price your product. The model you use depends on a lot of factors, particularly the nature of your product—single- or multiuser, low support needs or high, etc. But mostly the pricing model you select will depend on the market you're trying to reach and what will resonate with your prospects.

## Fixed Price

I think software shouldn't be harder to buy than it is to use. In the manufacturing systems market where E-Z-MRP is sold, pricing can be confusing. The systems are complex. So they're often sold by the module. The theory is that the customer will be happier buying only the features they need. But that leaves the customer wondering exactly which modules they should buy. And opens them up to sales pressure from a commission-based sales agent that may alienate them. It can be a difficult decision.

So for the E-Z-MRP system, I set a one-price policy. You can see the pricing policy at `www.E-Z-MRP.com/pricing.htm`. It's quite simple. You get everything for one price.

If your product is relatively simple, you won't have this problem. You'll be charging a flat price for the program. If your product has lots of options, however, you might consider this simple one-price scheme.

## Annual Subscription

Another approach is to charge your customers an annual, or monthly if you like, contract price. It's like renting the software. The company gets to expense the cost, and you create a dependable revenue stream. Of course, you have to have some way to "turn off" the program when the customer no longer needs it or stops paying.

The difficulty with this approach is, of course, that most people buying a solution believe they will be using that solution for a long time. So they will be comparing their total cost for using your application for a number of years with the fixed price of competitive products.

For you, the annual or monthly subscription fee means that you have to set up and run an airtight system for billing and collecting your fees.

The annual subscription approach can be appealing to certain customers if your application requires ongoing post-sales support. In that case, the monthly or annual cost includes the support, and it's easier for the prospect to rationalize. In fact, you could position the pricing as paying only for support—that there's no charge for the software.

## Pay per Seat

Most applications that are more complex than a simple single-user or utility program have a central database that is maintained and used by more than one user in a company. In this case, you can charge the customer by the number of people who need to use your application.

That charge can be a one-time fee, an annual fee for on-going maintenance and support, or both. The user can feel that they get certain cost-saving benefits from this approach, as a sitewide license (if you have one) would be prohibitively expensive. But they need to decide how many users they want. This can start conversations and debates inside a company that can slow down the decision to buy your product.

Also, you will need to have some way inside your application to control the number of users. And some automated way to increase the number of users if your customer decides they'd like to add another seat.

So while this approach may seem to offer users some flexibility in their purchasing decision, there are technical problems you need to solve.

## Pay per Use

There are a few applications that users might use only once or very infrequently. A health or psychological assessment would fall into this category. Or an analysis of financial condition such as retirement planning.

After users get the information or feedback they're looking for, they may never run the program again. Or they may run it at irregular intervals and appreciate only having to pay per use.

These users might be more amenable to paying a fee to get information as opposed to paying a charge to purchase software. From the users' side of the table, it looks like they are buying a service rather than a product.

This pricing model works particularly well for web-based applications where you can charge the user's credit card for each use of your program.

## Pay by Capacity

As you can see from the pricing of the E-Z-MRP system, there are two versions. One version limits the capacity of a critical data table—the Part Master table. And it sells for considerably less than the unrestricted version.

Since the target for this product is manufacturers in the startup to $20,000,000 range, a low-priced version helps startups get started with a system. At that level, the restriction is not material as the number of parts they have to manage is usually very low. As time goes on and they grow, they will eventually bump up against the restriction. At that point, however, they can upgrade to the unrestricted version for the difference in the price.

This approach can work for many applications where you encounter some price resistance. It's a way to get your product into the hands of the user. And it makes it easier for them to pay for it. They can pay in two smaller chunks instead of one large one.

The key is to find some restriction that will not interfere with your customer receiving the full benefit of the product. In the case of E-Z-MRP cited earlier, other than that one restriction on the capacity of the Part Master table, the restricted and unrestricted versions are identical.

A variation on this model is to restrict some of the functionality of the product. Again, you have to find functions that users who are just starting to use your product will not miss, but will require as they grow the business or grow into the product. This is a little trickier because it can easily evolve into paying by the module or function. Keep it simple. One restricted version and one unrestricted version makes the decision easier for your prospect.

## Give It Away?

Of course, I don't advocate that you give your product away for free. That business model was pretty thoroughly discredited by the dot-com bust of 2000. However, there is a whole audience out there in academia that you can expose your product to by providing a highly restricted version—one that's functional but only useful in a classroom setting.

This works, of course, only if your product addresses a subject or discipline that is taught on the college level. For example, the subject of manufacturing systems is widely taught in business schools. For them I created a version of E-Z-MRP in which the capacity of the Part Master table is restricted to 35 parts. Other than that one restriction, the full and educational version are the same.

This allows enough parts to create a small product but not enough to be useful in a real production environment. This version is provided for free to any educational institution that wants it to teach the principles of manufacturing systems.

The carrot here is that those students who learn the subject by using your software will one day graduate and get a job where they might want your product. It's a kind of long-range advertising program. Additionally, professors who do consulting on the side will be familiar with your product and will recommend it to their clients.

So if your product happens to be in one of those application areas that are taught in colleges and universities, a free or very low-cost educational version can pay big dividends.

There's one other situation in which you might consider giving away your software. If your application relies on data that change over time and requires you to supply an updated database to your users, you are probably going to charge your users for each update. Antivirus software comes to mind. Having an antivirus scanner is an essential tool in today's unfriendly Internet environment. But it's nearly useless without periodic updates of the virus library.

If you are developing an application whose primary function is to poll a database of information and give feedback to the user about this information, then you might consider giving away your software and charging for the data.

# Getting Paid: Setting Your Payment Policies

Once you've settled on a selling price, you also need to set a payment policy. Most companies will quote you **Net 30**. That means they will pay your invoice thirty days after it is presented to them. Of course, they will tell you that it takes thirty days for your invoice to work its way through their system. And of course, they could just as easily pay you in four days. Everyone just likes to hang on to their money as long as possible.

I always ask for **Net on Receipt**. That means they have to cut the check when they get the invoice. I feel lucky when a Net on Receipt invoice gets paid in less than two weeks.

Remember that the seller sets the terms. When I take a purchase order (PO) from a company, I always ask first what their standard terms are. Net 30 is the most common response. But, as a seller you don't have to accept this. I respond that my terms are Net on Receipt, and I'd like that entered in my vendor profile so that every time I get a PO from this company, those will be the terms.

Of course, Net 30 might be a condition of sale. The buyer will be sympathetic but "their hands are tied." They're not allowed to give any more liberal terms. If so, you'll have to suck it up.

There's a variation on this theme most commonly known as **2 10 Net 30**. This means that the company will pay in thirty days. But if they'll pay you in ten days, they can take a discount of 2 percent off the invoice total.

Companies who accept this kind of arrangement ALWAYS take the discount and usually, but not always, pay in the shorter time frame. So it's a way of getting paid more quickly and with less hassle and follow-up.

If you're shipping a product in a box you can go **COD** (cash on delivery). The shipper collects the customer's check when they deliver the goods and forwards it to you.

If you really don't trust your prospect, ask for **prepayment**. Of course, that raises suspicions in the mind of the buyer about your financial stability and your reliability as a long-term partner. So this is not a real popular approach.

Finally, there are credit cards. This form of payment is becoming more popular, even for purchases in the thousands of dollars. In order to take credit card payments, you need to establish a merchant account with a bank. It's not rocket science, but it's one of those onerous administrative tasks. And there are fees involved. Fees—multiple.

But it has the charming advantage of getting you paid right away. The middlemen will skim 2–3 percent off the top for the privilege, but you won't have any accounts receivable problem.

For The Sleep Advisor, which sells for $59.95, taking credit cards was absolutely required. For E-Z-MRP, at $9,800 a pop, it has rarely been an issue.

# Actually Getting Paid: Dealing with Your Receivables . . . and Their Payables

Accepting terms from a buyer means having accounts receivable—the most onerous part of running a business. You simply cannot wait idly for payment. Your account receivable is their account payable. Knowing a bit about how these systems work can make it easier for you to get to the right person and to talk their language.

In my experience, at least half the time something "goes wrong," and your payment doesn't arrive. Payables systems are set up 1) to avoid making erroneous payment, and 2) to avoid making payments.

OK, perhaps I am being a bit cynical here. But on more than one occasion, I have called up the payables department after thirty days, looking for my check, only to be told that I'm not scheduled for payment, but I can talk to the payables manager when she returns from vacation, or sick leave, or maternity leave.

Actually, one of the biggest problems with software, especially software delivered electronically, is the "receiver" problem. To pay a vendor's invoice, a payables clerk must have at least 1) the PO, 2) the invoice, and 3) some kind of receiving document showing that the goods were actually delivered and received. I used to have payments sit in limbo because there was no receiver. I delivered the software by hand or by e-mail. Or, even if mailed to the user, it never went through receiving. Getting a bill through Congress is easier than getting that receiver generated after the fact.

I have also known controllers who, in times of cash flow problems, simply reset all payment terms to Net 45 or Net 60. By the time you straighten out the problem, 45 or 60 days have gone by.

Oh well. Although I have been "stretched out" by accounting departments, I've never been stiffed. They'll all eventually honor their purchase order and your invoice. All you can do is make friends with the payables clerk, and recruit your purchasing agent as a friend and ally. And don't get mad or impatient. They'll only dig in their heels. Apply steady slow and friendly pressure, and eventually they'll cut loose with a check.

# Leasing and Self-Financing

In my experience, there seems to be no correlation between the price of software and amount of time spent by the prospect in agonizing over the payment. So, of course, you want to make it as painless as possible.

One of the most common ways to grease the skids is to spread out the payments. You can either make an arrangement with a leasing company or set up a payment schedule yourself.

As you can see on the E-Z-MRP pricing page, there is a lease plan available. This is a "lease to buy" plan in which the buyer owns the software license at the end of the lease period—just as if they had bought it outright.

The total payments are a bit higher than the cash price, but in return, the buyer gets less of a hit on their cash flow and might receive some favorable tax treatment. The leasing company will send you a check for the purchase price so you get all your money up front. And you don't have the administrative problem of collecting a payment every month from your customer.

If you can tolerate the paperwork and the reduction in your cash flow, you can self-finance—that is, set up a schedule of monthly payments with your customer. You can choose to charge more, just like the leasing company, or waive the finance charges if that will help close the deal. It's up to you.

Working with leasing companies is more popular with sellers when the variable costs of their product are high. With a lot of their working capital tied up in the finished product, they may need the full payment in order to finance the next round of manufacturing.

But since the variable costs of software are so low, you don't have a lot of money tied up in product you deliver. Having a self-financed lease option program in place might be a way to make some extra sales that you'd otherwise lose. It makes the purchasing decision easier for your customer. And you might end up covering your fixed costs with monthly lease payments. This smoothes out what might otherwise be a very sawtoothed revenue stream: feast one month, famine the next. Predictability in income allows you to plan for growth and expenses—a very comfortable position to be in.

# Annual Support: Creating an Annuity

Generally, you sell your product to a company one time. There are often no repeat sales within the same company, unless you are charging by the seat. Or, in the case of a single-user application, for each machine on which they want to run it.

But you can generate an ongoing stream of income by charging for ongoing support. This support includes updates to the software as they're made available and technical support—usually by phone or e-mail.

Annual support contracts generally run between 10 percent and 15 percent of the sales price. Of course, the customer has to feel the need for the support payment. In the case of E-Z-MRP, my stream of support payments never materialized because most users never have a question about the product after the first year of operation.

You can charge for updates to the product as they're made available. Release them once a year, and it's a de facto annual payment. But this means that, should a user decline to pay for an upgrade, you will have to support many previous versions of your product.

Of course, you can always set a policy that you will no longer support previous versions after a certain amount of time. But that smacks a bit of coercion and might be a big negative to your prospects. So, no, you're not required to support older versions of your software forever. But to the extent that your future sales depend on word of mouth, endorsements, and recommendations, well, yes, you do have to support them indefinitely.

Again, it depends on what the competition is doing and whether that kind of policy will work to your advantage or disadvantage. You have to balance the potential revenue against the potential loss of goodwill.

Since many software sales come by word of mouth, it is to your advantage to have every customer using the latest release of your product. To that extent, the goodwill you generate by providing your customer with free upgrades as they are released might more than offset the revenue you could generate by charging for them.

Finally, you can use your support program as a spiff during negotiations. Waive the ongoing support costs for one, two, or three years, and that might close the sale.

# And in Conclusion, My Friends . . .

I hope this chapter made a lot of sense to you. This chapter was all business—no techno-fun at all. If you want to be a software entrepreneur, more likely than not you love software. But you're going into business. The emphasis at some point is going to shift from "software" to "entrepreneur".

So if this chapter left you a little glassy-eyed, if you're thinking like a lot of people, "I just don't have a head for business," then you need to find someone to partner with who DOES have a head for business. The topics presented in this chapter and the next one are dry nuts-and-bolts considerations. But unless you can set up a business that runs profitably, the best software product ever created will fail as a business even as it succeeds as a problem-solving application.

# How They Did It: An Interview with Arthur Fuller

*In which Arthur Fuller—software developer, screenwriter, philosopher— talks about his long career in creating software products, tries to alert the gentle reader as to how it can go terribly wrong, and considers reentering the game with a new product.*

**Smolin**: So, Arthur, you're a software developer.

**Fuller**: Yes.

**Smolin**: And what on earth possessed you to become a software developer?

**Fuller**: Love of computing.

**Smolin**: I see you have a degree in philosophy from the University of Winnipeg, and when you got that degree, did you look in the paper for Applied Philosopher Wanted?

**Fuller**: No, actually, the reason I took philosophy—everyone I knew at that time who was older than me was not in a profession in which they took their degree. In other words, I knew some political scientists who were not politicians. I knew some historians who were not making history but rather studying people who did. So I thought I should take a degree which will teach me how to think. And then it wouldn't matter what I did.

**Smolin**: And that worked out pretty good, I assume.

**Fuller**: Well, it could have been better [*laughter*]. But, it worked across the board, yes. And then when I discovered computing, one thing led to another. It just seemed like the natural place where I should be.

**Smolin**: When did you start with that?

**Fuller**: I purchased my first computer on March 15, 1983—an Apple II. It came with a CPM card and it came with WordStar, dBase II, and SuperCalc. And the first thing I did with that computer was to upgrade it from 48K to 64K with a 16K RAM extension card.

**Smolin**: And then one day, I suppose, you created a program which eventually turned into a product. What was the genesis of that program? Was it a custom application for somebody?

**Fuller**: No, it was a build-it-at-home sandbox sort of thing, and it was because, as I may have mentioned previously, my first ambition was to be a screenwriter, and I guess you could consider me successful, although in that realm it means very little. I sold two out of approximately thirty-five screenplays.

**Smolin**: Uh-huh.

**Fuller**: Which that's not bad. On the other hand, it means that you—you work as a waiter and a house painter and stuff in between.

**Smolin:** And other menial jobs like programming?

**Fuller:** Yes. Well, no, I hadn't discovered programming at that time. I had been reading *Byte* magazine without a computer until I finally sold the first screenplay. Then, I had to go buy that Apple II.

**Smolin:** So the application that you eventually turned into a product— what was the nature of the application? What did it do?

**Fuller:** It was called FilmStar, and it was an entire in-the-box film production management system.

**Smolin:** And did you do that for your own entertainment to learn how to program, initially? Or did it spring full blown as an idea for a product?

**Fuller:** That's a tough line to draw. It was kinda a bit of both. I was in love with the film business. I wanted to be in the film business, although writers are not really in the film business, not like a grip is—those kind of people.

However, I took the time to type in all the union rates of the various unions, and when I started writing the notes using dBase II on the aforementioned Apple II, it took a long time because you could only open two files at once. So that meant it was very awkward. And then—this was way back when in the days of DOS—dBase compilers were beginning to emerge. And we got all of them. We, meaning I had a partner whose name is Peter Shatalow. So while we were creating this beast, the dBase components came out, and the first one that we got was from WordTech Systems. It was called dB Compiler. And it sort of worked. And then along came Clipper and that changed everything.

**Smolin:** Oh, I remember Clipper.

**Fuller:** It turns out that, we're off topic, but the original authors of Clipper are still some of my best friends.

**Smolin:** Oh.

**Fuller:** But at the time I didn't know them. I just, I was freelance writing as a way to pay the bills. And I worked for *Database Advisor Magazine*.

**Smolin:** Oh, I remember the name. They were in San Diego, weren't they?

**Fuller:** Yeah, it was. And that's, basically, how I learned how to program— by reading the code in the magazine, typing it into my computer, and then trying to change it to do stuff that I wanted it to do instead of, you know, the specific task it was intended to do.

**Smolin:** So there were two of you in a partnership?

**Fuller:** Yeah.

**Smolin:** And were you both programmers?

**Fuller:** Yeah. Although Peter was primarily a filmmaker who got addicted to programming, and I was primarily a philosopher who got addicted to programming but who wanted to be a screenplay writer. And back then,

I mean, all you could take were mainframe classes. So we just taught ourselves.

**Smolin**: Like many of us. So the idea right from the get-go was to make a product and sell it to people—

**Fuller**: In the film business.

**Smolin**: Initially though you didn't have a shrinkwrapped program? You were delivering it as a service?

**Fuller**: That's correct, yeah. Because it was too complicated to teach people how to use it. We had little or no money, so we often delivered it as a service rather than a shrinkwrapped program. We were on set, doing the reports, etc.

Now, as I mentioned to you, we made a serious error in that we designed it for the Canadian business, not the American business. We knew nothing about the American business, so we just designed it to become what we knew.

We had gotten a dozen or so customers, and took some of the money to visit a film exposition in Santa Monica. We rented a booth and presented our software.

And we discovered that the American film business works nothing like the Canadian business. Our entire model was inappropriate.

**Smolin**: You would think that, you know, film is film, and managing the sets is managing the sets. What was the big difference between the two?

**Fuller**: We designed an all-in-one package because that was how the Canadian business worked. The more mature American business had hard-edged definitions of job roles and wanted software to match that.

The Canadian business is vertically integrated. You're typically going to find a couple, a married couple or perhaps a slightly extended family who do everything. They are the producers, the fund raisers, the directors, the director of photography, the script writer—they're all in one tight little three or four person clique, so to speak. Whereas in America it's horizontally integrated. What you've got is people whose profession is I'm a first AD, a first assistant director. That's what I do. I'm not a director, I'm a first AD.

**Smolin**: So it's more corporate.

**Fuller**: I'm a DoP. I'm a Second DoP. DoP means director of photography. So the correct business plan, had we known it at the time, would have been to sell about ten modules rather than one all-encompassing program.

**Smolin**: So the first one you sold was to a Canadian company, I assume?

**Fuller**: Yeah, in fact, the only ones we sold were to Canadian companies. And the price was about $5,000.00.

**Smolin**: Canadian?

**Fuller:** Yes, which back then was—

**Smolin:** That's a piece of change.

**Fuller:** Yeah, however, now . . .

**Smolin:** So then you went to Hollywood and found out that the model you had—

**Fuller:** Nobody wanted to buy it.

**Smolin:** The design was not appropriate for the American market. So what did you do then?

**Fuller:** We returned to Toronto, went back to the drawing board, and saw that our integrated design was next to impossible to convert to a job-centered model. We shrank our focus and started to concentrate on the Canadian market and the Australian market because it's very similar.

**Smolin:** And did it work in Australia?

**Fuller:** We sold a couple.

**Smolin:** What year was the first one sold?

**Fuller:** Approximately 1986.

**Smolin:** And what kind of machine did it go on at that point? IBM PC?

**Fuller:** Oh, no. I could be wrong, but don't think the PC came out till about '88.

**Smolin:** So you were on—

**Fuller:** We were running on a CPM machine. The first editions, we put it on any CPM machine that the customer had. Then the IBM PC came out, and we ported it to DOS, which was actually trivial. It didn't take much at all because Clipper was there, and so it was just copy the codes and compile it, and away we were to the races.

**Smolin:** So when you sold to the places where you couldn't go personally and install, you delivered it parcel post?

**Fuller:** Effectively, yeah. It was actually FedEx, I believe, but anyway.

**Smolin:** And how long did it take people to fire it up and get it running to where they were getting some value from it?

**Fuller:** Initially, probably within a week, and then as we got better at it, within a day.

**Smolin:** Did you have a manual?

**Fuller:** Yeah.

**Smolin:** And how long did it take you to write that? Longer than the program, or less?

**Fuller:** Oh, way less, way less. Took maybe three weeks or so to write the manual.

**Smolin:** Oh. Well, yeah, you guys were writers.

**Fuller:** Well, I was, yeah. So that part was not trivial but not consequential either.

**Smolin:** It's a big hurdle for a lot of programmers. So this was a single-user product?

**Fuller:** No, no it was multiuser.

**Smolin:** Multiuser?

**Fuller:** Yes, from the get-go it was—I couldn't even imagine designing a single-user program.

**Smolin:** And the networks were pretty crude at that time.

**Fuller:** Yeah, but there were some things way back in the initial stages when we were still on CPM, there was a network called Molecular.

**Smolin:** I had a Molecular machine. It had about a 10-megabyte hard disk in it.

**Fuller:** Yeah.

**Smolin:** And it was networkable. Yeah, I had three, four terminals. We had terminals then.

**Fuller:** Exactly, and our stuff ran on that.

**Smolin:** I see. Boy, that brings back memories.

**Fuller:** From the get-go we thought, you know, how absurd to design in single-user, why not design out single-user and design in multiuser.

**Smolin:** So, the program itself, how long did that take to write?

**Fuller:** A couple of years, but that's not because we were working full time in the day, it's because we were writing at night and on weekends. And conceptually, I mean, there were, I mean, this is kind of ludicrous to talk about now, but there were about at least 100 tables, and we could only have two open at once. So a lot of the magic went into figuring out how to finesse that limitation. Then Clipper came along and it had ten tables open at once. So that caused a rewrite which was actually a dramatic simplification.

So we could, you know, we could throw away about 80 out of a 100 lines of code.

**Smolin:** Did you have any copy protection?

**Fuller:** We didn't have any protection at all. On the other hand, the Clipper product shipped as an executable. But because Clipper used a version of P-Code, there were ways to reverse engineer it. But we didn't think that the film market was into that, so we just didn't worry about it.

**Smolin:** Did you Beta test it?

**Fuller:** Yeah. Which, I mean, the Beta testers were our first users.

Smolin: Okay.

Fuller: There were about a half-a-dozen of them and they shook it down pretty thoroughly, told us what didn't work, told us what was clunky, and so on. And we went back to the woodshed and fixed it.

Smolin: How did you decide on an initial selling price of $5,000?

Fuller: There was no competition and so we just picked that number out of a hat. There were no business people in the company.

Smolin: Yeah, I see.

Fuller: That was the big problem [*laughter*]. All we had was an idea and wing and a prayer. So we just picked the number $5,000 because we thought that sounded, you know, good, and twenty-odd years ago that was actually a reasonable number.

Smolin: So you sold the product, but there was a lot of onsite support initially because you guys would go onsite for the production, for the shoot?

Fuller: Yeah, because way back then nobody really much knew how to use computers. We were definitely on the leading edge.

Smolin: So it was a, kind of, a hybrid product/service thing.

Fuller: Well, that's why it became a service. Because back then very few people could even type let alone understand the computer program. I mean, you know, we're going back to the initial days of Apple and the initial days of the IBM PC. The IBM PC did, you know, move into the mainstream and all that, and people began to learn how to type. But a lot of people, when you were trying to teach them how to use software, didn't know how to type. And, you know, we'd say, "Hold down the Shift key and press."

Smolin: Right. You say, "Hit any key to continue." And they say, "Where's the any key?"

Fuller: Exactly.

Smolin: So how long did FilmStar last?

Fuller: Perhaps, five years, maybe, at the max.

Smolin: Did it give rise to any other variations?

Fuller: No.

Smolin: No? Just put it on the shelf?

Fuller: It was way too specialized. We sold a few here and there, and eventually closed our doors. We didn't declare bankruptcy, but when the phone doesn't ring, eventually you get the message. However, what it did give rise to is that as we converted it first from dBase to WordTech dB Compiler to Clipper, I learned how to program.

Smolin: And your next product grew out of that experience?

**Fuller**: Then I began to write the next thing, which was not part of that FilmStar company. It was the product that got born as Artful.lib.

**Smolin**: Which was what kind of application? What did it do?

**Fuller**: It was not an application. It was an object-oriented library for Clipper developers. And so the customer ceased to be an end user. The customer became a programmer.

**Smolin**: I see. And how did you price that one?

**Fuller**: For that one I got some advice. The guy's name is David Erwin. And he was associated with that magazine, *DataBased Advisor*, in La Jolla [California].

**Smolin**: Yes, I remember him. My office was in La Jolla at that time.

**Fuller**: Well I hired him to give me some advice. And he created our ad and our propaganda and set the price point and so on.

**Smolin**: So, you had identified the market?

**Fuller**: I was already writing for *DataBased Advisor* and I was writing a book. I wrote one of the first books about Clipper, and I was writing this library which was basically gleaned out of stuff I had written for several clients. Then you see the repetition of, you know, you write this for this client and almost the same thing for that client and almost the same thing for the next client, and then you realize, hey, I could generalize this. And write objects.

Now, in the first couple of versions, Clipper wasn't object-oriented. It was clearly leaning in that direction, but I was using a product at the same time called Actor, which was one of the first, maybe the first, completely object-oriented products for Windows. So I learned the basics about Actor, about object-oriented programming by using Actor. And then I discovered that Clipper couldn't do it, so I kludged a way that it could. It was basically pointers to functions.

**Smolin**: So Artful.lib became a successful product.

**Fuller**: Yeah, it did. It became very successful . . . I was vaguely aware of a marketing maxim that says, "You have to appear in three successive issues" or "You have to buy 17 minutes of TV time" to make a penetration into the recipients' consciousness. I found enough money to finance our initial magazine ads, and sure enough it worked. In the first year, I sold more than half-a-million dollars' worth of product, and in the second and third sales went over a million. Not all profit, of course.

**Smolin**: How many years of life did it have?

**Fuller**: Through its various iterations, about seven.

**Smolin**: And it reached the end of its product life primarily because of what?

**Fuller:** Because of the emergence of Windows and our reluctance to see the tide coming. We lived in DOS too long. And did not see, you know, the tidal wave that Windows was going to prove.

**Smolin:** So, what happened next, as they say?

**Fuller:** Well, we devised ways of making our Artful.lib Clipper apps work in a DOS box in Windows. And we added a mouse product and this and that and the other thing. But basically, we were too busy to catch the tide. There's no pretty way to gloss it over. The world was changing, and we vaguely recognized it but were under too much pressure to do anything about it. The Clipper compiler was for DOS, not Windows, and Windows was just emerging as a serious player.

By this time, Nantucket Corporation was sold to Computer Associates. A "Clipper for Windows" was under development even before the sale, and I got a contract to write a book about it. The product had some beautiful aspects but was buggy beyond belief. The book got published, but the product went nowhere, and I lost a year developing code for a failed product. And that was the end of my second company. Once again, I closed the doors before having to declare bankruptcy, although this time it cost a house and a marriage.

After that, I retreated into contract programming. I became an expert in Microsoft Access first, then moved into Microsoft SQL Server. I continued to write for various publications while also doing contract development, with no thought of creating another package and another company to sell it. Which is how I got into, first of all, Access. I did a bunch of contract programming in Access all over the place, here, there, and everywhere.

**Smolin:** Uh-huh.

**Fuller:** And that, in turn, led to, mind you, now we're jump cutting to about the year 2000 when the first implementation of Access ADP came out. Actually, I was already into SQL before that, but with the Clipper's versions of the Access ADP format, I had done a couple of apps in Access plus ODBC, but that sucked.

**Smolin:** I know.

**Fuller:** It was not really in my mind a solution. It was a patch, and anyway I found myself into SQL. And as time went on, well, yeah, I was one of those pioneers of ADP. As soon as they released it, I dove in headlong. At that time, I did a couple of really significant Access apps with, like, 500 tables.

**Smolin:** So from 2000 to the present, you've been doing custom programming, database, and application development?

**Fuller:** Yeah.

**Smolin:** On a fee for service basis, basically?

**Fuller**: Yeah, almost entirely SQL Server. I've done a couple things in DB II and a couple of things in Oracle, but almost entirely in SQL Server.

**Smolin**: Any new products on the line here?

**Fuller**: Well, yeah. Now we get to the next product. A friend recommended me to a friend to do an application for horse riding stables.

**Smolin**: On a custom basis?

**Fuller**: Yeah. When I was eight years old, from when I was eight to sixteen, I had a job as a guide at a riding stable, and I loved horses.

**Smolin**: Uh-huh.

**Fuller**: I haven't been on a horse, well, with the exception of the last six months, I haven't been on a horse for thirty years or so. But I really love horses and, you know, I have a simpatico thing with them. And, anyway, this job fell into my lap, and it was just to write a custom app to manage horses and lessons, instructors, and this and that. It's not a complicated app. I mean, there's only—there's probably only about forty or fifty table sets. You know, given some of the things I've written, it's one-tenth as complex. I'm used to writing things that have 500 tables.

**Smolin**: Right.

**Fuller**: But anyway, this fell into my lap, and I love horses and I liked the people, and according to Canadian law in the absence of a clause that says, "I, the Contractor, own the code," then the person who writes it owns the code.

**Smolin**: Right. That's the same way it is here.

**Fuller**: Yeah. And so I said to the lady, Kelly, I said to her, "I think this has resale possibilities and, you know, although we didn't write in a clause, I'll give you a piece if you want one." And she just said, "Go for it, good luck." And, you know, in effect washed her hands of any possible royalties that might ensue.

And so now here we are having been twice burned and thrice shy, I'm thinking about this and I've investigated the market, and I have a friend named Michael who is a marketing guru and who is now, basically, retired. And he's affluent and he has no need to pursue the filthy lucre anymore.

He's very comfortable, but he's bored. And so he's been helping me look into this market, and we found out that there's only one competitor. And the irony is that the person who hired me to write this is a licensed user of the aforementioned competitor. And hates the software so much that she hired me to replace it.

**Smolin**: I see.

**Fuller**: So, I've had a peek at that product, and we ensured that everything in mine does what that one does, plus, plus, plus, plus. So that's where I stand at the moment, and I'm not really sure whether I'm going to dip my toe in this pond again. Because it turns out almost every time that you end up working 120 hours a week, and the last one cost me a house and a marriage [*laughter*]. Mind you, now that I have neither a house nor a marriage, it can't be that awful.

**Smolin:** Yeah, not much downside. So, if somebody came to you and said, "Arthur, I've got a fabulous idea for a product. I've got this program. I think I'm going to turn it into a product," what would your sagest piece of advice to a person be who's entering this arena for the first time? What is the biggest pitfall or the biggest risk you'd like to notify them of?

**Fuller:** The first thing is don't risk, entirely, your own money. Get financing somewhere. Get a partner, get something. But don't risk your house.

**Smolin:** Okay. That's it?

**Fuller:** And the second thing would be get somebody who knows something about business. Don't rely on your programming skill to win the day. That's not going to work.

The central problem is that I know nothing about business. I have devoted all my intellectual efforts to philosophy first, and then screenwriting, and then programming, and then database design and development. I know nothing about how to run a business, or effective marketing, and even worse, I hate selling.

What I have learned is that the success of a firm is defined by its weakest link. Should I proceed, I need partners with skill sets totally unrelated to mine. Loving to sit in the back room devising new algorithms is not enough. Wild-eyed ambitions are not enough. Lust for wealth and dates with Penelope Cruz are not enough. When I first began, a couple of guys in a garage did have a shot. Not now. Nothing less than a team of experts in various fields will do.

I guess that I'm talking myself out of trying this next venture, but the saddest part is that despite all my cynical arguments, I still feel like giving it a shot. What if? What if? Maybe I could get a date with Penelope Cruz.

Anyway, those would be my two lessons learned the hard way.

# 5

# Legal Matters

Legal matters. It can matter a lot. Yet many software developers, completely obsessed with trying to get their product to the starting line, or selling enough of it to keep the lights on, delay or avoid altogether dealing with legal matters. Many folks would rather get a rectal exam than have a conversation with a lawyer.

The whole legal thing seems to be such a waste of time: preparing for all kinds of eventualities that never happen, setting up systems and structures that no one ever looks at. Like insurance that you never make a claim on. Or seat belts that you very rarely need.

But as I said in the last chapter, "Plan for success." This means that some-day, hopefully, someone WILL be looking at your legalities because they will want to pay you a big chunk of dough for your product.

And on the downside, you might hear from someone who thinks you have done something wrong. And they'll want a big chunk of your dough as well.

And then there's that whole other industry that wants you as a partner—the illegal copy, software piracy business. You need to protect yourself from them if you can. To a lesser degree, this involves your users who may not be as, shall we say, sensitive about your property as you are.

So you have to cover all your legal bases. It's boring, tedious, absolutely no fun, and doesn't involve anything as entertaining as programming. And so I apologize for the length of this chapter and the dearth of pictures. But doing the legal thing and doing it right will increase your chances of success in many ways.

**Legal disclaimer**: do not rely on this chapter for legal advice. I'm not a lawyer and don't even play one on TV. The purpose of the information con-tained herein is to introduce you to the various legal topics you need to con-sider when bringing a software product to market. It is not a substitute for a consultation with a qualified attorney and/or tax accountant.

# How to Talk to a Lawyer

Legal matters are off-putting because of the sometimes, OK, often, confusing or obscure nature of the subject. And the language they use! Would you hire a programmer who talked like that?

As a community, software developers tend to be controlling types. And so we like precise, program-like answers to our questions. But, when we sit down to talk law with a lawyer, their answers never seem to have the satisfying precision we like. So we don't get that comfortable in-control feeling. And there seems to be so much basic stuff we don't know. We don't even know the right questions to ask. (Of course, ask a lawyer how comfortable they feel about talking to a programmer.)

However, if you've gotten this far creating a working software product, let me assure you that there's nothing going on in the legal world that you aren't capable of understanding. You just need to know the issues that require attention to set up and maintain a clean, street-legal business, protect your product, and cover your assets. To do it right, you will most likely need a lawyer—and sooner rather than later.

Let me digress a moment and put in a good word about lawyers, here. Lawyers are an easy target. The pundits have a lot of fun at their expense. People all the way back to Shakespeare have been heaping gratuitous vilification on this group. "The first thing we do, let's kill all the lawyers" says the often-quoted Dick the Butcher in King Henry IV. Of course, what Shakespeare was really underscoring was the importance of the part that lawyers play in a society based on laws. The quickest way to despotism, even then, was to remove the defenders of the law.

Certainly there are as many unethical and corrupt people among lawyers as there are among, say, the programming community. But arguably not more. So cut your lawyer some slack. They're as straight and competent as you are. And they're going to do a lot of good things for your business. End of sermon.

A good lawyer will advise you about and defend you against any problems that arise in the course of your business. A really good lawyer will see to it the problems don't occur in the first place. So you need to find a really good lawyer that you trust.

Finding the really good lawyer is not as difficult as it might seem. Referral is the absolute best way to find one if you don't already have one. Family, friends, and business colleagues are the best source.

You'll want one who specializes in business issues—what is called a "transactional lawyer"—as opposed to one who specializes in litigation or criminal law. A lawyer who also does trademarks and patents and can advise on issues of intellectual property will be a big plus for your business.

The really good lawyer should not charge you for an initial consultation. Think of it as a job interview or as evaluating a vendor. You don't pay people to make sales calls on **you**, do you?

Don't be shy about talking fees. Hourly rate means nothing. To compare apples and apples, you need to ask for the "out the door" estimate on a specific item. How much will it cost to incorporate? How much will it cost to do a trademark? Is this a firm quote or an estimate? Does the estimate include the filing and other fees you have to pay to the state or other agencies?

Bear in mind that, just like programming, things go wrong, and it often takes more time than one initially thought to get the job done right. The last time I renewed the trademark on E-Z-MRP, I was quoted around $400–$500. It ended up costing over $1,000 because the rules—and the technology—had changed since the last time I did it twenty years ago.

So, most lawyers will balk at giving you a firm quote for a job, the same way you'd balk at giving a client a firm quote for an ill-specified application. This is why the issue of trust is so critical to your selection of a lawyer. A referral's previous experience with a lawyer is the best criterion for making your selection.

# Who Owns Your Software?

This may seem pretty obvious. You wrote it (or paid to have it written). You own it, right? In general, yes. There is one potential exception to this, and that exception comes up quite often when turning a program into a product.

Many products begin their lives as a custom program written for a particular company and probably highly tailored to their specific requirements. But does that company own the rights to the program? This issue is covered under federal law in *The Copyright Act of 1976*, U.S. Code 17, sections 101–810. Generally, the author of a work owns the copyright or, in the words of section 201(a) of the act, "vests initially in the author or authors of the work." Seems only fair.

So, if you wrote the program as an independent contractor, then *in the absence of an express agreement assigning the rights to the person or company who hired you,* the rights to the program probably belong to you.

Even as an employee, under the language of the copyright act, you may still own the rights to the program. Following is the doctrine known as "work for hire," according to U.S. Code 17, section 101:

> *Works Made for Hire—(1) a work prepared by an employee within the scope of his or her employment; or (2) a work specially ordered or commissioned for use as a contribution to a collective work, as a part of a motion picture or other audiovisual work, as a translation, as a supplementary work, as a compilation, as an instructional text, as a test, as answer material for a test, or as an atlas, if the parties expressly agree in a written instrument signed by them that the work shall be considered a work made for hire.*

According to this doctrine, for the employer to have the rights to your work as an employee, three conditions have to be met: 1) the work has to be "specially ordered or commissioned," 2) the work has to fall within one of the nine categories listed, and 3) there must be a written agreement between the two parties that the work is to be considered a "work for hire."

Note that in (2) of the doctrine, software is not on the list. However, according to the explanation of the work for hire doctrine on the U.S. Copyright Office's web site (www.copyright.gov/circs/circ9.html), a software program created within the scope of employment is covered by that list.

Which—if you're in the situation where the program you want to turn into a product was initially created as a custom application for a specific company— means what? It means you need to consult with a lawyer on where the rights to the program lie. And you should probably clear this up before investing a lot of time in any other plan to make a product out of this program.

The same advice can be applied to you as the employer. If you had a custom application written for your company, either by employees or an outside firm or independent contractor, and are now thinking of turning it into a commercial product, again, a consultation with a lawyer would be a good idea. You need to clearly establish your rights to the software.

As an employer or business owner, it might seem unfair that, after all the money you paid to a programmer to have a custom application written for you, you don't own it and have the right to resell it.

As a programmer sitting on the other side of the table, however, it looks a bit different. One of the things that gives a good programmer leverage and efficiency is that, over the years, we all accumulate a bag of tricks—a personal library of forms and code that allow us to create working programs in a fraction of the time it would take to write them from scratch.

So, as I create one custom application after another, I'm building into each one common routines I pull from my personal kit bag. I certainly don't want ownership of that code to pass to my client. And I certainly don't want to lose the right to reuse that code on the next job.

So I always retain all the rights to the programs I write and never sign a contract that passes ownership of the rights to the client. If the client really wants to own the code, then I have to write it all from the ground up, which would take much, much longer. And most clients don't generally want that. Most clients are more interested in time and cost than issues of software ownership.

Note as a final caveat that this "work for hire" discussion centers around U.S. law. Your country's laws may vary.

If the subject interests you, simply Google "work for hire doctrine," and you'll get over 13,000 hits. Have fun.

# Never Sell Your Software

Now what's he on about? The whole point of reading this book is getting ready to sell huge amounts of software, no?

This is a legal distinction, but an important one. You never sell your software. You sell someone the right to use it. As pointed out in the previous section, if you sell them the software, then you're transferring your rights to the buyer. Hopefully, one day you **will** sell your software. Once. For millions. But for the moment, you want to retain ownership and just grant others permission to use it.

The right to use your software is outlined in a legal document called a **license**. You, the person granting the license, are the **licensor**. The person paying you for the privilege of using your software is the **licensee**.

The licensee is permitted to use your software as long as they adhere to the conditions outlined in the license. You know about this because you have agreed to many End User License Agreements ("EULAs" in the euphonious jargon of the computer business), each of which you have read thoroughly, being prudent enough not to ever agree to a document you haven't read. OK, you've never read any of them, have you? When installing a piece of software and the screen comes up asking whether you agree to the displayed license, you just click yes, don't you? I know I do.

Now might be a good time to get out those dime-store readers and actually read one of these masterpieces. If you have software-in-a-box, there's probably a printed copy of the EULA somewhere in the box or the manual. If you don't have one at the ready, you can read the sample software license in the Appendix. Have a cup of coffee handy.

Usually, a license, like any legal agreement, needs to be signed by both parties. For software, the license is sometimes wrapped up with the software—known as a **shrink-wrap license**—and you don't get to read it until you open the box but before you break the shrink-wrap seal. There's a warning that says if you don't agree with the terms of the license that you should return the product. Not returning the product is regarded as acceptance of the terms of the license.

Sometimes the license is presented to you as part of the installation process. This is called a **click-wrap license**. At that point you will be asked to click a control that indicates your acceptance or rejection of the terms of the license. Figure 5-1 shows an example of the installation screen for The Sleep Advisor.

Notice that as long as "No, I do not accept the terms in the license agreement" is selected, the "Next" box is grayed out—disabled; the user cannot proceed with the installation of the program until they select "Yes, I accept the terms in the license agreement."

Accepting the terms of the agreement implies that the user has scrolled down the document and read the terms, as unlikely as that may seem.

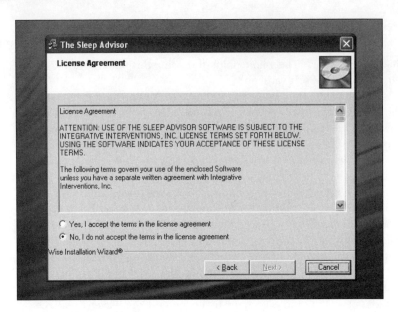

**Figure 5-1.** Software License Acceptance screen

So, as part of your process of converting your program into a product, you need to decide on the text of your license and how it's going to be presented.

However you get your user to accept the terms of your license, you'll have to create one. Or have it written by a lawyer. Or cobble it together from other licenses like many of us have done.

There are some fairly standard paragraphs you need to include. The license for E-Z-MRP granted by Beach Access Software in the Appendix is printed in the E-Z-MRP manual. The first couple of paragraphs cover the contents of the manual followed by the actual license agreement itself:

- **No Warranty**: Covers me in case I've made some bonehead mistake in the documentation.

- **Copyright Notice**: Covers the contents of the manual.

- **Trademarks**: Notifies the reader of the trademark status of the product name.

- **License Agreement**: Dictates users must agree to abide by all the terms of the license to use the software. I agree to give them their money back in case they don't want to.

- **License Grant**: Where I actually give my OK. E-Z-MRP, like most commercial applications these days, can be run over a network, and it is anticipated that, because of the nature of the application, it will have multiple users. Beach Access Software grants a "site license," discussed earlier in Chapter 4. So the grant includes the phrase "single working location." If your software is to be restricted to a single machine, or to be used on a per-seat basis, you need to incorporate language limiting the scope of the license to the pricing scheme you have adopted.

- **Ownership**: Makes it perfectly clear that the license does not transfer any ownership of the product.

- **Copies**: Restricts making copies of the product to backup or archival purposes, and warns against spreading copies around in the public domain.

- **No Disassembly**: Prohibits the licensee from stealing your intellectual property by disassembling or decompiling your software. You cannot, of course, prevent someone from knocking off your product by "reverse engineering," that is, building a clone with the same kinds of features and functions, just by looking at the screens and reports and the fields and tables in the database.

  Most products do not have algorithms or other proprietary routines that cannot be discerned merely by looking at the product from the outside. There's no mystery about an accounting system, for example, or a manufacturing system.

  This clause becomes more operative in a product like The Sleep Advisor, an expert system that identifies sleep problems based on a complex formula connecting the user's responses to an assessment identifying a list of sleep problems. In this case, there is value in the code that you would not want to have knocked off.

- **Transfer**: Allows the license to be transferred. Fielder's choice here. But if a company changes name or ownership or is bought out, the new owners will want to be able to carry on business using your product. So this will give them the option of transferring the license to the new entity.

- **Termination**: Specifies that you will terminate this license if they fail to comply with any of the license terms. And that they must destroy the software. To which they'll probably reply, "Yeah. You and what army?" Which is what keeps the courts in business.

- **"As Is" Warranty Statement**: I love this part.

  1. **Disclaimer**: Wherein you make no claims about your software working correctly. Or even working at all. Can you believe anyone actually agrees to this? Would you buy a car that, according to the manufacturer, "May not work correctly. May not work at all. Not guaranteed to run on any specific kind of road"?

2. **Limitation of Liability**: In which you state that, in light of the Disclaimer, should your user suffer any damages from the use of your software, you have no responsibility to pay for said damages. (Car manufacturer: "We told you the car might not work right. If the brakes don't work and you run into a wall, don't come crying to us.")

3. **Use at Your Own Risk**: In light of the first two paragraphs, you tell the user "Should the Software prove defective, you assume the entire cost of all service, repair, or correction." Wow. Do you know of any other product or service that can get away with that?

- **Governing Law**: Indicates the state where you do business or, if different, the state where your lawyer is licensed to practice.

- **Consent to Jurisdiction, Venue, and Service**: Dictates that should the user want to press any claim against you, they have to come to your town to do it. This doesn't stop them from filing a claim against you in their own hometown and forcing you to go there and ask for a change of venue. But it may slow them down a bit.

Doesn't the foregoing make you want to go back and look at some of those licenses to see what you've actually agreed to?

The primary purpose of a license, in my opinion, is not to provide fodder for a lawsuit. Most companies do not want to base any part of their business on an illegal copy of software. In my experience, any company caught with an illegal copy of my software couldn't get a check to me fast enough.

On the other side of the table, if you find someone using an illegal copy of your software, you're probably not going to spend the time or money to pursue them in court. Since your damages are probably limited to the cost of the software, and you're probably not going to recover your attorney's fees, there's just not enough money involved.

And most companies, if you sell them a defective product, don't have the time, energy, money, interest, or damages to come after you legally. They'll just get rid of you and your software.

Almost all people are honest. Almost all play by the rules. The primary purpose of your license is to lay down the rules for using your software. So craft a license that is clear and thorough about your expectations for the use of your product. Then, of course, give it to your lawyer.

# The Business Format

You have several options for how you want to form your business, the most common being sole proprietor, partnership, LLC, and corporation. Herein follows a very brief description of each—just enough to start you searching the Web for more information.

How you elect to form your business entity should be based on discussions with both your lawyer and your tax accountant. No tax accountant, you say? Been using TurboTax since your undergraduate days? Well, life is about to become a little more complicated.

A good lawyer will keep your nose clean. A good accountant will keep more of your money in your pocket. Get yourself one of each.

## Sole Proprietor

This is by far the simplest and least expensive option. This is because there is no legal difference between you and your company. So there are very few or no legal formalities.

Filing taxes is also easy because all of the business income and expenses are declared on your personal tax return using Schedule C.

So all of the income of the company is your income. On the other hand, all of the debts of the company are your debts. You also have no protection of your personal assets from creditors or anyone making claims against your company. Should someone sue you and win, all of your personal assets can be used to satisfy the claim. This can include your home and retirement accounts.

Legally you should register a fictitious business name or DBA ("doing business as"). Usually this means running an ad in the business notices section of your newspaper's want ads. That will allow you to go to the bank and open an account under your business name.

So the startup is cheap and easy. However, as your business grows, there are some drawbacks to a sole proprietorship. You can't sell shares in your company. So raising money can be difficult. It's also harder to get bank financing. And as the company gets bigger, the risks grow. It can be difficult to hire employees. And again, your personal assets are at risk for the errors or misdeeds of an employee.

## Partnership

This is essentially a sole proprietorship with more than one proprietor. The partners agree to run the business together and share the profits and losses. Like a sole proprietorship, a partnership is not a taxable entity. So the profits (or losses) flow directly into the personal returns of the partners in proportion to their ownership.

As in a sole proprietorship, there is no protection of personal assets. Each partner is jointly and independently liable for the debts of the partnership as well as the acts of the other partners.

Because there is more than one person involved, you should most certainly have an operating agreement between or among you regarding your partnership. You should also have a buy-sell agreement—a kind of prenuptial agreement—specifying who can buy the interest of a partner who wants out (or was forced out, by dying, for example), and what events will trigger a buyout. The purpose of the buy-sell agreement is to ensure that everyone is treated fairly and that the business will continue smoothly. As you can imagine, these kinds of agreements can be fairly complicated and are always tailored to the specific conditions of the partners. You can find sample buy-sell agreements online if you're curious.

The documents required by a partnership will most certainly require a lawyer. Depending on complexity, and how much disagreement is generated between the partners over the terms of the agreement, partnership agreements can run several thousand dollars.

## Limited Liability Company

A limited liability company (LLC—sometimes referred to incorrectly as a limited liability corporation, although it is not a corporation) combines features of sole proprietorships, partnerships, and corporations. Instead of partners or shareholders, LLC owners are called members. You can have any number of members.

The biggest advantage of an LLC over a sole proprietorship or partnership is limited liability. The LLC exists as a separate entity, so the members' personal assets cannot be used to satisfy the debts of the LLC.

LLCs are easy to run. They don't require the formalities of a corporation, and the profits flow through to the members, avoiding the double taxation of corporate and individual taxes.

You will need a couple of documents: 1) Articles of Organization, which you will need to file with your secretary of state, and 2) an Operating Agreement, specifying terms of ownership, responsibilities of the various members, and profit sharing.

So, setting up an LLC is a bit more complicated and expensive than a sole proprietorship or partnership. You can learn to do it yourself and it will probably cost less than $200. You can probably learn to do your own root canal as well. A lawyer will charge you on the order of $2,000 to do the job, and it will get done right.

## Corporations

A corporation is a legal entity that exists separate and apart from its owners. The word has its roots in the Latin *corporare*, meaning to form into a body. It has many of the same rights as a person. It can sue and be sued. It can sign contracts, hire agents or employees, buy, own, and sell assets, and govern its own affairs through by-laws that it can make, modify, and repeal.

The ownership of a corporation is divided into shares, all or part of which are distributed to the shareholders when the corporation is formed. More can be sold or issued later to others who then become "shareholders" in the corporation. One of the great advantages of a corporation is that the shares can be transferred from one person to another without affecting the legal status of the corporation. So the corporation continues on as a legal entity regardless of any shareholder's withdrawal or death.

Finally, and perhaps most importantly, the corporation provides you as a shareholder with limited liability. That is, your personal assets cannot be used to satisfy any debt or judgment against a corporation in which you own shares. And you're not liable as a shareholder for the criminal acts of the corporation.

For tax purposes, you can choose to be a C corporation or an S corporation. C corporations pay federal corporate taxes, which currently range in the U.S. between 15 percent and 35 percent of net income. S corporations do not pay federal taxes. The profits (and losses) of the corporations flow directly into the personal tax returns of the shareholders.

A full discussion of the advantages and disadvantages of incorporating is beyond the scope of this book. Only a qualified tax accountant and an attorney can tell you if it is the most advantageous business form for you and your partners, if any.

A corporation is more expensive to set up initially and to maintain. In addition to annual filing fees, there is a separate corporate tax return that has to be prepared by your accountant. There are also annual corporate formalities that must be done to keep your corporation street-legal.

Check the Web, and you'll find lots of sites for do-it-yourself incorporating, usually under $100. The same advice about do-it-yourself LLCs applies to corporations. Don't do it. A lawyer will charge you on the order of $1,000 to $1,500 for a simple incorporation. Given what you will have invested in your product in time and money, and that you've planned for success and intend to get rich and famous with your software, this is chump change.

# Insuring Success

More things to worry about. Insurance. I'll make this brief. You're not unfamiliar with insurance, having at various times bought auto, home, and medical insurance policies.

So, if you've rented some office space, you absolutely need a general liability policy that protects you from someone who walks in, falls down, and breaks their arm, not to mention fire, theft, and vandalism.

But the bigger issue for software developers is the question of product and professional liability and whether you should seek this kind of coverage. What you need to know and perhaps more than you want to know about software product liability is clearly spelled out in a document titled "Software Product Liability" by Jody Armour of the University of Pittsburgh School of Law. It is available online at `www.sei.cmu.edu/pub/documents/93.reports/pdf/tr13.93.pdf`, and if product or professional liability is a concern for you, I recommend reading it.

If the success of your business and hence your family and/or partners' families' economic well-being depends on both or all of you being present and healthy, then you might want to consider life insurance and disability insurance.

Seek the advice of a reliable insurance agent—preferably an independent agent who can represent many different companies—and learn what you can about the different types of coverage you may need.

In the end, you will make the final decision about buying insurance. Remember, to a man with a hammer, everything looks like a nail. I've rarely had an insurance agent recommend against buying a policy. It's not that they just want the commission. They believe in the product.

# What If You Get Hit By a Truck? Software Escrow

Because I spent so many years as a "lone ranger" software developer, more than once I was asked the question "What if you get hit by a truck?"—a metaphorical way of asking what happens if they call one day and find I've disappeared, gone out of business, or run off to Cancun with the housekeeper.

The real question they're asking is how do they maintain the application in the event of a problem—an application that may be critical to the operation of their company. In other words, under what conditions might they be able to get their hands on the source code? The more knowledgeable among them asks if the source code has been **escrowed**.

**Software escrow** means giving a copy of your source code to a third party to be released to all of your customers in certain defined events. The most common event that will trigger the release of your source code is going out of business. Other conditions that may be written into the escrow agreement might include the failure to maintain or update your program per the terms of your license agreement or the failure to provide timely technical support.

Do you need to escrow your source code? This depends on the nature of your application. If it will cost your customer a large amount of time and money to replace your product, incurring the costs of conversion and training to learn a replacement application, they might feel more comfortable knowing the source code for your product is in escrow. The more "mission critical" your application is to your customer, the more likely that they will want the security of knowing that they can get the source code in the event there is a problem with the program that you cannot or do not correct in a timely manner.

So for a relatively simple and inexpensive application that could be easily replaced, source code escrow will probably not result in any additional sales. For your customers, it's simply not a consideration.

The need to escrow your software source code is also a function of the size and history of your company. When you're just starting out and may be only a one-man shop, or have only a few people working, and very little track record, knowing that your software's source code is available might give a potential customer the additional confidence they need to buy your product.

It will cost on the order of $1,000 to $2,000 a year to escrow your source code. Think of it as a marketing cost, one of those pesky "fixed" costs from Chapter 4. If you're selling an application that runs to five figures, and it gives you the edge to close a few additional sales, it's cheap enough.

The procedures and terms of the escrow among the three parties—you, the licensee, and the escrow company—are defined and governed by the escrow agreement. It should spell out in detail

- The procedures for depositing your source code in escrow (it needs to be kept current with the latest version of the product, of course).

- The events or conditions triggering release of the source code, and the parties to whom the source code is to be released.

- A license for the source granting the licensee use of the source code and conditions for keeping it confidential. Even though you are no longer maintaining the product, it may still have value, and you may still want to sell the rights to the product at some point.

- Some language that indemnifies the escrow company and limits their liability in the event someone sues them in a dispute over this escrow.

You know what comes next here. This is not a do-it-yourself job. Enlist the aid of your really good lawyer in fashioning an escrow agreement that accomplishes its dual purpose—1) protecting your rights to your product and your source code, and 2) giving your customers the measure of confidence necessary to invest in your product.

# Copyrights

To protect the intellectual value in your software, you want to have copyright protection. The owner of a copyright generally has the right to

- Duplicate or reproduce copies of the work.

- Create other products based on the copyrighted work.

- Distribute and sell copies to the public.

- Perform the work publicly (not a big issue in software).

- Display the work publicly.

or to authorize someone else to do these things. Anyone who does any of the preceding without the permission of the copyright owner is violating the copyright, and that is an illegal act.

Copyright protection for software exists from the time the first line of code is written. Again, the "work for hire" doctrine, which was discussed earlier in this chapter, may affect who is the owner of the copyright. But the protection still exists for the copyright owner, whoever that may be.

To secure a copyright, no publication or registration is required. The copyright is yours automatically when you create the work. Even the familiar notice of copyright has been eliminated as a requirement to secure your copyright. So, for once, no lawyer is needed.

However, use of a copyright notice may strengthen your claim in the case of infringement. The defendant will find it much more difficult to base their defense on "innocent infringement"—that is, that they were unaware that they were violating a copyright—if the copyright notice is displayed. Note that on the opening forms of both E-Z-MRP and The Sleep Advisor, there is a copyright notice.

The protection endures for seventy years after the author's death. That should give you (and your heirs) plenty of time to exploit your software.

You can register your copyright with the U.S. Copyright Office. Although it is not a legal requirement, there are several advantages to doing so.

One of the best sources of information about copyrights is the web site of the U.S. Copyright Office: `www.copyright.gov/`. There you can find pages about copyright basics, frequently asked questions, current fees, and, for the less literate, even a kind of comic book presentation, "Taking the Mystery Out of Copyright."

# Trademarks

Trademarks do not add functionality or real value to your software for your users. But they can enhance the intangible value of your product—the goodwill associated with the mark—by associating the mark with your products. To the extent that your product reflects high standards or quality and professionalism, the mark comes to be associated with those values. To someone who may be interested in acquiring your company, this could be very important.

You probably think of a trademark as a logo. And many times they are. But it can also be a name (E-Z-MRP®) or a word or words (The Sleep Advisor®), or a series of letters (like IBM), or even a sound like the NBC chimes.

You get initial rights in a trademark similar to a copyright—simply by using it. To get federal rights, you have to have a sale of the product with the trademark attached—a legitimate sale as part of a real sales and marketing program (not a copy to your brother-in-law).

Of course, you need to be sure that someone else has not used that mark first. Or something similar. Otherwise you may find yourself in a legal tussle with them.

Rights to a trademark can also be established by registering it with the United States Patent and Trademark Office (USPTO). It strengthens your rights to the mark because granting of the trademark registration by the USPTO presumes that it is valid and doesn't infringe on anyone else's mark. It also allows you to sue infringers in federal court and recover damages and costs.

You can learn more than you want to know about trademarks at the excellent USPTO web site: `www.uspto.gov/main/trademarks.htm`.

After you study up on trademarks, assuming you want one for your product—you know what's coming next. Call your really good lawyer. Sure, the instructions on the USPTO site make it seem like you COULD do it yourself. But you already have a job, don't you? And it's probably not being a trademark attorney. If you want to get a trademark to enhance the value of your product and business, it pays to have it done right.

# There Be Pirates Out There . . .

Back in the bad old days at the beginning of the personal computer software business, there was a widespread lack of knowledge about propriety and ethics of software ownership. The first programs were games and useful utility programs for the hobbyist, and those got passed around pretty freely.

Then, software for businesses began to reach the market. Ashton Tate's dBase II, Borland's Turbo Pascal and Sidekick, Visicorp's VisiCalc, and MicroPro's WordStar, among many others, helped move the personal computer out of the game room and into the office.

Still, the software was simple to copy, and copies were relatively untraceable. And many people did not really understand what was wrong with copying a program to run on two or three computers in the same office. Those who did understand had the same attitude toward their copies that music sharers and downloaders have today.

During this time, we spent a lot of hours trying to figure out how to stop or reduce the number of pirated copies of our software. Every scheme to control piracy had its drawbacks, however. Every one of them created a problem of some kind for the user and so impacted, to some degree, the attractiveness of the product in the marketplace.

There were hardware keys that plugged into the parallel port on the back of the computer that had to be present for the software to run. There were programs that required the original disk to be in the disk drive to run the program. There were ways to record things on diskettes and CDs that would not be copied by a generic disk copy program. There were counters on the diskette that limited the number of times a program was installed.

Limiting the number of times a product can be installed was a failure—not technologically, but because of the way it alienated customers. Given the nature of Windows, it is not unusual for someone to have to reload their entire system repeatedly. When you run out of installs, you have to call the manufacturer and convince them that you're not a crook. Bad public relations.

None of these schemes were immune from being hacked and defeated. All created the impression in the buyer's mind that they were not to be trusted. Many felt that, as long as they adhered to the terms of the license, they should not have any restrictions on doing what they wanted with the software they had bought and paid for.

In the end, we decided that we would just sell it faster than they could steal it and never look back. There was no percentage in trying to control the copies.

The seriousness of the problem depends to a large degree on the cost and complexity of the product you're selling, and how important it is to the user to have product support from the manufacturer.

For a utility program or consumer-based product like The Sleep Advisor, something in the $50–$100 price range, there's not much you can do. Even if you have your software "call home" as a way to identify users of your product—an approach many users find intrusive and a violation of their privacy—you can't begin to take legal action. Your damages aren't great enough to bother with. On the upside, there is more awareness these days about the ethics and legalities of software ownership, and more and more people are playing by the rules.

Your application might provide its own internal restraints against piracy because of price, complexity, and/or the need for developer support.

On the price front, if you pay $3,000 for software, how likely are you to give a copy to a friend? Of course, employees leaving the company can always add a copy of the product to the shopping bag of office supplies they're stealing.

So then there's the next line of defense—complexity—which implies the need for support from the software developer or vendor. Particularly in "mission critical" applications—programs that a customer depends on for the success of their business—no one wants to take a chance of failing because they based their business on a stolen product for which they cannot get support.

Complexity also creates another barrier to piracy. A product that by its nature is multiuser means the pirate has to put everyone on alert who uses the product never to call the manufacturer. Many products, like E-Z-MRP, have the manufacturer's name and contact information right on the opening form. So the employer has to involve all the employees in a conspiracy to defraud the software manufacturer. This means every employee who leaves the company under less-than-favorable conditions becomes a potential whistleblower.

So you want to measure the time and energy you put into piracy deterrence against the sales you might lose because of the hoops you make the honest customer jump through just to turn on your software.

For The Sleep Advisor, there is no practical copy protection scheme. Requiring the CD to be in the machine is no solution. CD copying software comes with Windows.

For E-Z-MRP, I adopted the "product key" approach. People are accustomed to this from installing Microsoft and other products. So the idea has built-in acceptance. You can embed lots of information in a product key. The most useful data I embed in the E-Z-MRP key is the expiration date. You can hide the date by converting the numeric data into letters. Pick twelve letters in sequence, say, L through W. L then becomes January, M is February, and so on. The year can be managed similarly by starting with a random letter like F for 2007. 2008 becomes G. When you reach Z, loop around to A. If your product lasts for more than 26 years, you'll have a nice problem to solve.

Scatter this date information in noncontiguous characters of your key to make it a little harder to break, and have several positions in your key that contain placeholders that have no meaning.

Using this approach, you can embed lots of information in the product key, including a serial number. Another useful piece of data is the version or release number. This would make it impossible for someone with a key for an earlier version to give their key to someone with a later version, and vice versa.

So you need to write a routine to "encode" the key given the source information—expiration date, version, serial number, etc.—and a routine to "decode" a key to recover the original information. Then you can use the encoding routine in your internal customer registration and tracking program to create the product key. The decoding routine gets embedded into the opening form of your application.

You can reduce the probability that someone will be able to "hack" your key by adding in a checksum digit to the key. The simplest way to do this is to take the numeric value of each of the ASCII characters in your key, sum them, and put the last digit somewhere in your key. Any alteration of your key by the user in an attempt to decode your key results in a different checksum digit. When that happens, the decoding routine generates a message that the license key has been corrupted and instructs the user to contact the manufacturer for a new key.

The expiration date provides some great advantages. The primary one is that you can send someone a copy of your product to evaluate, set the expiration date for thirty days, and you don't have to worry about the evaluator making copies of your product. In fact, you can encourage them to do so and spread your product around to as many people as might be interested in it.

Registered users of E-Z-MRP get a product key that is good for a year. Evaluators get a key that expires in thirty to sixty days. Forty-five days before their license expires, they begin to get a notice every time they start their system that their license is running out and they need to contact Beach Access Software for an updated key, as shown in Figure 5-2.

Using this approach, users' licenses can be extended for any length of time you wish. Simply put the expiration date into your key encoder routine and e-mail the key that's generated to your user.

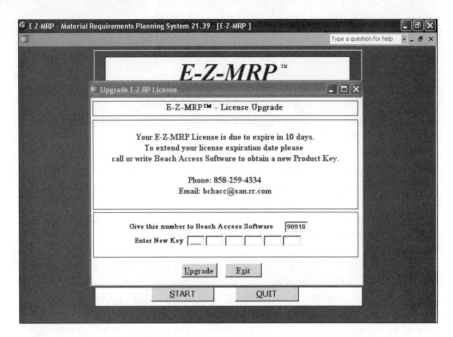

**Figure 5-2.** License Upgrade form

One way to game this system is obviously for the user to set their clock/calendar back so that the computer date is never later than the expiration date. Then, it would seem, the license would never run out. One way to defeat this scheme is to store in a local table the date of last access. If the date they last started the program is greater than the computer's current date, indicating that someone may have monkeyed with the calendar, the program will not start.

Yes, the user could set the calendar back permanently, but more and more, having an accurate clock/calendar in the computer is necessary for a variety of applications. For a date-centric application like manufacturing planning and execution, having your computer's calendar set to a bogus date permanently is completely impractical. The same goes for accounting applications, contact management, and many others. It also means that the date/time stamp on every file in your computer will be bogus.

It's more and more common to have the software "phone home"—call in to a web site to register the software. This adds another layer of protection for your application. It is not, however, without its cost. You have to develop and maintain (in the light of a rapidly changing technology) the function that does this, and it has to be as easy and transparent as possible. You have to be prepared to provide manual support to users who have firewalls or other outgoing restrictions on communication (more and more common) and/or who are probably not technologically adept. And you have to be willing to pay the price for whatever negative feedback you get from your users about their computer contacting your computer without them being in control.

The Chinese have a saying, "Locks are for the honest man." Back in the day, we often used the flimsy rationalization that anyone who went to the trouble of stealing our software was not going to buy it anyway, so we didn't really lose a sale. And to some degree that is still true.

At the end of the day, some will get sold and some will get stolen. In the words of the oft quoted Serenity Prayer, " . . . grant me the serenity to accept the things I cannot change. . . ." In other words, do what you can and then don't lose any sleep over it. As the Chinese also say, "Living well is the best revenge."

So here you are at the end of the longest and arguably one of the most valuable chapters in the book. You made it. Hopefully, this chapter has provided a useful introduction to the various legal issues you need to consider when setting up shop. And there certainly are a lot of them. But invest a fraction of the effort and expense in legal matters that you're putting into your software, and you'll sleep better. If nothing else, you'll be well rested.

# How They Did It: An Interview with Barry Matfield

*Barry Matfield, the cofounder of SageKey Software (www.sagekey.com), began his adventure in product development a bit differently. Rather than being pulled in by an idea, he dropped out of the regular work world and went looking for a problem to solve.*

**Smolin:** Barry, can you give me a little background on yourself? Where did you come from and how did you become a software developer?

**Matfield:** I'm an electronic engineer by background. And that gave me a good understanding of hardware. And I've been, in my professional career, around computers most of my adult life. I worked many years in the oil patch [in Canada] working on digital signal processing. And then after the oil industry let me go, I hung up a shingle and started programming, and it's just something I love doing. And you know things moved forward from there.

**Smolin:** Though you weren't happy being an engineer in the oil patch?

**Matfield:** Well, you know, I did a lot of different jobs, but I just got to the point where I felt cramped by working for large organizations. I rose up through the management ranks and the managed groups. But I found that limiting because I couldn't choose the people who I was working with, and I had to take whomever I was assigned. And large organizations have policies that, you know, sometimes will get . . . well, let's say were counter to my own values. For a long time, when I worked at Volvo, I felt actually a bit like a fish out of water. I didn't feel like my values were very well aligned with the company. You know, as I got to know myself better, it became more and more of an issue for me.

**Smolin:** So you dropped out and moved over to where you are now.

**Matfield:** I moved into a little backwater. It was a gut life choice decision to move somewhere which was attractive, with lower pay, although the quality of life is higher. And then my wife and I tried to figure out, you know, OK, we're here now, what are we going to do? I always liked doing programming, so I hung up a shingle and started doing contract work and I think actually, you know, I read an Access book from start to finish and a VB [Visual Basic] book from start to finish, and then I was loaded and dangerous [*laughter*].

**Smolin:** So at that point you began to do just custom database and application development and contract work?

**Matfield:** Yes, here in the valley where we live. Then I saw this little problem Microsoft had with its Access runtime packager.

**Smolin:** What was the problem that you saw?

**Matfield**: Well, it was their installer. The people who want to create commercial products from Access, Microsoft provided them an installer to install a runtime version of Access and that was buggy. So I reverse engineered—perhaps a little bit too strong a term—but I, you know, figured out what their installer was doing and remapped it into a generic installation tool, hunting down the bugs and fixing them. At the end I had built an installer that did a good job of installing the Access runtime on a wide range of machines.

But, I didn't do the exercise with a commercial product in mind. I did it because I was interested in the challenge. But something else had driven me in that direction. I just took a look on the newsgroups and looking at the programmer's newsgroups to see what people are complaining about— you know, their weaknesses that they're complaining about—and then used that to focus my attention.

So I could see that they were complaining about the runtime Access installer that wasn't working properly and that would be worth providing a solution. So I thought that, you know, that they had a need for this.

**Smolin**: Great. The runtime is a way to package a product that doesn't require a copy of Microsoft Access, correct?

**Matfield**: Yeah, thank you for clarifying. It's a stripped-down version of Microsoft Access that doesn't have the design view, and it'll run an Access-based application on a machine that doesn't have Access on it already.

**Smolin**: So you did this more or less as a challenge and to learn. Did you use the Wise installer as a basis for that script then?

**Matfield**: I did, yeah. Yeah, I started with the Wise. A friend of mine had shown me the old version of Wise—that was Wise 5 at the time; they're on version 10 now. I thought it kind of looked like a cool area. I was always kind of interested in how things were behind the scenes—engineer, you know. So you know that fit with my natural passion for taking things apart and putting them back together again, and seeing how things worked.

**Smolin**: So then once you had an Access runtime installation script that worked, what did you do with it?

**Matfield**: Well, there were two newsgroups where Access programmers discussed various issues. So I just posted a note onto these newsgroups. I put together a rinky-dink web site. I grabbed a number out of the hat as to how much to charge for it, and we started getting, you know, five to ten sales a week.

**Smolin**: How much did you charge for it initially?

**Matfield**: $195.

**Smolin**: And so the orders began coming in. Did you have to do anything to make it a product from a program? In other words, you had sort of a raw solution that worked for you. But to put it out there, did you have to do anything to it, modify it, package it, make it easier, or is it just a script that fell into the Wise installer?

**Matfield**: That's a good question. I tried to stand in the shoes of somebody who didn't know Wise particularly well and who did not know this issue very well. So I tried to make the scripts as self-explanatory as possible and to make the path, you know, for a user, as simple as possible. Mostly by adding a lot of comments to guide the user through customizing it to package their own product.

So it was focused, and self-explanatory, and it looked professional, and it was customer-centric rather than programmer-centric. I didn't really know if I had the solution they all wanted when I first released it, and I was actually quite nervous about the idea of working as a solution provider to programmers. I thought the programming community would actually be quite demanding, you know. The programmers that I had interacted with were quite pragmatic. So I was quite afraid. I thought actually I was going to see a really tough crowd and I found quite the opposite. Which surprised me. People were very grateful for this solution.

My philosophy was that an outstanding company is built through outstanding customer service, which is an old adage that came from Tom Peters' book that he wrote called *In Search of Excellence* back in the '80s. So I figured that out, I'll do whatever it takes to support my customers and to just build a product that was clean and easy to use. I didn't see myself selling a product, I saw myself selling a solution. So the key was to be there to help people through any problems that they had. And there was an educational component—I was enjoying talking to people on the phone. So I didn't really care about how much time it drew, and customers would feed back other issues around the Access runtime problem that I hadn't been aware of. So I would fix that and then rerelease the product. I was releasing minor version changes, sometimes weekly when it first started off.

**Smolin**: When did you sell the first one? Do you remember when it was?

**Matfield**: January or February 1996.

**Smolin**: And what version of Access was that for?

**Matfield**: Access 97?

**Smolin**: Right.

**Matfield**: Oh, in that case it would have been probably 1997—

**Smolin**: So did you have other products which evolved from that first script?

**Matfield**: Yes, I started considering myself as an installation specialist. Then I started listening to what customers were asking for. There were other complex installation issues back at that time. They don't exist today, but the people wanted that quality script that solved some of the problems that Microsoft left behind. So I just basically looked for any area where, you know, a commercial supported script would have provided a solution.

And, as it turns out, there were many. There was MDAC and MSDE, which is the free version of SQL Server. There were some Palm scripts and then the different versions of Access as they came out. What happened was we started getting a very good reputation for support, and the newsgroups spoke well of us. So any time anybody ran into this issue—we actually had customers acting as our representatives, recommending us to other programmers. Pretty well everything was word of mouth, which is one of the nice things about the programming community.

**Smolin**: So you pretty much started this thing on a shoestring. Did you have to put any hard dollars into this before it began to sell?

**Matfield**: I left Mobil with a year's salary. So both my wife and I had a year's salary from our jobs in Calgary. So the whole thing was bootstrapped by ourselves.

**Smolin**: What do you do about copy protection or pirating?

**Matfield**: Well, you know, I thought about that for a while. And my philosophy was that people were buying a service, not a product. You know, I didn't do much about that apart from taking a couple of license agreements—I looked at the one at Wise and one from InstallShield—and merging them together and made one up for this product. I found that the customer base I was dealing with was honest and ethical. And so I don't think we have a lot of trouble about people stealing the product. You do get a small amount of people who try sometimes to buy the product with bad credit cards. Occasionally, we get calls in for support from people who haven't purchased it.

We priced the product reasonably, and the support we offer is part of the price, and that's what people want, they want a solution. I would like to say though that there are different bands of customers. There was an experiment that IBM ran in the '70s which had an unexpected result. Back in the '70s, IBM owned a large part of the computer market, and they were supplying hardware and software and turnkey solutions. And some areas, some business areas, some sales areas were high-performing areas and cooking, and other ones were low-performing areas and lagging. So they would flip the salespeople over. They'd take the high-performing salespeople and put them in low-performing areas, and they'd put low-performing salesmen in high-performing areas. What happened was that the sales after two or three years were about the same, and then the people—the high-performing salespeople had mortgages and car payments and so forth and had an expectation, a set salary, and so they did whatever it took to get the salary back up to their previous levels. What they didn't expect is that the low-performing people would actually sabotage the sales accounts to get their salaries down to the levels that they were comfortable with.

So this introduced the idea of comfort zones to IBM—that everybody operates within a band of comfort, be it around how much they're willing to pay for something to provide for them with a solution. That's where areas of comfort zones come into play in pricing software.

What I observed when we started up is that at $195, we tended to attract the nickel-and-dime crowd. People in that comfort band might navigate to shareware, want something for nothing, people that have a kind of hobbyist kind of attitude. We used to get a lot of credit card vouchers. Now we hardly get any credit card vouchers since raising the price—people who pay by credit card and they don't have the funds. But back then you know it wasn't uncommon for us to have somebody buy a product, and then you know their credit card would be tapped out.

**Smolin**: So you raised the price and found that you had fewer problems doing business?

**Matfield**: Well, yeah. We actually—after about a year and half, I hired a business analyst/consultant. He was a generic business analyst. He didn't know the software industry per se, but he had a good reputation in the valley for helping businesses improve themselves, and he did a thorough analysis of our business. Anyway, one of the recommendations that the consultant made was to raise our product price. I was actually quite terrified to do that. I thought our customers would just disappear overnight. I was surprised to find that it didn't even have a blip on our sales volume. So we went from $195 to about $325 overnight, and you know, there wasn't even a blip in the sales volume.

**Smolin**: But you were working with a better class of people.

**Matfield**: Well, essentially that's what happened. We filtered out the nickel-and-dime crowd and we attracted people who were looking for a more serious product—

**Smolin**: Serious developers.

**Matfield**: Yeah, and we since then increased our prices more than once and generally have found that we have not changed the sale volume. Well, in some cases actually an increase in price has increased the volume.

**Smolin**: So you've expanded the product line quite a bit, as I see on the web site. Have you had any that have tanked?

**Matfield**: Oh yeah, and you know, they've not so much tanked that, you know, they probably haven't even paid the cost of the development. I didn't see that as necessarily a failure. I just saw it as, you know, I was interested in trying this or that concept, and some of them had less blatant need than others.

**Smolin**: Was it because it was a smaller market, or did you misgauge the market size or segment?

**Matfield**: Well, one good example is the Palm Pilot. They were kicking out so many versions, we ended up with half-a-dozen different versions of the Palm Pilot runtime script. I'm sure we didn't break even on those, but we learned a lot about the Palm.

By this time there were four or five of us working together in the company, and we'd moved from the basement into an office building. So it was like we were a real company by then. Some of these products that tanked, they didn't require a lot of development time, so it was no longer high risk.

**Smolin**: OK. So, many of my questions really don't apply to you because you're providing not a turnkey application or a vertical solution, but—I don't know how we would define it—an auxiliary program or function that gets built into something else. In this case, the script goes into the Wise installer, or which other installers are you covering now?

**Matfield**: We had InstallShield for a while, which we have dropped now. MSI is probably half of what we sell.

**Smolin**: So you don't have manuals per se or do you? Do you provide documentation for your scripts?

**Matfield**: We have help—CHM files—for all of our product.

**Smolin**: So what's the mix, would you say now, of product to service?

**Matfield**: About 85 percent custom programming and 15 percent product.

**Smolin**: So you're still mostly a custom software house?

**Matfield**: Well, we weren't initially, but we are now. Initially we were basically providing product and supporting that product. You know, we would do custom—we built and stored customs for people, but it was all very tightly bound around the product, and you know people were coming to us because of the product and then asking for the supporting services around it.

**Smolin**: What is your official product support policy?

**Matfield**: Well, we—at first it was done with no limits. But then after time we started limiting it to three months and then asking to pay for support. Now we have a full-time person for support. He's a programmer who does all the tech support and does most of the product updates. You know, we probably don't sell more than a dozen tech support incidents a year. So we're pretty flexible, and we just use it when something that clearly comes up above and beyond what's a reasonable expectation for support. We'll use that to kind of limit what people are asking for, for free.

**Smolin**: If somebody came to you and said, "BARRY, I've got an idea for a product. I got a raw program or just an idea. I want to make a product out of this," what would your advice be for them? What would be their biggest pitfall or risk or problem? Or what would the one thing be that you would tell them to help them be successful and bring a product to market?

**Matfield**: I think the key thing is to research the market and understand it very well before you do any work. The first product we tried to do that with when we were trying to become a larger company, we looked at building a security system that was based around a device driver. We became experts in the technology. It was very challenging, and we learned a lot about device drivers and how the cache works and low-level stuff in the computer—in other words, it was wonderful. You know, we were going to the boundaries for us. We were pushing the boundaries of what was going on inside the OS and things. And then—it was—oh we probably had fifteen months worth of work into it before we realized that the idea had already been patented [*Laughter*].

**Smolin:** OK, so—market research first.

**Matfield:** Well, yeah, and before we realized it was patented, and we had this idea and we didn't know what the market was. You know, there is a lot of innovation that occurs specifically where people don't know what the market is, and they just do it because it seems like a good idea.

So I would say marketing and understanding the market, understanding what the market wants before even getting obsessed with an idea is the most important thing.

# Some Final Considerations

If you've come this far, I'll assume you remain undaunted by the number and magnitude of the tasks facing you in converting your raw program into a finished product. So, I'd like to introduce a few final topics to which you should give some serious attention.

## When to Stop Programming

This is a bit of a digression. But it's a subject of critical importance that doesn't fit neatly into any of the previous chapters, so I present it here for your consideration.

The subject reminds me of the story of the old man sitting on his porch whittling, detailing, and polishing a beautiful wooden boat. When his grandson asked him, "When will it be done?" the old man replied, "When they take it away from me."

It's both a natural and quite expected result of the software development process that the project grows and changes while it's in progress. This happens with every client for whom I create custom software. At first they have a rough idea of what they want their system to do. As they see the various forms and reports taking shape, more and more possibilities occur to them, and "feature creep" begins to set in. Of course, in the end, it's their nickel, but I always try to engage them in some discussion about the costs (both in dollars and in the added operational complexity) and the benefits of their latest brainstorm.

In commercial product development, I have worked with more than one client who never seemed to quite want to finish the development phase. As the program took shape, more possibilities appeared for useful (and some not so useful) features and functions to be added. There were new reports and variations on old ones. There were enhancements of existing functions. There was always a list of changes, additions, enhancements, deletions, etc. that never all seemed to get done.

You will likely have the same experience as your product takes shape. Like Achilles in Xeno's paradox, it seems that you will never manage to catch the tortoise as your "to do" list grows longer and longer. The urge to create the best product in the world is a laudable one. But there's a trap here. Time is not infinite. Neither is your money. At some point you have to call it quits, stop programming, and package your product for market.

If you're a lone ranger programmer, there's no one to "take it away from you." You are your own client, and you can go on forever, enhancing, polishing, testing, gathering input from your beta testers, and adding to your product every suggestion they, you, or anyone else has for making it "the next killer app."

If you're working with a partner or two, eventually you'll have a discussion, an argument, or a battle to the death over features and functions—which are needed, which are nice but not necessary, which are superfluous, which add more operational burden than value to your product, and which are totally bonehead ideas.

What to do?

# The Version Two List

The solution is simple. Make a Version Two List. This is also known as the "It Would Be Really Nice But . . . " list, and the "We Can't Afford to Do That Right Now . . . " list. It's also known as the "That's a Stupid Idea but We'll Throw Him a Bone and Hope the Feeling Passes" list. This then becomes the "to do" list for Version Two of your product.

When should you start your Version Two List? You should start it at the same time you're making your Version One List.

Back in Chapter 2, I talked about developing a more or less detailed system specification describing exactly what your product does. In the process of doing that, you defined the features and functions of your product in serious debate with either yourself or your partners.

Perhaps this was the first time the conflict arose among the partners (or among your various personalities) about the cost of adding a feature versus the benefit of having it in the software. Bear in mind that, in addition to time and economic considerations, there is a tradeoff between comprehensiveness and complexity. The more features you add to your product, the more complex, harder to learn, and even intimidating it is to a prospective customer.

At some point, it becomes necessary to "draw a line" around your product. You have to decide which features will be in the first release product and which will be left for another day.

So, as you are making your (more or less) detailed product definition, start the Version Two List—things you think are a good idea but need to be left out of Version One because of time and/or money and/or design pressures.

If you're a lone ranger, this will mollify the anal, obsessive side of you and will alleviate the anxiety of the business side of you.

If you're working with partners, you know that people often get their egos caught up in their proposals. I have found the Version Two List gives folks a face-saving way to a compromise. Those in favor get their idea recognized, valued, and listed for future inclusion as time and resources allow. Those opposed will be satisfied with having the motion tabled for the moment.

However you resolve the problems, be ready to draw a final boundary around Version One of your product, including the features and functions that are essential and deferring to Version Two of your software a whole host of desirable additions.

You WILL have to make compromises on your ideal system. You will NOT be releasing the product you ultimately want. You WILL have a Version Two. But keep your eye on the goal—which is, first and foremost, to pay the rent. You can't play if you can't pay.

# Custom Tailored or Off the Rack?

One of the policy decisions you have to consider before launch is whether or not you are going to provide custom modifications to your customers. In some cases, the answer will be obvious. Customers of a low-priced ($100–$1000), high-volume product will not be amenable to paying you $50–$200 per hour to modify their application. The cost-benefit ratio simply is not in their favor.

If your product is fairly high priced (five figures and up) and volume is not great, there will be a strong temptation to modify your product to meet a specific customer's requirement. No off-the-shelf program completely satisfies anyone. Purchasing canned software always means a compromise by the customer between the cost of the program and the completeness of the solution.

Sometimes the user's requirements are so unique that no off-the-shelf product will satisfy their needs. When requirements trump cost, a 100 percent custom-written application is necessary. In between 100 percent off-the-shelf and 100 percent custom is a whole range of tempting alternatives.

Everyone who evaluates your product will give you a list of things they'd like to see that your program doesn't do and will drop broad hints about getting the go-ahead to purchase if only one or another feature could somehow be included.

So let's divide modifications into two classes. The first kind is generic; that is, anybody who uses your software would be happy to see that feature and find it useful—a report sorted on a field you didn't think to put into the original specification, for example. The other kind of modification is specific to the customer, and no one else would ever want to see it—the company logo at the top of each report, for example.

99999999999

I used to have a policy that if a modification was requested by one customer, it was a custom chargeable item. If two customers asked for it, it became generic and was included at no charge in the next release.

You don't have to charge for a chargeable item. But it's important to let the customer know what the modification is worth. You can always waive the charge to close the deal. Everybody likes to get something for nothing.

But the trap is that if you make a custom modification to one of your sites, it has to be maintained. When you release Version Two of your product, you're going to have to incorporate those custom modifications into the copy of the product you send to that customer. You could end up having to maintain many unique versions of your product. You want to avoid that (duh).

This is where the beauty of the registered serialized product with product key described earlier really comes to the fore. You can tie custom features, functions, forms, and reports to a specific serial number and activate or deactivate them with a line of code. Simply compare the serial number of the system to the serial number of the custom feature, activating it if there's a match, leaving it hidden if there isn't.

For example, one E-Z-MRP customer wanted a button on the Purchase Order form to send an e-mail to the vendor. So the button was included on the form, and the code behind the button was written to send the e-mail. But the button was made invisible. When the form opens, a line of code is run:

```
If InStr(1, gstrRegisteredName, "Pro Flowers") <> 0 Then
Me.cmdEmail.Visible = True
```

Here `gstrRegisteredName` is a global variable holding the name of the customer to whom this copy is registered. Only a system registered to "Pro Flowers" will show the e-mail button.

So custom modifications built into the standard product are invisible to all but the customer who requested (and, hopefully, paid) for them. So it travels with each upgrade and new release. So you wind up with only one version to maintain. Of course, your application does end up carrying around a bit of extra baggage. But, in my experience, the extra few kilobytes or even megabytes generally don't make any appreciable delay in loading and starting your application. Inconveniencing a few electrons is a small price to pay for having only one version of your package to maintain while providing sale-closing custom modifications.

# Manual Labor

I now come to perhaps the most horrifying job in all of software development—writing the user manual.

Documentation is the ugly stepchild of the software business. Nobody wants to do it. However, unless the operation of your application is so completely obvious, intuitive, and user-stupid that even an engineer could run it, you WILL need a user manual.

The primary difficulty in writing an effective user manual is that it requires some different skills—skills that are not always found among programmers.

Primary among these missing skills is the ability to write complete, coherent, grammatically correct sentences, and then string these sentences together in a logical sequence. I could go on for a bit here about the dismal state of public education that gives rise to remedial writing classes in our great universities, but I won't.

The second problem facing the manual writer is being too familiar with the subject. To write a good user manual, you have to sit in the place of the reader who, at the start, knows little or nothing about your application. It is too easy to skip over information that is so familiar to you that it doesn't even register consciously.

You might think that this sentence

*Begin a new contact record and enter the person's first and last names.*

is a pretty clear instruction, especially when accompanied by a screenshot of the form with the Add button highlighted. However, what is really needed is

*Begin a new contact record by clicking the button in the lower-left corner of the screen labeled "Add". The cursor will shift to the Last Name field. Enter the contact's last name and press the Enter key. The cursor will shift to the First Name field. Enter the contact's first name, and press Enter.*

Now for half your readers, the first instruction will suffice. For the other half, many will need some of the instructions in the second version. Some will need all of that information. The outliers will call you and ask whether they should press the Enter key when they finish entering the information in the First Name field.

Tech support: "OK. Now press any key to continue."

Outlier: "Where's the any key?"

So my first piece of advice on manual writing is to be wordy. Proceed carefully, asking yourself at every point whether you have skipped over something that is obvious to you but would leave your reader in the dark. In the preceding example, you've been entering the last name and pressing Enter for months. You could do it in your sleep. But you leave that tidbit out at your peril. You will get calls asking what to do next. Not a lot, but enough to make you wonder how some people find their way to work three days in a row.

So—and here's the hard part—when you sit down to write the manual, you have to take an absolutely fresh look at the program, and write as if you were seeing the program for the first time. So you won't forget to tell them to press the Enter key.

This is not easy. It's a skill you have to work at to develop. But paper is cheap. Electrons are even cheaper. In a user manual, it's hard to be too wordy or too redundant.

The best manuals are loaded with pictures—screenshots with callouts, sample reports, etc. Figures break up long passages of text and reassure the user that what they're seeing on the screen is what they actually should be seeing.

Do not worry about talking down to your reader. People are not offended by overly simple, detailed instructions. Actually, they're often flattered. It makes them feel smart to know that **they** don't need that level of detail to run your application.

The best manual writer is someone hired in from the outside who has excellent writing skills and does not know your application. But, given the practicalities of most software development by individuals or small teams, bringing in a person solely to write the manual probably won't happen. So that leaves you to do the deed.

I don't hold myself out as the world's best manual writer. But I have written a couple. One of them is online at `http://e-z-mrp.com/manual.htm`. You can download it and have a look. It's not bad. The download is in PDF format. But if you want the original Word document to see how the actual formatting goes, contact me through the publisher with your e-mail address, and I'll see that you get one. Since I nearly committed suicide creating this oeuvre, I'm always grateful when anyone looks at it.

## How to Get Started Writing Your User Manual

Before you begin writing, identify your audience. How much technical knowledge will they have? Or lack? Are you writing for programmers? For professionals? For clerical? White collar? Blue collar? Highly educated? High-school dropouts?

The audience you target will determine many of the decisions you will make about format, content, and language. Speaking of language, nothing is worse for a reader or a manual than to use a term with which the reader is unfamiliar or has not been previously defined. Making a list of technical terms and definitions before you start will help avoid this pitfall. And the list can become a glossary, adding even more value to your manual and product.

Once you have identified your audience, write the table of contents. Creating the table of contents should always be the first step in writing your manual. The table of contents is, in effect, an outline or specification. And, just as in product design, a detailed specification is the best place to start. The *E-Z-MRP User Manual* table of contents goes three levels deep, but the outline can go further—as deep as you want. The more detail you put into your outline, the easier it will be to write the manual. Once the outline is complete, writing the manual becomes a manageable task of filling in each section.

Before you begin writing, however, decide on your format—font and font size for headings, subheadings, sub-subheadings, figure captions, table captions, and report captions. Also decide on your page margins and line spacing.

If you're good enough with your word processor, make a template. If you're not, use one of the prebuilt templates in your word processor. If you are consistent in your use of heads, subheads, figure captions, etc., you can automate the creation of the table of contents. Microsoft Word, for example, has a feature that creates tables of contents, and lists of figures and tables. As you add, delete, and change contents, updating the table of contents and lists of figures with the new page numbers becomes a push-button affair, eliminating one really nasty manual writing job. But it keys off of specific formats for each, hence the need for preplanning and consistency. A template, of course, will maintain this discipline for you.

Your page layout should have lots of air—blank space. It's easy on the eyes, easy for your reader to find just the piece of information they're looking for. Use wide margins, and generous headers and footers. And skip lines between sections and paragraphs.

And I recommend no smaller than 10-point type. I use 10.5-point type in the *E-Z-MRP User Manual*. If your target audience is generally over 40, 11-point or even 12-point type wouldn't hurt.

There are some strong opinions about serif versus sans serif typefaces. I have one. I use sans serif. I find it cleaner and easier to read. Times New Roman is . . . well . . . ugly. But it's the staple font of your daily newspaper, so it can't be all that bad. But the Web is mostly sans serif, and they can't all be wrong.

An exhaustive study of the controversy was done and much more than you want or need to know about serif versus sans serif can be found at `www.alexpoole.info/academic/literaturereview.html`. The executive summary? There's no definitive winner. So pick what you like. But don't do your whole manual in script or Comic Sans just because it looks cool. Just make it a standard font like Arial or Times New Roman, which have both high readability and high legibility.

## What to Say

In Speech 101, we learned how to structure a speech to inform:

1. Tell them what you're going to tell them.

2. Tell them.

3. Tell them what you told them.

The same guideline can be applied to a nice, clear, wordy manual. Introduce the chapter or section with an outline of topics to be covered and close it with a summary of items discussed.

Nothing says it like pictures. Use lots of pictures and graphics. One picture can also replace several paragraphs of prose. It's easy to make screenshots of your product in action—forms and reports—and sprinkle them liberally throughout your manual.

Callouts—boxes with descriptions pointing to various controls or fields on a form or report—work particularly well for screenshots (see Figure 6-1). And when the user sees on the screen what you've printed in the manual, they know they're on the right track.

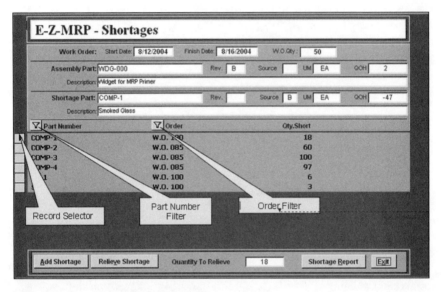

**Figure 6-1.** Screenshot with callouts

Pictures and graphics also break up lengthy sections of text, making your manual more visually appealing. Which is important if you want to induce your customer to read the manual instead of calling you for answers.

Whatever you write, try to make it entertaining and enjoyable to read. A little light humor can go a long way to making a boring topic approachable. Some writers think that a casual style detracts from the professionalism and "dignity" of their opus. Ask yourself what you would rather read, and then write like that.

## When to Start Programming . . . Again

One valuable but frustrating consequence of writing a detailed manual is that it can reveal weaknesses or holes in your product. If you are writing a description of a function and it becomes difficult to express precisely why or how the function is used, that is a red flag. If you can't write about it clearly, you can bet the user won't be able to run it successfully.

If you come to a part of the description of a feature or function and find yourself wanting to write about something that simply isn't there—a command button that you forgot, for example—that's even more problematical.

So now that you're all done programming and probably much of the way through Beta testing, you have to go back and rewrite a chunk of your program—maybe a big chunk. Then the rewritten parts need to be sent through testing again. It can really play hob with your schedule. It can be frustrating. It can be exasperating. Yes, you can add these things to the Version Two List. But don't cut corners at this point. The extra effort will pay off.

## Reference or Tutorial?

There are two functions for a user manual, and a good manual will include them both, if necessary. Your manual can be used as a tutorial, teaching through scripts and examples, or as a reference document.

There are two kinds of tutorials.

The purpose of the first one is to teach the reader about the application as it's used apart from the software. In other words, you could run an accounting system manually using a thirteen-column green pad and a quill pen, but until you understand debits and credits and the other basics of accounting, you're not going to make much progress. So an accounting system manual might contain a tutorial covering the basics of the double-entry accounting system.

Here, your audience is important. If you're selling to accountants, this kind of tutorial would be unnecessary. If you're selling to first-time business owners, this explanation might be essential.

The second kind of tutorial teaches the user how to use your application by actually walking them through the operation of each function step by step, using an actual example, and having the user enter and report this sample data.

As the user is led through the operational steps, the tutorial explains what the various fields on each form are for, what the different controls do, and what the data on the reports tells the user.

This kind of tutorial is very tedious to write. It involves creating some sample data first, and then painstakingly analyzing the precise steps the user must execute to get the desired results. It must be even more unambiguous than the wordy "Add a contact" instruction discussed earlier, since the user will be pushing the keys in response to your instructions. You don't want to mislead them.

On the other hand, this kind of tutorial is easy to edit. Just sit someone down at the keyboard who is unfamiliar with your application, and watch them as they read your manual and go through the steps, noting every place they stumble over an instruction.

Once your user masters the operation of your application, they will have very little need to do the tutorial again. However, they'll have questions about how to use certain features of your application. At that point, your manual switches from tutorial to reference manual. There's no sharp line between the two kinds of information. What you want to do is make it easy for them to find what they're looking for. A detailed table of contents is helpful. An index is even more helpful.

## Back Matters

In the back of your manual, you might want to include an index and/or a glossary.

An index is especially useful if your manual is intended for use as a reference document. If the table of contents isn't detailed enough to get the user quickly to the page with the information they're looking for, then an index is strongly recommended.

A glossary is another element that ranges from useful to essential, if you are introducing terms that the typical user might not know. The first time the term is used in the text, draw the reader's attention to the fact that it appears in the glossary with some consistent format—italics, bold, underline, or some combination. Just be consistent.

## Online or Hard Copy

Printing out your manual and putting it in a lovely silk-screened binder is a nice touch—particularly if the user is paying big bucks for your product. It adds the perception of value and saves your customers the time and trouble of printing and binding your manual themselves.

As you know from your own experience, fewer and fewer products are being shipped with hard-copy manuals. Mostly, they're included on the distribution CD and get copied into a folder during the installation process.

An electronic form of your manual can be especially handy if delivered in a form that allows the user to click a table of contents entry and go directly to the page they're looking for. Microsoft Word and Adobe Reader have features like this which make it easy to navigate around a document. With an electronic form of the manual, your users can also do a text search for a key word or phrase.

However, a minor point in favor of a hard-copy manual is that it serves as a deterrent to pirates. Delivering a copied CD with no manual is hardly worth bothering with. Copying and delivering the manual as well? Well, maybe that's also not worth bothering with.

So printing and delivering a manual with your product is one of those minor policy decisions that needs to be thought through before you finish your project.

### *Online Help . . . Or Not*

You also have to decide whether or not to have online help with help files. Having a written manual makes this job much easier. You can cut and paste the text from your manual into the help files and use your index for the help search function. There are a lot of commercial help authoring products available. And several free ones.

Microsoft offers a free solution in their Microsoft HTML Help Workshop, available as a free download: `www.microsoft.com/downloads/details.` `aspx?familyid=00535334-c8a6-452f-9aa0-d597d16580cc&displaylang=en`.

The Microsoft HTML Help Workshop uses application programming interface (API) commands to create the kind of help files you are used to seeing with context-sensitive help and keyword lookup, and a help window with style and formatting options. There are two compilers for the help files you author—one that creates HLP files and another one that creates CHM (HTML) files. Many third-party help authoring products require these compilers.

If you have never designed a help system before, you can learn a great deal about how to design and create a help system at the Microsoft Developer Network (MSDN) page: `http://msdn2.microsoft.com/en-us/library/` `ms670169%28VS.85%29.aspx`.

There are ways other than the classic help file to provide forms of online help. Control tip text, where a few words of description pop up when your mouse hovers over a control—can provide just the hint of explanation the user needs to clear up confusion or ambiguity about the function of a control or the contents of a text box. Small pop-up forms with explanatory text can be displayed when the user double-clicks or presses a specific combination of keys (like Ctrl+H).

Your application may benefit greatly from online help. However, in general, the need for online help is inversely related to how clear, unambiguous, and simple your application is to run. If you find yourself concluding that your application needs online help, first go back and question why. Can the user interface be reengineered to be simpler or more intuitive?

Help files are useful, but using them disrupts the flow of work. If you can engineer a product that absolutely doesn't need online help, you will save yourself a lot of work and money and probably end up with a better product.

# It's a Wrap: Packaging Your Product

Finally, your product is ready to deliver. You've done everything your Beta testers have asked—within reason. You've written a terrific user manual. You've got a Version Two List as long as your arm.

One thing you probably learned in the testing process, however, is how completely inept some users are when it comes to technology. Now, that's not a crime. I can drive a car, but I can't put one together. I can run your software once I get to the main menu. Why should I have to know about files and folders and registering DLLs and installing fonts and how to copy stuff to my network drive?

When I first released E-Z-MRP for Windows, I sent everything in a ZIP file. After all, the installation process was dead simple.

**1.** Create a folder on your C drive named C:\E-Z-MRP.

**2.** Unzip all of the files in the ZIP file into that folder.

**3.** Right-click the MDE file and drag it to your desktop to make a shortcut.

**4.** Double-click the shortcut to start the program.

I don't install odd fonts, register DLLs, make weird registry entries, or any of the other things that more complex products need to do in order to be properly installed.

After all, there were only half-a-dozen files—the program, three demo databases to play with, the manual, and an icon file. This couldn't be that difficult.

But at least half the prospects got stumped by step one. Even the question "Do you have Microsoft Access 2000 or later?" was often met by a pregnant pause. Many times the user would run E-Z-MRP right from the ZIP file instead of unzipping and saving it in a folder. And of course, being read-only, the program crapped out right away, leaving me, once again, to walk the user through the process on the telephone—AFTER I had figured out what they had done (or failed to do). Users will never tell you what they've actually done.

The number of different problems users encountered with what looked to me to be a stupefyingly easy process would have provided endless entertainment, if it was not affecting sales. Negatively.

In short order I realized that I had to package my product with a professional-looking installation that would not only make the installation easy, but also follow the conventions people were used to seeing in other third-party software they had installed on their own computer. E-Z-MRP is now delivered in an executable setup file. When they run the setup file, they get the familiar looking screen you see in Figure 6-2, followed by the screen in Figure 6-3.

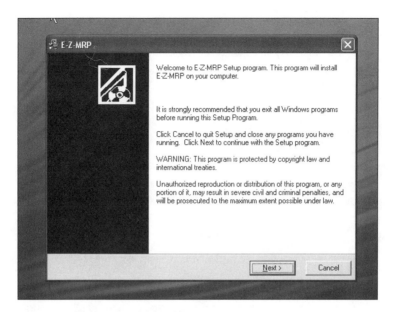

**Figure 6-2.** Opening installation screen

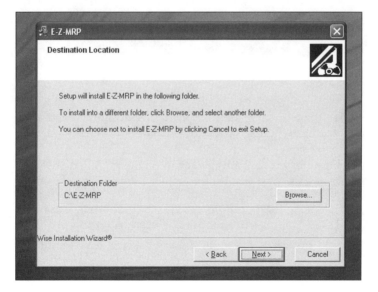

**Figure 6-3.** Selecting an install folder

Here, if the user doesn't understand folders, they can just click Next to accept the default folder.

The Sleep Advisor has a similar install process including a "click-wrap" license agreement, where the Next button is not active until the user agrees to accept the terms of the license (see Figure 6-4).

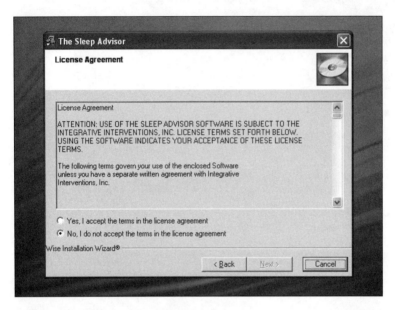

**Figure 6-4.** "Click-wrap" license agreement

In both of these products, the installation program does all the work for the user including placing a shortcut on the user's desktop using the product icon.

Although there are many commercial packagers on the market, there are two ways to package your product that I can recommend—one free, the other a bit pricey.

The first method is to use Microsoft's Windows Installer. It's free. And it's worth every penny—that is, it's not as powerful and flexible as the leading commercial products. After all, if it were, there wouldn't be a market for the others. But it fits everyone's budget and may be perfectly adequate for your purposes.

There are two other widely used commercial products. One is the Wise Installation Studio (the Wise for Windows Installer and Wise Installation System product lines have been discontinued) (`www.wisesolutions.com/Products/Installations.aspx`). The other is InstallShield from Macrovision (`www.macrovision.com/products/installation/installshield.htm`). I'm sure you have used both of them from the customer side.

Personally, I use the Wise system, but both products are excellent. The toughest part of the Wise system is learning the scripting language to make your installation behave exactly as you want it to. But I finessed that whole problem by purchasing a script from SageKey (`www.sagekey.com/`), a company that provides high-quality scripts for Access runtimes, .NET Framework, Satellite Forms, Palm Pilot, and MSDE-based applications.

The combination of Wise and SageKey isn't cheap. But, using the SageKey script, it only took me about an hour to configure a professional, bulletproof Access runtime installation package for The Sleep Advisor. I could have written the script myself, but it would have taken tens, perhaps as much as a couple hundred, hours to learn the scripting language, write, and test my script. So looked at that way, the Wise/SageKey combination was very inexpensive.

# The Last Word: How to Eat an Elephant

Thank you for reading to the end. I hope that it has been valuable, at least in parts, and that if you're not feeling particularly optimistic after reading this book, at least I hope you have a feeling that you know what you're up against.

I remember a teacher I approached once, feeling overwhelmed with a huge project. "Do you know how to eat an elephant?" he asked. "No," I replied. "One bite at a time, Rocky. One bite at a time."

So go back and skim through this book again, making a "to do" list of all the things that need doing in order to get your product ready for market. Then just do them one at a time.

I hope that learning about the number and complexity of the tasks before you has not put you off your lunch. On the contrary, I hope you see now a clear path to the finish line, the many hurdles notwithstanding. And that having this path will energize you and your partners to bring your project to a successful conclusion.

# How They Did It: An Interview with Steve Capistrant of Symphony Information Services

*Sometimes there is little mystery about the genesis of a product. Created as a custom application, the second and third sales of the same type of program often trigger the logical response: "I think we have a product here!" Steve Capistrant's advice: beware of success. You can pay a heavy price if you spread yourself too thinly and lose focus on what's really important.*

**Smolin**: Steve, can you tell me a little bit about your company—Symphony Information Services.

**Capistrant**: Symphony Information Services is a software development company that I started eleven years ago. It was originally designed to do custom database development because the nonprofit groups that I was working with didn't have any software that did what they needed to do. By the year 2000, we realized that we were rebuilding the wheel and doing the same things over and over again. So we consolidated all our good stuff into one product and then concentrated on selling that, which turned out to be a good approach.

**Smolin**: So in 1996 you started the company to provide customer software development for nonprofits.

**Capistrant**: Yes.

**Smolin**: And how did you happen to get into the nonprofit arena?

**Capistrant**: I have a degree in urban planning and had worked a lot in United Way and other kinds of planning agencies in social service planning capacities. So, you get to know the crowd that you're working with, and you have personal contacts. You tell them that you're doing database software, and they begin to ask for solutions.

**Smolin**: So you became familiar with nonprofits because you were working in the area. And how did you get into programming?

**Capistrant**: [*Laughter*] I—what do I call it?—by curiosity. I didn't touch a computer until I was in graduate school. I got my first job at a bank, lying that I knew how to use computers. On the job I realized that the most interesting thing that people did, to me, seemed liked databases. I just learned by doing—and a lot of times using Internet searches—and then became good at it. So I'm totally self-taught. That's good and bad. I have hired some people with formal degrees in the subject, and I feel they do know some important things that I don't. So I need to recognize the value of that. But that's where I came from.

**Smolin**: Well, that's kind of how I got into it too.

**Capistrant**: That's what I kind of thought.

**Smolin**: Well, I started in high school, but that's a different story. That was back when computers were still steam powered. In any event, you started doing custom work for this nonprofit sector, and after you'd done a bunch of projects, you saw a possibility of creating a product? Is that how it went?

**Capistrant**: Innovation, not only for their benefit but for my benefit. It's just annoying to have to re-create code.

**Smolin**: So that product turned out to be Federation. Why did you name it Federation?

**Capistrant**: Because it brought together a lot of functions that all these nonprofits had to do. Everyone had a little database that handled fund raising, and a little database that handled event management. What I wanted was to put it all together as a completely integrated thing, centered around people, your clients or your donors. I just thought clumping all these other areas together sounded good—so I looked for some word that had some meaning in that way and just picked Federation.

**Smolin**: OK.

**Capistrant**: I wasn't too smart. I should have picked something that was available as a domain on the Internet, and that wasn't. I have plans to change the name to a different one that I actually found a domain for.

**Smolin**: So this Federation was the first product you commercialized?

**Capistrant**: Yes.

**Smolin**: I assume this is a multiuser application.

**Capistrant**: Yes.

**Smolin**: Is it written in Microsoft Access?

**Capistrant**: Yes.

**Smolin**: And why did you pick Access for that?

**Capistrant**: I used to work in Paradox. And then I, when I came across Access 2.0 and it was hullabalooed by the press. I mean, you know, I don't like supporting the big evil empire. But I wanted to work with a system that had a 99 percent chance of being supported over the future. So I didn't want to go with a product that might, you know, vanish one day.

**Smolin**: So how long did it take—from the time you decided, "Let's make a product out of this," until you were ready to sell it to the first user?

**Capistrant**: About three months because all the buttons were there. We just had to build a user interface and menu system that allowed you to navigate to those subzones, but still keep a consistent person table and a consistent organization table.

**Smolin**: Did you write a manual to go with it?

Capistrant: Yes, we have a manual. It's about 188 pages. I don't know that anybody reads it.

Smolin: Nobody reads my manual. And I almost committed suicide writing it [*laughter*], so I'm always grateful if somebody refers to it. How long did it take to do the manual?

Capistrant: That took an exorbitant amount of time. I did it in bits and pieces, but if I had to add it up—

Smolin: Longer than to put the program together?

Capistrant: No. Over a week's worth of time if I had to add it all up.

Smolin: Did you have to put a lot of money into it to get it started up, or was it mostly sweat equity? You know, from the day you decided you want to make a product until you were ready to sell the first one.

Capistrant: I guess I did but not cash so much as just bodies. I had to either do it myself and not make any money programming or have someone on staff write some stuff and have them not do any programming. So, yeah, we invested money by just the loss of work.

Smolin: And then did you Beta test it?

Capistrant: No, we broke all the rules there. We just threw it on a customer and let them find the problems. But they were a nice customer. I wasn't smart enough to Beta test. I didn't forego it. I didn't know that that was, you know, the rules of the road.

Smolin: So the first person you gave it to tolerated the problems that are inherent in every new piece of software, I suppose.

Capistrant: They did, but, you know, you treat them really well. Because they're doing your Beta testing for you. And if you're really responsive to them, they're pretty happy. So I just was very careful to be responsive to them and cleaned up a lot of the initial problems.

Smolin: Do you have any copy protection for the program?

Capistrant: Well, no, and it's been a concern for a while. I've met with lawyers and talked about copyrights versus trademarks versus service marks, and I actually don't really know where that ended up. For a while we just sort of kept everything on MDEs [compiled version of an Access program], so it's not to easy to break into the code itself. And that was my copyright protection.

Smolin: Well, I'm thinking of not copyrights so much as copies, pirated copies. What do you do about people pirating the software, using an illegal copy?

Capistrant: Well, it has a built-in time bomb. It's sold as a subscription, and it will deactivate after the specified period of time, like a month, or a quarter, or a year. And at that point, someone has to call our shop to get an opening code. So if I don't know who they are, then obviously they've pirated.

And it's a pretty complex little bit of code. It generates a random number each time, and there's a hidden mathematical algorithm that we run on this side, and give them a number that they type in and they're good to go. If a really smart programmer looked through this, they could figure out the algorithm. But all the little pieces are scattered around in different tables and places in the database.

**Smolin**: How much do you sell it for?

**Capistrant**: We used to sell it as a product for somewhere between $4,000 and $7,000, which was great when we got the hit, so it was like getting a big shot in the arm. But it really hurt when sales lagged. I had to think of overhead, you know, the staff and the office, and so when we'd run low, times I would be really sucking wind. So, I decided that the best thing to do with this would be to sell it as a service, as a subscription. And by doing that, it makes it a lot more attractive to get into because the user thinks, "Oh, all I do is start at $40 a month, and that's it?" So it makes it very easy for people to bite.

**Smolin**: So now you sell it, you sell it as a subscription service, not as a product.

**Capistrant**: I do.

**Smolin**: So what they pay per month depends on the modules that they get?

**Capistrant**: Yes, the pricing system is based on the combination of modules and number of concurrent users. And I advertise the pricing quite clearly. There's a spreadsheet on the web site that they can download and use to figure out the math themselves. And it works out pretty well. Most people are pretty pleased by that price. You know, it all ranges anywhere from $32 to $200 a month.

So then, that's what I want to do. I want to build up a subscription base, and that's money that keeps on flowing in as long as I, you know, keep on good terms with those customers.

**Smolin**: So Federation was first released when?

**Capistrant**: Spring 2000.

**Smolin**: And you do updates on a regular basis?

**Capistrant**: Constantly. In one sense I still treat it as custom software because if someone wants me to build them a new set of reports or a new table—

**Smolin**: Some new function.

**Capistrant**: A new function, new module, I'm a sucker for new business, and so I will do it. And I have a way of upgrading the version number at the minor level, and sometimes the release will only go to one person because it's a very minor change. But, on a significant scale? The ones that actually get packaged and tested? About once a month.

So it's pretty frequent. And the thing that I've always been happy about is that 90 percent of the development cost of this has been customer driven.

**Smolin**: So do the custom modifications that you make generally become part of the standard package?

**Capistrant**: Yes, and that's what people like about it, too. But every time that something is added, I'm very careful to not lose something else. I'm also very careful to make it turn off if they don't want it.

**Smolin**: Right.

**Capistrant**: So they have a lot of flexibility in turning off features that are either irrelevant or annoying.

**Smolin**: So you distribute this by download from your web site, right?

**Capistrant**: I distribute through an FTP site. I give them an e-mail and say, "Here." Each customer has a private FTP folder, and they download it from there. If they need a new version or a fix or a bug fix, they download from there.

And the other thing that's related to that is that I use GoToMeeting from Citrix to support my customers remotely. I can actually install it, and my fingers can be on their keyboard and on their mouse, and instead of going through the horrible pain of explaining how to do something, I can actually do it for them.

**Smolin**: So you're not using a commercial installer like Wise?

**Capistrant**: We tried doing that and it works, but the problem with the database, especially the multiuser database, is that it just doesn't install on one machine. So you have the difference between where the back end resides and where the front end resides, and we've never figured out a way to make that intuitive. So I've given up on that and just tell them, "I'll help you install it. That's part of the package."

**Smolin**: How long does it take the typical user to implement the product, get up and running?

**Capistrant**: To physically install it takes fifteen minutes. You just create the folders in the right places, copy the files in, and you're done. Make sure the front and back end links are proper, and we're good to go. The thing I've often underestimated is how complicated it is to someone who is seeing it for the first time. I think it's intuitive because I've looked at it every day for seven years.

**Smolin**: Right.

**Capistrant**: But as life is, people get overwhelmed pretty quickly, and it's a complex program. There's many, many features. I keep forgetting that they need a lot of hand holding. I'd say that one of our biggest oversights is, you know, not highlighting that at the sale time.

There's a rule of thumb that says implementation and training time costs should be 100 percent of the product cost, not just a three-hour session, hand them the user's manual . . .

**Smolin**: So do you do any on onsite training?

**Capistrant**: Yes, at least locally. I think I've gone as far as 200 miles, but I really hate it—the loss of time with driving is horrible.

And I'm telling that more and more to people, "Look, I'm going to charge you for driving." Hopefully then it's at full programmer's rate because I'm losing focus big time.

**Smolin**: When you brought the product to market for the first time, what was, would you say, the biggest problem that you faced in getting it rolling—from the time you decided you were going to make Federation a product until you were ready to sell the first, or install the one?

**Capistrant**: I think the biggest problem was realizing that it's going to have to be modular, and people are going to have to be able to turn things on and off. It's all going to be the same code. The only way to pull this off was to make everything table driven. So we had to rethink a lot of our menuing system to be a completely table-driven thing with parent and child relationships and be able to configure it quickly for a customer.

And then the other thing really hard at first was making changes to the data structure—the back end. Front-end updates are easy. Here's the new file. Back-end updates are a chore because they are using it every minute of the day. They don't want to send it to you.

So we would manually do it and keep track of what the changes were, but that was horrible, and then finally we got it automated. We give them an updater which they open up, they browse and point to their data file, and it just takes them from whatever version they're at now to the current version.

**Smolin**: So then, with Federation up and running and making you some money, how long was it before the second product—Auction Central? What caused that to come into being?

**Capistrant**: Oh, just my personal involvement with church and school activities. I just built something because it was needed at a silent auction at church. And it totally transformed the way people did it, and they were all excited because checkout was not a hassle anymore. So I realized that the program was pretty useful. I cleaned it up a bit. It's by no means anywhere the size and complexity of Federation—but it's a cute little program that does a lot of things for silent auction. There's a lot of churches out there, and a lot of schools out there.

**Smolin**: So you identified the market first, and then you went after creating the product and packaging it?

**Capistrant**: No, not really. I mean I did it on my own, for my own purposes. But then I guess I realized that it could be a product.

**Smolin:** Oh, so you developed Auction Central first as a custom program for your own use, and then you decided to commercialize it?

**Capistrant:** Yeah.

**Smolin:** And do you price this one the same way, you know—

**Capistrant:** No, this one has traditional product pricing. It's only a few hundred dollars.

**Smolin:** How did you decide on the sales price?

**Capistrant:** [*Long pause*] Dart board? I don't know.

**Smolin:** OK. [*Laughter*] I'm getting a lot of those answers.

**Capistrant:** I just thought about the typical user of this, the customers of this thing and what they'd be willing to pay. And I just took a guess at what the market would bear. So that's how I priced it. I think I'd love to charge more for it, but I can't charge less for it either because it's still, you know, I can't do a $29 product.

**Smolin:** Right, you have to sell thousands of them.

**Capistrant:** Especially with database stuff there's a lot of follow-up and support.

**Smolin:** But that wasn't the end. Then you developed another product called Critters for municipalities to track animal licenses. Where did that one come from?

**Capistrant:** That one was a custom program initially. There was a local municipality that hired us to make one from scratch because he wanted a system to do just that. And then by chance one day, we got another customer who asked for the same thing and I thought "Well, there's a trend here." So we cleaned it up a little bit and made it a little more packaged. And then we got another one that asked for the exact same thing. So we said, "OK, this is product worthy." By that time, we knew all the tricks about, you know, menuing and making it a protected product.

**Smolin:** Yeah, and how's it going?

**Capistrant:** Well, there's not a lot of sales because I don't advertise it, and we're so busy dealing with Federation issues that I don't advertise anything, really. All the Federation stuff seems to come by word of mouth. I don't actually advertise Auction Central either, but a surprising number of people just find it by surfing the Internet.

I'm getting the feeling that we may be spread a little too thin. The last year and a half has been really stressful on the company. We've been trying to do too many things, you know, do web programming and other product development.

**Smolin:** So you would warn software entrepreneurs about getting spread too thin or taking on too many things?

**Capistrant**: The business has become really different in the last several months. I have realized that, I think, I just need to focus. I have a product that's good enough and road tested enough to be really exploded if I advertise. And spreading myself on one-off projects, you know, dollar-per-hour stuff, is sort of a waste of time if I have this product opportunity.

**Smolin**: What if somebody came to you and said, "Steve, I got a terrific idea for a product. I got some ideas, maybe some code done. It's a little custom program. I think it'll be a great thing. I see you've done this. What advice would you have for me, or better yet, what kind of warning would you have for me about what the biggest risk is that I'm facing, or what should I avoid, or what should I be aware of that I don't know even enough to ask the question?"

**Capistrant**: Well, first of all, I'd ask if they were married [*laughter*].

**Smolin**: Because they may lose that partnership?

**Capistrant**: Well, because it's a huge strain. Starting anything new, it is just a monster strain on time, and your wife becomes very disgruntled. It's not a good thing. So I'd advise people who are single, "Great. Go ahead do anything you want." But I'd give a lot of caution to married people [*laughter*].

**Smolin**: I see. All right, that's a good piece of advice.

# How They Did It: An Interview with Reuben Cummings of Government Finance Consultants

*Reuben Cummings, the cofounder of Government Finance Consultants (www.gfconsultants.com), shows why a program doesn't have to be a block-buster to be successful. The father-and-son team demonstrate how to build a successful business by providing a solution to a well-defined problem in a niche market. As is often the case in software product development, success is a partnership between expertise in an application area and expertise in programming. One partner understands the problem, the other partner understands how to turn the solution into an effective program.*

**Smolin:** Reuben, you wrote to me in your e-mail that you're a lone ranger programmer. How did you get into the software game?

**Cummings:** My father retired from the state of Indiana government in 1993 and started consulting. So I started writing some simple applications for him to make it easier. And then at some point that turned into making them really easy to use. Then I moved into writing databases in Access.

**Smolin:** How did you happen to pick Access for a platform?

**Cummings:** You know, I don't really know, to be honest with you. I have a cousin in Indy. I was talking to him; I don't really know why we picked it. I was teaching myself VB at the same time. So I started playing with Access. Access, you know, the interface is easy. You can focus on coding rather than interface issues.

**Smolin:** So which program was it that you decided to make into a product?

**Cummings:** It was for counties to complete their annual report for financing.

**Smolin:** That's the product labeled CAR that I see on the product links on your web site [www.gfconsultants.com]?

**Cummings:** Yeah, County Annual Report.

**Smolin:** Did you initially do this as a custom job for the county?

**Cummings:** No, it was just an issue that we knew existed. People spend weeks and weeks and weeks doing this. So we just started from scratch and created that to fill a little hole for them.

**Smolin:** Did you have an order in hand, or did you just decide to do it and see if you could find somebody to—

**Cummings:** We just did it. There were no orders. We had talked to some auditors that we knew, and they had expressed an interest. But there were no orders. We had no guarantee on anything.

**Smolin**: And so how long did it take to develop this?

**Cummings**: I would say it was probably a two-month project. It was a pretty simple application. But that was my first one. I had to learn a lot. The hardest part was making reports. There are some reports there that are pretty complicated. Some of them took quite a while to figure out.

**Smolin**: How did you promote it? Was it strictly for county governments?

**Cummings**: Well that, well there's two versions of that one, the County Annual Report and the City and County Report. They're similar, but there are different requirements out of each of them. So I took it and a split it, you know, I spent a whole week copying it and making changes to the other one.

So we just started out with just going to the people we knew and dealt with a lot anyways. And that way then they all start talking to each other, and it went from there.

**Smolin**: So it was mostly word of mouth?

**Cummings**: We sent out letters and went to conferences and so forth. But mostly word of mouth.

**Smolin**: So then the city one grew out of the county one. And there's enough similarity from one city or county to the next that this annual report, the annual report program satisfies their need?

**Cummings**: Yes.

**Smolin**: And do you still promote the product now?

**Cummings**: We don't promote that one any more because the whole time we were doing it, we were communicating with what's called the State Board of Accounts, who oversee the annual reports. They kept assuring us they weren't going to do anything, so we kept building, selling, and selling. And finally at one of their annual auditors conferences, they gave away a free version of it. So there's just not been a market since then.

**Smolin**: The free version that the county came up with, was it a knock-off of yours?

**Cummings**: No, it wasn't similar at all. Terrible program [*laughter*]. Terrible in most people's opinions. Even people I talk to now, they say it's terrible, but, you know, it's free. So it's hard to get them to spend the money on ours.

**Smolin**: Well, anything that's free is always worth it, as they say. Do you remember what year that was that you started with that?

**Cummings**: That would have been about—oh, that was the fall of '99 probably. I had quit my full-time job in May of '99, the week my son was born, and then started writing that software to have it ready for January of 2000, I believe.

**Smolin**: And was that Access 97 at the time?

**Cummings:** That was 2000.

**Smolin:** 2000. Did you have to update it for XP or 2003?

**Cummings:** I still do everything in 2000.

**Smolin:** Is this single or multiuser?

**Cummings:** Multiuser. Usually it's only one or two. But one of my offices has seven users I think. It typically is two or three.

**Smolin:** Do you have any copy protection on this, or how do you control distribution?

**Cummings:** The database is just an MDB. You know, it resides in the server or wherever they want to put it. The front end I convert to an MDE before I ship it out. They don't have to log in or anything. There's no user accounts or anything.

**Smolin:** Are pirated copies of any concern to you?

**Cummings:** No because in my experience, well, typically my experience even with clients is when they get a new computer, they just try to copy the front end over to the new computer. As far as I know, I don't have any problem with piracy.

**Smolin:** Do you have a manual that goes with the product or online help?

**Cummings:** We have a manual for everything we have.

**Smolin:** And did it take longer or less time to write the manual than the software?

**Cummings:** Well, I don't actually write the manuals. My father, who's a partner—what we have is a business with two divisions type of deal, a software division and a consulting division. He's really in charge of consulting; I'm really in charge of software, but we do both. And he does the manual.

I write the software, so in my opinion it's best for me not to write the manual. So he goes through the software then and just plays with it and learns it, finds problems with it, and he writes the manual because he's more of the user than I am.

**Smolin:** So what do you charge for the annual report application?

**Cummings:** I have no idea [*laughter*]. You know the product's been around so long, but we don't sell it anymore hardly. I do know we get $500 a year for it—

**Smolin:** In support.

**Cummings:** Yes. If you look on the web site, you can see our biggest two right now. We have a thing called CHARTS and on the product page, if you go to the download page, you'll see Auto Excise. Those are our biggest two right now. CHARTS will sell for $6,000, and we charge $1,500 a year for support. Now some of the people are shocked by this. And when we talk about support, their clients are even shocked by it.

We charge $1,500, and that covers all phone calls, all trips, e-mails, whatever. They never get charged another dime. Unless they do something to the database that's their fault and I have to fix it, I cover that. If they have a problem with their database, they can ZIP it and send me the data, and I'll look at it and say, "We need to change this record and do this etc., etc.," and tell them, you know, that's included in their fee. Most people don't believe we do it that way. They don't think it's enough. But you know, it's enough for me.

**Smolin**: Did you trademark any of these products?

**Cummings**: No.

**Smolin**: So at the moment—

**Cummings**: I'd be interested in hearing about it if you're doing it [*laughter*]!

**Smolin**: So I'm looking at your web site, and there's six products there now. You said you did CAR first, and then which was the second one?

**Cummings**: The Annual Budget Preparation was I believe the second one. That was because my father's primary business was developing budgets for county government. Every year, you know, county government will have a thing that will say how much I'd like to have to spend next year. Well, it goes through a process, and you determine how much your property tax is. He did that for 31 years for the state. He'd go to counties and help them do it. And then he retired, and he started doing it from the other side.

And so the next project was the budget. So now he can take a county's budget, put it all in. He gets to do the revenue estimate, and this figures the tax rate. And prints the whole deal—legal publications and all—everything for the council to sign. So it takes a budget process from two weeks to a good one night to get that done.

**Smolin**: So you wrote the program and he did the design?

**Cummings**: Yeah, he specified what he wanted it to do, how everything works. How the math works, what the math should report, and I made it all happen.

**Smolin**: And that's strictly for county governments?

**Cummings**: Almost anybody can use that one, any government usually can use that one, in Indiana at least.

**Smolin**: Do you sell these products outside of Indiana?

**Cummings**: We don't sell any out of Indiana right now.

**Smolin**: How did you promote this second product? Did you go to the people that already had the annual report program?

**Cummings**: Yeah, we just kind of gave them a package deal.

**Smolin**: Yeah.

**Cummings:** There's one for additional corporations. We call it ADP. It's a package deal; those three together.

**Smolin:** I don't see that one on the web site.

**Cummings:** Well, it's probably not, but there's not really that much sale, you know it's kind of something we include. It's something we use more internally. But we do provide it if you want it.

**Smolin:** So, in addition to selling product, you provide services.

**Cummings:** Yeah.

**Smolin:** And what's the mix there between service and product?

**Cummings:** It's probably half and half. Even with our product CHARTS, a lot of our work on it will be, you know, service related. Somebody will call in and they'll have an issue because they need a new account number, a new project they're going to start. So you talk it through with them. The system will handle any way you want to do it; it's just a matter of how you want to track it.

**Smolin:** Do you provide custom modifications for these products?

**Cummings:** No, I deal with all like clients in a certain software package, like CHARTS. It's almost all county highways. It could be city street departments, and so forth, with all the same basic needs and wants. If one county calls me and says, "Can you add this seal, or can you add this record?" I'll add it, and the next step is they all get it. At some point someone else wants it too. My experience is they all want it. That's why it's kind of a combo customization. We customize because, yeah, if you want something, if it's reasonable, I'll put it in, but everybody gets it too.

**Smolin:** OK, so it becomes a part of the standard package?

**Cummings:** Yeah, I don't want to get into worrying about versions, who am I talking to, and all that kind of stuff. It would be harder to update.

**Smolin:** So it seems like you had a well-defined market for the product and contacts so that you could reach them. You knew who you were going to and what the problem was you were trying to solve. What would you say the biggest problem was creating a product versus customized program, a product that you want to sell canned to a market? What kind of problems did you encounter getting from the idea that you wanted to make standard products to the point where you were ready to sell standard products?

**Cummings:** The biggest problem I had is, because we're not in the field everyday doing the work, I think the toughest thing is to visualize what the need is and how best to meet that need. And then turn that around into something that most easily fills that need. A lot of software I run across, being from competitors or noncompetitors in other fields of software and county government even, does the job but, you know, in my mind there are programmers—I don't know how I can say this—there's, in my mind, programmers and then people who write software for people.

What I'm saying is, if there's a programmer sitting in a back room somewhere that's told what to do, he has no idea what the people really see. He's always thinking from the point of making it the best software he can that can do the job. He's not thinking of the poor lady sitting in the county highway office that only wants to put her time sheets in so then she can get her payroll turned in to the auditor and get her invoices paid. I think that's the thing, in my mind, determine that need, and then work on creating something that meets the need—that's what we focus on.

I'm not a trained programmer. I'm totally self-taught. My dad's 73, I believe, you know, so he's not about to become a computer expert. So nobody's a computer expert in our company—so we just make it so it works. It isn't fancy, the code's not the best, but it sure does the job, you know.

**Smolin**: Well, you know, there's a saying among programmers, "A good program is one that works." Nobody looks under the hood.

**Cummings**: Right, I believe that 100 percent. People ask me all the time, CHARTS, for example, "Well is CHARTS finished yet?" It's hard for me to say. You know, they always want to hear yes. I say none of my software's finished. There's no reason to finish it. I always want to add something; I always have ideas.

**Smolin**: It evolves all the time.

**Cummings**: Technically it's never finished, no. If I finish it, that means I'm not working anymore.

**Smolin**: OK, I hear that. So if somebody came to you and said, "Reuben, I got an idea for a product. I think it would be a good thing to do, and I think I'm going to sit down and write a program and see if I can sell a bunch of them," what would your best piece of advice be for them on what to avoid doing wrong or what to do right? What's the most important thing that you would tell somebody who's just at the starting line?

**Cummings**: To understand database structure and to get what you want into that database in the most efficient way. That's something I learned in those first couple things I did. The first couple of databases I designed, it was hard to go back and make a change because of the way I first structured it. But now I've learned to just really sit down and map out to best handle the data. So now I can deal with expanding my database in any direction depending on how I want or how the clients want to add data. And there's no concern or worry.

# Appendix:
# Sample Software License

## E-Z-MRP® Material Requirements Planning System—User's Guide

The software described in this manual is furnished under a license agreement and may be used only in accordance with the terms of the agreement.

Information in this document is subject to change without notice. Companies, names, and data used in examples herein are fictitious unless otherwise noted. No part of this document may be reproduced or transmitted in any form or by any means, electronic or mechanical, for any purpose without the express written permission of Beach Access Software.

NO WARRANTY. The technical documentation is being delivered to you AS IS, and Beach Access Software makes no warranty as to its accuracy or use. Any use of the technical documentation or the information contained therein is at the risk of the user. Documentation may contain technical or other inaccuracies or typographical errors. Beach Access Software reserves the right to make changes without notice.

### Copyright Notice

### Trademarks

E-Z-MRP® is the registered trademark of Beach Access Software.

Other product and company names herein may be the trademarks of their respective owners.

## License Agreement

ATTENTION: USE OF THE **E-Z-MRP®** SOFTWARE IS SUBJECT TO
THE BEACH ACCESS SOFTWARE LICENSE TERMS SET FORTH
BELOW. USING THE SOFTWARE INDICATES YOUR ACCEPTANCE
OF THESE LICENSE TERMS. IF YOU DO NOT ACCEPT THESE
LICENSE TERMS, YOU MUST RETURN THE SOFTWARE FOR A
FULL REFUND.

The following terms govern your use of the enclosed Software unless you have
a separate written agreement with BEACH ACCESS SOFTWARE.

**License Grant.** BEACH ACCESS SOFTWARE grants you a license to Use
one copy of the Software. "Use" means storing, loading, installing, executing,
or displaying the Software. You may not modify the Software or disable any
licensing or control features of the Software. You may copy the Software in
machine-readable form solely for backup purposes or use within a single
working location.

**Ownership.** The Software is owned and copyrighted by BEACH ACCESS
SOFTWARE. Your license confers no title or ownership in the Software and is
not a sale of any rights in the Software.

**Copies.** You may only make copies of the Software for archival purposes or
when copying is an essential step in the authorized Use of the Software. You
must reproduce all copyright notices in the original Software on all copies or
adaptations. You may not copy the Software onto any bulletin board, web
page, or similar system.

**No Disassembly.** You may not disassemble or decompile the Software unless
BEACH ACCESS SOFTWARE's prior written consent is obtained. In some
jurisdictions, BEACH ACCESS SOFTWARE's consent may not be required
for disassembly or decompilation. Upon request, you will provide BEACH
ACCESS SOFTWARE with reasonably detailed information regarding any
disassembly or decompilation. You may not decrypt the Software unless
decryption is a necessary part of the operation of the Software.

**Transfer.** Your license will automatically terminate upon any transfer of the
Software. Upon transfer, you must deliver the Software, including any copies
and related documentation, to the transferee. The transferee must accept
these License Terms as a condition to the transfer.

**Termination.** BEACH ACCESS SOFTWARE may terminate your license
upon notice for failure to comply with any of these License Terms. Upon termination, you must immediately destroy the Software, together with all copies,
adaptations, and merged portions in any form.

## *Beach Access Software "As Is" Warranty Statement.*

1. DISCLAIMER: TO THE EXTENT ALLOWED BY LOCAL LAW, THIS BEACH ACCESS SOFTWARE PRODUCT ("SOFTWARE") IS PROVIDED TO YOU "AS IS" WITHOUT WARRANTIES OR CONDITIONS OF ANY KIND, WHETHER ORAL OR WRITTEN, EXPRESS OR IMPLIED. BEACH ACCESS SOFTWARE SPECIFICALLY DISCLAIMS ANY IMPLIED WARRANTIES OR CONDITIONS OF MERCHANTABILITY, SATISFACTORY QUALITY, NON-INFRINGEMENT, AND FITNESS FOR A PARTICULAR PURPOSE. Some countries, states, and provinces do not allow exclusion of implied warranties or conditions, so the above exclusion may not apply to you. You may have other rights that vary from country to country, state to state, or province to province.

2. LIMITATION OF LIABILITY: EXCEPT TO THE EXTENT PROHIBITED BY LOCAL LAW, IN NO EVENT WILL BEACH ACCESS SOFTWARE OR ITS SUBSIDIARIES, AFFILIATES, OR SUPPLIERS BE LIABLE FOR DIRECT, SPECIAL, INCIDENTAL, CONSEQUENTIAL, OR OTHER DAMAGES (INCLUDING LOST PROFIT, LOST DATA, OR DOWNTIME COSTS), ARISING OUT OF THE USE, INABILITY TO USE, OR THE RESULTS OF USE OF THE SOFTWARE, WHETHER BASED IN WARRANTY, CONTRACT, TORT, OR OTHER LEGAL THEORY, AND WHETHER OR NOT ADVISED OF THE POSSIBILITY OF SUCH DAMAGES.

3. Your use of the Software is entirely at your own risk. Should the Software prove defective, you assume the entire cost of all service, repair, or correction. Some countries, states, and provinces do not allow the exclusion or limitation of liability for incidental or consequential damages, so the above limitation may not apply to you.

4. NOTE: EXCEPT TO THE EXTENT ALLOWED BY LOCAL LAW, THESE WARRANTY TERMS DO NOT EXCLUDE, RESTRICT, OR MODIFY, AND ARE IN ADDITION TO, THE MANDATORY STATUTORY RIGHTS APPLICABLE TO THE LICENSE OF THE SOFTWARE TO YOU.

**Governing Law.** This agreement shall be governed by the law of the State of California.

**Consent to Jurisdiction, Venue, and Service.** Customer consents and agrees that all legal proceedings relating to the subject matter of this agreement shall be maintained in courts sitting within San Diego County, California, and Customer consents and agrees that jurisdiction and venue for such proceedings shall lie exclusively with such courts. Service of process in any such proceeding may be made by certified mail, return receipt requested, addressed to the party where it is to receive notice.

*Beach Access Software*
*13614 Boquita Drive • Del Mar, CA 92014*
*Phone: 858-259-4334 • Fax: 858-259-4471*
*E-mail: info@e-z-mrp.com*

# Index

## A

Access *see* Microsoft Access
Access installer
    market definition, 152
Access runtime packager, 149
    copy protection, 151
    customer service, 150
    pricing, 149, 152
accessing data *see* data access
add ons
    BidFax, 16
    PMS-II, 15
administrators
    data access levels, 38
advertising, 16
Annual Budget Preparation, 181
annual subscription pricing, 112
appearance *see* product appearance
Apple
    product specification, 46
application design
    defining database, 31
    defining outputs, 30
applications, horizontal/vertical, 8
Artful.lib, 125, 126
atomic-level data, 31
Auction Central, 175
    pricing, 176
author *see* Smolin, Rocky
average selling price, 106, 107

## B

backgrounds
    type and background colors, 76
BarTracks Permissions Management
    form, 40
Beach Access Software, 1
    copyright notice, 185
    license agreement, 185–188
    trademarks, 185
    warranty, 187
Bejeweled Software Company, 48
Beta testing *see* testing
BidFax, 12
    add ons, 16
    bugs, 18
    commercial installers, 18
    copy protection, 13
    costs and revenues, 13
    custom modifications, 20
    development time, 12
    implementation time, 19
    interfacing with third-party
      databases, 16
    lifespan, 20
    multiproduct package, 15
    networks, 15
    pricing, 14
    programming, 13
    programming language, 13
    sale of, 14

secure keys, 14
software distribution, 16
support revenue, 15
testing, 12
trademarks, 17
training, 18
user manual, 17
break-even point, 106–107
bugs
BidFax, 18
Jewelry Designer Manager, 54
PMS-II, 18
testing, 89
business focus
Federation, 176
business formats, 136–139
corporations, 138
limited liability company, 138
partnership, 137
sole proprietor, 137
business knowledge, 128
business rules and processes
identifying user requirements, 28
output specification, 28
product specification, 36–37
Buzzsaw, 20

## C

C-Basic (CB86)
BidFax, 13
PMS-II, 11
Capistrant, Steve
interview with, 170–177
Carlton, Barbara
interview with, 48–59
CHARTS, 182
custom modifications, 182
pricing, 180
versions, 182
click-wrap license, 133
Clipper, 120, 123, 125
Artful.lib, 126
color
aesthetics in color selection, 75
consistency in reports, 72

functionality in color selection, 76
selecting color for product
appearance, 75–78
type and background colors, 76
comments
product development, 63
commercial installers, 18
Access runtime packager, 149
Federation, 174
SageKey scripts, 54
Wise Installation System, 68
competition
BidFax, 16-17
effect on pricing, 108–109
consistency
product appearance, 69–74
forms, 69–72
operation, 73–74
reports, 72–73
control tip text, 165
copy protection, 143–147
Access runtime packager, 151
BidFax, 13-14
County Annual Report, 180
E-Z-MRP, 145, 186
expiration date, 145
Federation, 172
FilmStar, 123
hard copy manuals, 164
license agreement, 135
PMS-II, 14
product key, 145
Sleep Advisor, 144
technical support, 144
Wedding Management for
Professionals, 94
copyright
Beach Access Software, 185
Federation, 172
Jewelry Designer Manager, 52
legal matters, 141–142
license agreement, 134
opening (first) form, 66
software ownership, 131–132
corporations, 138
costs *see* expenses

County Annual Report, 178
  copy protection, 180
  pricing, 180
  product development, 179
  reports, 179
  user manual, 180
  versions, 179
Craft Manager, 57, 58
critical path project management
    systems, 10
Critters, 176
Cummings, Ruben
  interview with, 178–183
currency
  international formatting, 85
custom modifications
  BidFax, 20
  CHARTS, 182
  Federation, 174
  Jewelry Designer Manager, 57
  PMS-II, 19
  pricing, 157
  software development, 157–158
  versions, controlling number of,
    158
  Wedding Management for
    Professionals, 99
customer service
  Access runtime packager, 150
customers
  Jewelry Designer Manager, 49
  perceived value of product,
    107–108
  PMS-II add ons, 16
  Wedding Management for
    Professionals, 94


**D**

data
  information and, 29-30
data access
  administrator, 38
  controlling data access, 37–41
  fields/functions, 39
    level of control to create, 41
    levels of access, 38
data fields see fields
data inputs see inputs
data storage
  atomic-level data, 31
  final storage specification, 35
  grouping data items in relational
    tables, 32–34
  product specification, 30–35
  storing historical data, 34
  storing un-normalized data, 34
database normalization see
    normalization
databases, 30
  application design, 31
  interfacing BidFax with third-
    party databases, 16
dates
  consistency in operation, 74
  international formatting, 85
decreasing quantities
  consistency in operation, 74
design considerations see product
    specification
developers
  hiring programmers, 62–65
development
  see also programming
  software development, 6
disassembling software
  license agreement, 135
  E-Z-MRP, 186
disclaimers
  license agreement, 135
distribution see software distribution
DocketWorks
  consistency in forms, 71
  functionality in color selection, 76
documentation see user manual
"Don't show this form again" check
    box
  opening (first) form, 68

# E

E-Z-MRP, 6
  Bill of Materials Menu, 42
  consistency in forms, 69
  consistency in operation, 73
  controlling data access, 38, 39
  copy protection, 145
  copyright notice, 185
  developing product for foreign
    languages, 80, 81
  error trapping and reporting, 87
  identifying user requirements, 28
  lateral navigation buttons, 44
  license agreement, 134, 185–188
  login form, 38
  Main Menu, 42
  navigation outline for, 45
  opening (first) form, 66
  output specification, 27
  packaging products, 166
  pay by capacity pricing, 114
  pricing, 112
  product definition, 24
  technical support pricing, 118
  trademarks, 185
  User Maintenance form, 39
  user preferences, 78
  warranty, 187
educational versions
  pricing, 114
enhancements
  version two list, 156
  when to stop programming, 155
errors
  trapping and reporting, 87–88
escrow
  software escrow, 140
expenses, 104
  fixed costs, 104, 106
  variable costs, 104, 106
expiration date
  copy protection, 145
external data inputs, 36

# F

feature creep
  version two list, 156
  when to stop programming, 155
Federation, 171
  business focus, 176
  commercial installers, 174
  copy protection, 172
  copyright, 172
  custom modifications, 174
  distribution, 174
  GoToMeeting, Citrix, 174
  pricing, 173
  product development, 171
  testing, 172
  training users, 175
  updates, 173
  user manual, 171
  versions, 173, 175
fields
  controlling data access, 39
  final storage specification, 35
FilmStar, 120
  copy protection, 123
  networks, 123
  pricing, 121, 124
  software development, 123
  technical support, 124
  testing, 123
  user manual, 122
filtering criteria
  consistency in reports, 73
financing software products, 128
first (opening) form
  product appearance, 66–68
fixed costs, 104
  break-even point, 106–107
  software, 106
fixed price pricing, 112
fonts
  consistency in forms, 70
  consistency in reports, 72
  sans serif font, 75
  selecting fonts, 74

serif font, 74
type and background colors, 76
foreign languages
    developing product for, 79–85
    international formatting, 85
forms
    consistency, 69–72, 74
        fonts, 70
        icons, 72
        menu bar, 69, 71
        text labels, 72
    data inputs, 35
    opening (first) form, 66–68
    sizing for product appearance, 86
Fuller, Arthur
    interview with, 119–128
functions
    controlling data access, 39

**G**

GoToMeeting, Citrix
    Federation, 174
Government Finance Consultants,
    178
gross margin, 105
gross profit, 105

**H**

hard copy manuals
    copy protection and, 164
help, 165
hiring programmers, 62–65
horizontal application, 8
horizontal integration, 121

**I**

icons
    consistency in forms, 72
implementation time
    BidFax, 19
    Jewelry Designer Manager, 56
    PMS-II, 19

increasing quantities
    consistency in operation, 74
information
    data and, 29, 30
    outputs providing, 30
inputs
    external data, 36
    product specification, 35–36
installation
    Access runtime packager, 150
    Jewelry Designer Manager, 54
    packaging products, 166
    Wedding Management for
        Professionals, 98
installer scripts, 153
installers *see* commercial installers
InstallShield
    packaging products, 168
insurance
    legal matters, 139
    software escrow, 140–141
international formatting, 85
interviews
    Capistrant, Steve, 170–177
    Carlton, Barbara, 48–59
    Cummings, Ruben, 178–183
    Fuller, Arthur, 119–128
    Matfield, Barry, 148–154
    Murphy, Jackie and Doug, 91–102
    Vanderpool, Al, 10–21
intros
    opening (first) form, 68
investment
    Jewelry Designer Manager, 52

**J**

Jewelry Designer Manager, 48
    background, 49
    bugs, 54
    copyright, 52
    custom modifications, 57
    customers, 49
    function of product, 48
    implementation time, 56

installation, 54
investment, 52
licensing, 50, 53
market definition, 49
market research, 54
networks, 50
pricing, 50, 53
product development, 58
programming languages, 51
security, 51, 52
software development, 51
software distribution, 50
support revenue, 53
technical support, 53, 54
testing, 51
trademarks, 55
training users, 56
updates, 56
user manual, 56
versions, 50, 53

**K**

keyboard
using mouse or keyboard, 88

**L**

languages *see* programming
lateral navigation buttons, 44
lawyers, 130
lease plan payments, 117
legal matters
Beach Access Software warranty,
187
business formats, 136–139
copyright, 131–132, 141–142
corporations, 138
disclaimer, 129
individual owner unable to
support software, 140
insurance, 139
introduction, 129
lawyers, 130
liability, 139

licensing software, 133–136
limited liability company, 138
partnership, 137
quotes for legal work, 131
software escrow, 140–141
software ownership, 131–132
sole proprietor, 137
trademarks, 142–143
liability
Beach Access Software warranty,
187
legal matters, 139
license agreement, 136
licensee, 133
licensing, 133, 134
click-wrap license, 133
disassembling software, 135
disclaimers, 135
E-Z-MRP license agreement,
185–188
governing law, 136
Jewelry Designer Manager, 50, 53
limitation of liability, 136
opening (first) form, 66
Show Producer, 102
shrink-wrap license, 133
software ownership, 133–136
terminating license, 135
transferring license, 135
use at own risk, 136
licensor, 133
lifespan
BidFax, 20
PMS-II, 11
limited liability company, 138
Loading program message
opening (first) form, 68

**M**

Manual *see* user manual
market definition, 20
Access installer, 152
Artful.lib, 125
Jewelry Designer Manager, 49

PMS-II, 11
Show Producer, 100
market research
  BidFax, 17
  interview with Barry Matfield, 153
  Jewelry Designer Manager, 54
  Wedding Management for
    Professionals, 97
marketing
  PMS-II, 16
  Wedding Management for
    Professionals, 96
Matfield, Barry
  interview with, 148–154
menu bar, consistency in forms
  DocketWorks, 71
  E-Z-MRP, 69
Microsoft Access
  Wedding Management for
    Professionals, 92
Microsoft HTML Help Workshop,
    165
modifications *see* custom
    modifications
mouse
  using mouse or keyboard, 88
multiuser system
  *see also* networks
  user preferences, 78
Murphy, Jackie and Doug
  interview with, 91–102
Murphy's Creativity, 91

**N**

naming rules/conventions
  product development, 63
navigation
  E-Z-MRP, 45
  flow of processes, 42
  lateral navigation buttons, 44
  product specification, 41–46
  vertical and lateral movement, 44
Net 30 payments terms, 115

net margin, 105
Net on Receipt payments terms, 115
net profit, 105
networks
  BidFax and PMS-II, 15
  FilmStar, 123
  Jewelry Designer Manager, 50
  product specification, 46
  Wedding Management for
    Professionals, 93
normalization
  database normalization, 32–34
  when to un-normalize databases,
    34
numeric fields
  consistency in operation, 74
  international formatting, 85

**O**

online help, 165
opening (first) form
  "Don't show this form again"
    check box, 68
  E-Z-MRP, 66
  intros, 68
  Loading program message, 68
  product appearance, 66–68
  Sleep Advisor, 67
  Wise Installation System, 68
operating systems
  product specification, 46
operation
  consistency in product
    appearance, 73–74
output specification, 26–29
  business rules and processes, 28
  E-Z-MRP, 27
  identifying user requirements, 27
  level of detail required, 26
  overcomplication, 30
  reports, 27
  Sleep Advisor, 26

outputs
  defining, 30
  information provided by, 30
  overwhelming users with, 29
ownership
  E-Z-MRP license agreement, 186

**P**

packaging products
  E-Z-MRP, 166
  Sleep Advisor, 168
  software development, 165–169
  Windows Installer, 168
palette
  selecting color for product
    appearance, 75–78
Palm Pilot runtime script, 152
partnership, 137
passwords
  controlling data access, 38
pay by capacity/seat/use pricing, 113
payments, 115–117
  leasing and self-financing, 117
  receivables and payables, 116
  setting payment policies, 115–116
piracy
  copy protection, 143–147
platforms
  product specification, 46
  Wedding Management for
    Professionals, 92, 96
PMS-II, 10
  add ons, 15
  bugs, 18
  commercial installers, 18
  copy protection, 14
  custom modifications, 19
  early days, 5
  implementation time, 19
  lifespan, 11
  marketing, 16
  networks, 15
  pricing, 14
  programming, 11, 13

support revenue, 12, 15
system updates, 18
training users, 18
user manual, 17
versions, 19
preferences
  foreign language selection, 82
  global preferences, 79
  user preferences for product
    appearance, 78–79
prepayments, 115
pricing
  *see also* payments; software
    distribution
  Access runtime packager, 149, 152
  Artful.lib, 125
  Auction Central, 176
  average selling price, 106-107
  BidFax, 14, 16
  break-even point, 106–107
  CHARTS, 180
  competition and, 108–109
  County Annual Report, 180
  custom modifications, 157
  educational versions, 114
  Federation, 173
  FilmStar, 121, 124
  Jewelry Designer Manager, 50, 53
  methods of distribution, 107
  perceived value of product,
    107–108
  PMS-II, 14
  revenue curve, 110–111
  Show Producer, 100
  technical support, 117–118
  useful terminology, 103
  Wedding Management for
    Professionals, 94, 95
pricing options
  annual subscription, 112
  fixed price, 112
  pay by capacity/seat/use, 113
  zero cost, 114
processes
  navigation, 42
  product specification, 36–37

Sleep Advisor, 36
product appearance
  consistency, 69–74
    forms, 69–72
    operation, 73–74
    reports, 72–73
  developing product for foreign
    languages, 79–85
  error trapping and reporting,
    87–88
  opening (first) form, 66–68
  screen resizing code, 86
  screen resolution, 86
  selecting color, 75–78
  selecting fonts, 74
  sizing forms for, 86
  testing, 89–90
  user preferences, 78–79
  using mouse or keyboard, 88
product development
  *see also* software development
  comments, 63
  commitment, 127
  County Annual Report, 179
  error trapping and reporting,
    87–88
  Federation, 171
  for foreign languages, 80
  hiring programmers, 62–65
  Jewelry Designer Manager, 58
  naming rules/conventions, 63
  product definition, 23–24
  testing, 89–90
product key
  copy protection, 145
  custom modifications, 158
product specification
  business rules and processes, 36
  controlling data access, 37–41
  data storage, 30–35
  database normalization, 32–34
  inputs, 35–36
  navigation, 41–46
  outputs, 26–29
  platforms, 46

storing historical data, 34
  summarized, 46
  systems analysis, 24–26
  users and programmers, 26
product support *see* technical support
products *see* software products
profit, 105
programmers, hiring, 62, 65
programming
  BidFax, 12, 13
  developing product for foreign
    languages, 79–85
  identifying programming
    omissions, 162
  Jewelry Designer Manager, 51
  PMS-II, 11
  product specification, 46, 61
  when to stop programming,
    155–156
project management systems
  PMS-II, 10

**R**

receivables, 116
Regional and Language Options
  dialog box, 85
relational databases
  normalization, 32
relationships between tables
  final storage specification, 35
reports
  application design, 31
  consistency in product
    appearance, 72–73
  County Annual Report, 179
  error trapping and reporting,
    87–88
  forms and data inputs, 36
  identifying user requirements, 28
  output specification, 27
  overwhelming users with, 30
revenue, 103
revenue curve, 110–111

# S

SageKey scripts
  Jewelry Designer Manager, 54
  packaging products, 169
SageKey Software, 148
sans serif font, 75
scheduling, 11
  PMS-II add ons, 15
screen resizing code, 86
screen resolution
  product appearance, 86
scrollbars
  sizing forms for product
    appearance, 86
secure keys
  BidFax, 14
security
  controlling data access, 37–41
  Jewelry Designer Manager, 51, 52
self-financing payments, 117
selling price *see* pricing
serif font, 74
Show Producer, 100
  licensing, 102
  market definition, 100
  pricing, 100
  software development time, 100
shrink-wrap license, 133
Sleep Advisor, 6
  controlling data access, 37
  copy protection, 144
  license agreement, 133
  opening (first) form, 67
  output specification, 26
  packaging products, 168
  processes, 36
  product definition, 24
Smolin, Rocky
  computing/programming
    background, 4
  reasons for being a programmer,
    4–7
  reasons for writing this book, 1–4

software development
  *see also* product development
  action items, list of, 3
  becoming software developer, 10,
    48
  charging for initial appraisal, 2
  custom modifications, 157–158
  FilmStar, 123
  getting started, 7
  initial questions, 2
  Jewelry Designer Manager, 51
  online help, 165
  packaging the product, 165–169
  reviewing current situation, 2
  Show Producer, 100
  user manual, 158–165
    audience for manual, 160
    getting started writing, 160–161
    getting the message over, 161
    reference or tutorial, 163
    table of contents, 160
  versions, 156–157
  Wedding Management for
    Professionals, 92
  when to stop programming,
    155–156
  working as a team, 6
software distribution
  *see also* pricing
  BidFax, 14, 16
  Federation, 174
  Jewelry Designer Manager, 50
software escrow, 140–141
softwear license *see* licensing
software ownership
  legal matters, 131–132
  license agreement, 135
  licensing software, 133–136
software products
  Artful.lib, 125
  break-even point, 106–107
  competition and pricing, 108–109
  costs/margins/profits, 103–106
  E-Z-MRP, 6

FilmStar, 120
financing, 128
  individual owner unable to
    support software, 140
  Jewelry Designer Manager, 48
  payments for, 115–117
  perceived value of, 107–108
  pricing options, 112–115
  revenue curve, 110–111
  Sleep Advisor, 6
  technical support pricing, 117–118
sole proprietor, 137
sorting criteria
  consistency in reports, 73
source code
  software escrow, 140
Stone, Jack, 2
storing data *see* data storage
support *see* technical support
support revenue
  BidFax, 15
  Jewelry Designer Manager, 53
  PMS-II, 12, 15
Symphony Information Services, 170
system design *see* product
    specification
system updates *see* updates
systems analysis
  data storage, 30–35
  identifying user requirements, 27
  inputs, 35–36
  outputs, 26–29
  processes, 36–37
  product specification, 24–26

## T

tables, 30
  final storage specification, 35
target market *see* market definition
technical support
  copy protection through, 144
  FilmStar, 124
  installer scripts, 153

Jewelry Designer Manager, 53, 54
  opening (first) form, 67
  PMS-II custom modifications, 19
  pricing, 117–118
  Wedding Management for
    Professionals, 96
technology
  product specification, 46
terminology, 19
testing
  Bidfax, 12
  Federation, 172
  FilmStar, 123
  identifying users for, 28
  Jewelry Designer Manager, 51
  product appearance, 89–90
  recruiting Beta testers, 89
  requirement for, 101
  Wedding Management for
    Professionals, 97
text labels
  consistency in forms, 72
The Sleep Advisor *see* Sleep Advisor
time
  international formatting, 85
to do list
  version two list, 156
  when to stop programming, 156
trademarks, 142–143
  BidFax, 17
  E-Z-MRP, 185
  Jewelry Designer Manager, 55
  license agreement, 134
  Wedding Management for
    Professionals, 97
training users
  BidFax, 18
  Federation, 175
  Jewelry Designer Manager, 56
  PMS-II, 18
  Wedding Management for
    Professionals, 99
typefaces
  selecting fonts, 74
  type and background colors, 76

# U

updates
Federation, 173
Jewelry Designer Manager, 56
PMS-II, 18
Wedding Management for
Professionals, 98
upgrades
*see also* versions
charging for, 118
use at own risk
license agreement, 136
user manual
audience for manual, 160
BidFax, 17
cost of maintaining/distributing
hard-copy manual, 17
County Annual Report, 180
Federation, 171
FilmStar, 122
getting started writing, 160–161
getting the message over, 161
identifying programming
omissions, 162
index and glossary, 164
installer scripts, 153
Jewelry Designer Manager, 56
navigating around electronic
documents, 164
online help, 165
online or hard copy, 164
PMS-II, 17
reference or tutorial, 163
software development, 158–165
table of contents, 160
Wedding Management for
Professionals, 98
user preferences
product appearance, 78–79
users
*see also* training users
controlling data access, 37
data access levels, 38
identifying user requirements, 27
navigation, 45

packaging products for, 166
product specification, 26
Wedding Management for
Professionals, 94

# V

Vanderpool, Al
interview with, 10–21
variable costs, 104
break-even point, 106
software, 106
VBErrorHandler
error trapping and reporting, 87
versions
CHARTS, 182
County Annual Report, 179
custom modifications, 158
educational versions, pricing, 114
Federation, 173, 175
Jewelry Designer Manager, 50, 53
opening (first) form, 67
pay by capacity versions, pricing,
113
PMS-II, 19
software development, 156–157
Wedding Management for
Professionals, 94, 97, 99
vertical application, 8
vertically integration, 121
Vista
Visual Basic compatibility, 92

# W

warranty
license agreement, 134
E-Z-MRP, 187
web-compatibility
product specification, 46
Wedding Management for
Professionals
choosing Microsoft Access, 92
copy protection, 94
custom modifications, 99

customers, 94
inspiration for product, 91
installation, 98
market research, 97
marketing, 96
networking, 93
platforms, 92, 96
pricing, 94, 95
technical support, 96
testing, 97
trademarks, 97
training users, 99
updates, 98
user manual, 98
users, 94
versions, 94, 97, 99

Windows
    product specification, 46
    Regional and Language Options
        dialog box, 85
Windows Installer
    packaging products, 168
Wise Installation System
    opening (first) form, 68
    packaging products, 168

## Z

zero cost pricing, 114

# You Need the Companion eBook

**Your purchase of this book entitles you to buy the companion PDF-version eBook for only $10. Take the weightless companion with you anywhere.**

We believe this Apress title will prove so indispensable that you'll want to carry it with you everywhere, which is why we are offering the companion eBook (in PDF format) for $10 to customers who purchase this book now. Convenient and fully searchable, the PDF version of any content-rich, page-heavy Apress book makes a valuable addition to your programming library. You can easily find and copy code—or perform examples by quickly toggling between instructions and the application. Even simultaneously tackling a donut, diet soda, and complex code becomes simplified with hands-free eBooks!

Once you purchase your book, getting the $10 companion eBook is simple:

❶ Visit **www.apress.com/promo/tendollars/**.

❷ Complete a basic registration form to receive a randomly generated question about this title.

❸ Answer the question correctly in 60 seconds, and you will receive a promotional code to redeem for the $10.00 eBook.

## Apress®
### THE EXPERT'S VOICE™

2855 TELEGRAPH AVENUE | SUITE 600 | BERKELEY, CA 94705